the
wilderness
israel's ultimate wandering

RAMON BENNETT

SHEKINAH

Citrus Heights   —   Jerusalem

First printing February 2013

Cover photograph: Taken by the author in the Wilderness of Judea, which extends from Jerusalem (altitude, 1,000 meters) down to the Dead Sea – the lowest point on earth.

Published and Distributed in the United States by:
Shekinah Books,
8049 Butternut Drive, Citrus Heights, California 95621, U.S.A.
Tel: (916) 877-0449. Email: rose@shekinahbooks.net.

Distributed in Israel by:
Ramon Bennett,
P.O. Box 37111, Jerusalem 91370.
Email: armofsalvation@mac.com.

In New Zealand, contact:
Michael Bahjejian,
210 Collingwood Street,
P.O. Box 1483 Hamilton.
Tel.: (07) 834-1128. Email: michaelba@clear.net.nz.

In the United Kingdom, contact:
John and Yvonne Hellewell,
5 Greenhill Ave., Hellaby, Rotherham, South Yorkshire S66 8HE.
Tel.: (0170) 954-4198. Email: Yvonne.Hellewell@tesco.net.

Shekinah Books is a division of Arm of Salvation Ministries headquartered in Jerusalem, Israel. Further information can be found at: www.ShekinahBooks.com

Printed in the United States of America

Indeed before the day was, I am He; And there is no one who can deliver out of My hand; I work, and who will reverse it? (Isaiah 43:13).

Dedication

For the *Lᴏʀᴅ God of Abraham, Isaac and Israel*
(1 Kings 18:36).

Contents

One

Four Thousand Friendless Years

The writing of this book began in 2003. Owing to debilitating pain in the author's left hip the writing did not progress well and the half-written book was put aside in favor of an urgent hip-replacement. The book was picked up again in 2007 and what had been written previously was rewritten. Then, due to a spinal surgeon diagnosing that the author had actually broken his neck forty years earlier in a horse-riding accident, the writing was put aside once more. Spinal surgery was performed and a prosthesis was inserted into the author's neck and his years-long history of headaches came to an end. Following recuperation from the neck surgery it was found that the author had advanced carpel tunnel syndrome in both hands and again underwent surgery, one hand at a time.

In November 2011, the author became virtually obsessed with the desire to complete the book and tackled the project with gusto. Not feeling comfortable with what had been rewritten four years earlier the author discarded everything, keeping only the original idea, and began writing afresh.

In December 2011, after making good progress with the book, the author suffered a major heart attack while addressing a meeting in England, this required two stents to be inserted into his heart's aorta. One week out from the hospital the author collapsed again, this time from internal bleeding from side-effects of proscribed heart medications. Needless to say, those new setbacks not only kept him confined to England for an extended period, but also put another halt to the writing of this book.

In March 2012 the author was finally able to concentrate upon completing what he had begun nine years earlier. The contents and nature has made it a difficult book to write, and with so much overt opposition to the writing of it the author feels that it must be important.

To everything there is a season, a time for every purpose under heaven (Ecclesiastes 3:1).

The chapter you are reading was intended to be part of an Author's Preface; however, due to the importance of its content and the propensity of many readers to skip prefaces and introductions, the author himself opted to skip having either a preface or an introduction. What was earlier written for the intended preface was edited and added to and finally morphed into this first chapter, which sets the tone for the entire book.

This is the author's fifth book dealing with the biblical place of Israel, the decades-long conflict with her neighbors, and the antagonism toward her by the so-called international community of nations. While it was fully intended for each of the author's five books on Israel to stand alone, a clear-cut continuity throughout all five has transpired – this was not by man's design, it is solely the work of *"the Holy One of Israel"* (Psalm 57:1).

In light of the obvious opposition to the birthing of this book – opposition that has shown no sign of abating even as the author made the inevitable last-minute changes – he dares to ask if, apart from the Bible, is it possible that the author's fifth book could be the last word on Israel and the nations?

The author's first book, *When Day and Night Cease: A prophetic study of world events and how prophecy concerning Israel affects the nations, the Church, and you*, which is scheduled to go into a fourth edition, is an overview of everything concerning the biblical place of the nation of Israel. It lists biblical prophecies and their fulfillments; the events that must take place before the coming of Jesus, our Lord and King; the Church's role in worldwide antisemitism;[1] and God Almighty's master plan for Jews and Christians.

As we journey through the book you are now reading we must, of necessity, traverse some patches of territory familiar to *When Day And Night Cease* for biblical prophecies are still being fulfilled today and the world's anti-Israel clamor is rising to a crescendo.

The second book, *SAGA: Israel And The Demise Of The Nations*, was perhaps a book a decade or more ahead of its time when it was first published in the early 1990s and is extremely pertinent for today. *SAGA* is a call to national repentance. *SAGA* deals with the biblical nations that were judged by the LORD, the Master of the universe, along with the nature of the sins that brought about their particular judgments, which caused either their destruction or total extinction.

A thread common to all the judged nations was a hostile treatment of or attitude toward Israel, whom the LORD calls *"the dearly beloved of My soul"* (Jeremiah 12:7). Using the same formulated list of sins that ultimately destroyed those early nations, the author included media reports from around the world to document the sins of many modern nations, sins that show for a certainty that today's modern nations will be and are being judged for the same reasons as the former biblical nations were.

Readers should be aware that the LORD's weightier judgements do not necessarily fall immediately upon a nation following its sin against Him – and ultimately, all sins are against God personally:

> *"Against You, You only, have I sinned, and done this evil in Your sight – that You may be found just when You speak, and blameless when You judge"*
> (Psalms 51.4).

His judgements can take hundreds of years before they fall, as is made clear in the case of the Amorite nation:

> *Then He said to Abram: "Know certainly that your descendants will be strangers in a land that is not theirs, and will serve them, and they will afflict them four hundred years. And also the nation whom they serve I will judge; afterward they shall come out with great possessions. Now as for you, you shall go to your fathers in peace; you shall be buried at a good old age. But **in the fourth generation they shall return** here, for the iniquity of the Amorites is not yet complete"* (Genesis 15:13-16).

Most readers of the Bible are aware of the Israelites being slaves in Egypt for more than four hundred years – four hundred and thirty *"years to the day"* (Exodus 12:41), but few readers ever question why the Israelites were required to spend those years in Egypt when the LORD, several centuries earlier, had repeatedly promised them the land of Canaan as an inheritance. The answer to that question can readily be found in the Scriptures, but we must first make a short detour.

Generally, Bible teaching sets the duration of a generation at forty years, but this is very misleading and mostly inaccurate. The *Oxford English Dictionary,* arguably the world's premier dictionary, defines a generation as "the interval of time between the birth of the parents and that of their children." We are here dealing with Abram, later renamed to Abraham, and the Bible tells us that Isaac is Abraham's *"only son"* (Genesis 22:2, 12). Ishmael, Abraham's son by Hagar the Egyptian, is not recognized here due to him being the fruit from a work of the flesh – God recognizes works of the Spirit, not those of the flesh.

The Bible also tells us that Abraham was *"one hundred years old"* when Isaac was born (Genesis 21:5), therefore, at that time, Abraham's generation was one hundred years – far longer than the forty years that a biblical generation is usually taught to be.

Returning to our passage of Scripture in Genesis 15 we understand that the Israelites would be afflicted for four hundred years and *"in the fourth generation"* they would return to Canaan – four of Abraham's generations being 4 x 100 = 400 – *"for the iniquity of the Amorites is not yet complete."* The Israelites, of necessity, had to go into Egypt for all those long and bitter years – into *"the iron furnace"* (Jeremiah 11:4), because the iniquity, or sin, of the Amorites was not at the level where the LORD was willing to annihilate them. After the Israelites returned to Canaan following their four hundred and thirty-year sojourn in Egypt, the Amorites were annihilated through Israel's military campaigns, but it was the Lord who actually exterminated the Amorite nation:

> *Yet it was I who destroyed the Amorite before them,*
> *whose height was like the height of the cedars, and*

he was as strong as the oaks; yet I destroyed his fruit
above and his roots beneath (Amos 2:9).

Also Egypt, to whom the Israelites were enslaved, was judged and destroyed (Exodus 10:7) just as the LORD said it would be.

Many nations are under judgement today. That God's judgments are actually falling is confirmed by the number and variety of catastrophes making headlines in the world's media. Unfortunately, most inhabitants of our planet, including many professing Christians, consider the LORD's judgements fitting for others, never for themselves or their nations. The reason for so many countries experiencing catastrophes and dire economic difficulties at this time is directly linked to Israel having so few friends today; later chapters will make this abundantly clear. But the author desires to make it perfectly clear that, as each day draws us nearer to the end of time, the catastrophes now being experienced will increase, both in frequency and severity.

Scripture challenges us to understand with our hearts that it is the LORD, *"the Holy One of Israel,"* who holds complete sway over the 'natural' forces of heaven and earth and sea:

Thus says the LORD, who gives the sun for light by
day, and the fixed order of the moon and the stars for
light by night, who stirs up the sea so that its waves
roar; the LORD of hosts is His name
(Jeremiah 31:35).

And did not the Master of the universe forewarn us of what will take place as we approach the end of this age?:

And there will be signs in the sun, in the moon, and
in the stars; and on the earth distress of nations, with
perplexity, the sea and the waves roaring
(Luke 21:25).

The catastrophes striking nations today are often reported as the worst in recorded history. Many are said to be caused by a weather system called *El Niño*, which is the Spanish term used to designate "The Christ Child" – the Lord Jesus. It is obvious to the author that God Almighty is sending a clear message to the world and to the sleeping Church that His Son is, as it were, on His way back to rule and reign from Jerusalem. The end of the age casts its ominous shadow in the doorway of time.

Today's judgments upon nations, however, are only the fore-warnings of the more dire judgments that are to come. The great judgments that shall befall all unrepentant nations are graphically imaged in the last book of the Bible, the Book of Revelation. The purpose of judgment is to bring repentance that leads to life:

> *For when Your judgments are in the earth, the inhabitants of the world will learn righteousness*
> (Isaiah 26:9b).

The final phase of the LORD's plan for mankind is for the righteous – those in an intimate relationship with Jesus – to inherit eternal life and to live that life in God's glorious presence. The unrighteous shall inherit eternal damnation away from the majesty of the *"Creator"* and *"Possessor of heaven and earth"* (Genesis 14:19). If there is any doubt in the reader's mind concerning the intimate nature of his or her relationship with Jesus, the matter should be settled immediately by calling upon Him before proceeding further. Do not, as Roman Procurator Antonius Felix did, put the decision off until a more *"convenient time"* (Acts 24:25). Time, as we understand it, is running out. Yesterday cannot be recalled, tomorrow cannot be assured, only today is ours.

The author's third book, *Philistine: The Great Deception*, is based upon biblical prophecies dealing with Israel's abortive "peace process" with the Arab world, most especially the Palestinians. This book lays out the background of the Arab-Israeli conflict and the so-called Oslo "peace process," brokered by the 'do-good' country of Norway, a "peace" that in just four years took more Israeli lives than did the previous fifteen years in a state of war.

The Palestinians have no real intention of making peace with Israel and apparently have never had intentions of making peace with the Jewish state. For longer than the seventeen years (at the time of writing) of the "peace talks" with Israel, Palestinian leaders have twisted and turned every-which-way in order to avoid serious negotiations that might have had a ghost's chance of leading to peace. Peace was never a goal for the Palestinians, the destruction of Israel is the goal – by any road, by any means. Indeed, the Palestinian aspiration is not to establish a state of their own, but to dismantle a state of others.

Philistine documents historical facts and is supported by over fifteen hundred quotations and references, facts which the international pro-Arab, anti-Israel brigade blindly refuses to acknowledge. The book presents Islam as being the determinant factor in the Israeli-Arab conflict. *Philistine* was written at a time when there was a taboo by writers and publishers on presenting either the Qur'an or the Muslim religion in a negative light due to Muslim death threats, of which not a few have been made against the author.

It is unsurprising, therefore, that would-be Western negotiators cannot bring an end to the Israeli-Arab conflict when they fail to even begin to understand the first cause of the conflict or to accept established facts.

The author's fourth book, *The Wall: Prophecy, Politics, and Middle East "Peace,"* describes the end of Israel's "peace process" with the Palestinians as foretold in biblical prophecy. It also majors on political factors brought about by the pressure of international politics – policies forced upon Israel solely for the financial and political profit of the nations involved, never for the sake of peace alone.

The people who profess aspirations of resolving the Arab-Israeli conflict – the president of the United States, Barack Hussein Obama, being a prime example – are the very ones who perpetuate it. There is no peace, will be no peace, can be no peace until Jesus, the *"Prince of Peace"* (Isaiah 9:6), returns to rule and reign from Jerusalem.

This present book, *The Wilderness: Israel's Ultimate Wandering*, the author's fifth on the history and biblical destiny of Israel,[2] details the LORD's ultimate dealings with His special people as laid out in biblical prophecy. The reader will see the LORD, the *"Mighty One of Israel"* (Isaiah 1:24), restoring His wayward children and fulfilling the chosen nation's destiny, albeit not without many tears and a great deal of pain. The information included between the covers of this book shows the grave danger almost all nations face due to their inherent hostility toward Israel and their lust for mammon, which blinds the eyes of justice.

It needs to be boldly declared to the leaders of Western and non-Western nations alike that, unless their attitudes change toward Israel, they may have signed their own nation's death warrant. And let them not forget that long ago the LORD made an irrefutable promise concerning the nation of Israel:

> *Thus says the LORD, who gives the sun for a light by day, the ordinances of the moon and the stars for a light by night, who disturbs the sea, and its waves roar (The LORD of hosts is His name):* **"If those ordinances depart from before Me," says the LORD, "then the seed of Israel shall also cease from being a nation before Me** *forever"* (Jeremiah 31:35-36).

Thus we understand that Israel is as eternal as day and night, which will doubtless be most disappointing to those tirelessly planning and working for Israel's demise. At the same time it needs to be pointed out to world leaders that Jerusalem, Israel's capital – *"the city of the great King"* (Psalms 48:2), is the only city on this planet with an eternal future (Revelation 3:12, 21:2), and those leaders would do well to internalize this fact. Another fact that should not be lightly dismissed is that ninety-six percent of all of the Bible – both the Old and the New Testaments – is directed to or about the Jews. Therefore let it be understood that Israel is on center stage of world events and is the principle actor, all other nations have only bit roles.

World leaders holding atheistic and agnostic views concerning the existence of *"Almighty God"* (Genesis 17:1), who believe the Bible to be a mere book of myths and fairytales, probably amuse Him:

> *He who sits in the heavens shall laugh; the LORD shall hold them in derision* (Psalms 2:4).

Unbelief does not in any way diminish the LORD's power or the accuracy of His Word, it merely shows non-believers to be blockheads: *"The **fool** has said in his heart, there is no God"* (Psalms 14:1, 53:1). No doubt the LORD had that line included twice for the benefit of fools who may have missed it the first time around.

Israel today is trudging a lonely, desolate road. It has been a four-thousand-years-long road. With each passing day, with each new step, her road becomes increasingly lonelier, more difficult, and very much more dangerous. It is said that there is a calm before every storm; for Israel, however, the relative calm of her modern war-torn sixty-four-year history is ending and a brutal hurricane is blowing in on the four winds. With so few friends and so many enemies, Israel's future looks miserable. But, Israel is the *"apple"* of the LORD's *"eye"* (Zechariah 2:8) and has a *"destiny"* to fulfill (Lamentations 1:9). The LORD will ensure she fulfills it.

---

[1] In the use of "antisemitism" the author follows historian Yehuda Bauer and agrees that "anti-Semitism," or "anti-semitism" is an "absurd construction, since there is no such thing as 'Semitism' to which it might be opposed." (Jerome A. Chanes, *Antisemitism in America Today: Outspoken Experts Explodes the Myths.* New York: Carol, 1995, p. xv). Arabs are the Jews' cousins and are, therefore, semitic also., The Arab nations, however, are fanatical in their hatred of Jews and repeatedly declare that they will finish what Adolf Hitler began; yet smugly say they cannot be antisemitic because they themselves are semites.

[2] Due to the prevailing anti-Israel sentiments throughout the Western world, books by Ramon Bennett are often difficult to obtain. All titles can be purchased from the distributors: Shekinah Books, California, U.S.A. In the first instance send an email to <rose@shekinahbooks.net>.

— *two* —

Israel, And The God Of Israel

Not too many days pass by in which the nation of Israel is not mentioned within the pages of the world's major newspapers – very often on the front pages – or found among the lead stories of television and radio news networks. This is not coincidence, it is part of Israel's divine destiny. *"God Most High, Possessor of heaven and earth"* (Genesis 14:19, 22) is *"the Holy One of Israel"* (2 Kings 19:22). He is also *"the Mighty One of Israel"* (Isaiah 1:24), and He brooks the predominantly biased and often overtly hostile reporting against His people Israel because it plays a role in the fulfillment of His inheritance's destiny.

Rarely are articles published in a daily newspaper concerning Israel that are equitable, but one such rarity was an article that appeared in the *Los Angeles Times* on May 26, 1968, almost twelve months following Israel's startling, lightening-fast military victory over five armies, three of which were each better equipped and greater in troop numbers than Israel.

The premise before the armies locked horns was that the Arabs were going to drive the Jews into the sea. One Arab commander told *Time* magazine that the Arab world "did not expect there to be one single Israeli survivor at war's end."

Often, things in our lives do not go quite the way we had been expecting. The 1967 Six-Day War certainly did not go the way the Arabs had expected. Israel was not driven into the sea and and the loss of life and equipment among the Arab armies was catastrophic. On the first day of the war Israel completely annihilated the Egyptian, Syrian and Jordanian air forces and the next five days saw the total decimation of their armies, together with those of Iraq and Lebanon. (We now know that the Soviet Union was the actual instigator of that war and had planned to bomb Israel's nuclear reactor in Dimona. The war did not go the way the Soviet Union expected either, and it aborted its plans.[1])

Israel captured some fifty-two thousand square kilometers (twenty thousand square miles) of enemy territory during the war. Israel, holding such large areas of Arab lands, thought she would be able to return the lands in exchange for a lasting peace with the Arab world. When Israel made its "land for peace" offer, things did not go the way she had hoped. The Arab summit in Khartoum, Sudan, then issued the now famous statement known as the Three No's:

> No peace with Israel!; No recognition of Israel!; No negotiations with Israel.

Thus Israel still holds much of those former Arab lands today.

Anwar Sadat became president of Egypt in 1970. Three years later he launched the October Yom Kippur War against Israel in tandem with Syria but, again, the war strayed from its planned path and did not go the way Egypt and Syria expected. Ten days after the surprise invasion of Israel on the Jewish nation's most solemn religious day, the Israel Defense Force had driven all aggressor armies from her land and in twenty days were knocking at the gates of the cities of Damascus and Cairo.

The Soviet Union, which had hegemonic power throughout the Arab world and the Middle East at that time, threatened to strike Israel with a nuclear bomb if the Israel Defense Force did not pull back. The United States was allied with Israel but had no stomach for a nuclear confrontation with the Soviet Union. Henry Kissinger, then President Richard Nixon's National Security Advisor and Secretary of State, endeavored to pressure Israel into halting her advance and end the war, but Israel repeatedly refused.

Kissinger withheld urgently needed spare parts from Israel, even threatened to provide weapons to the Arab armies for use against Israel. Nixon, who had never shown himself friendly toward Israel, withstood Kissinger and ordered a massive airlift of military equipment and spare parts to Israel. Caught between a rock and a hard place, between alienating her strongest and closest ally or stopping short of her military objectives, Israel opted for the latter and pulled back, but not before Egypt, Syria and another twelve Arab armies who had joined the fray, had all suffered humiliating and devastating defeats.

President Anwar Sadat was riding a wave of pacifist sentiment from among his war-weary people and they had no more heart to make war. Sadat subsequently came to Israel in November 1977 declaring:

No more war!

A peace treaty was signed between Egypt and Israel in 1979. Israel ceded to Egypt all the Egyptian lands captured in 1967 and 1973. Sadat's reward for making peace with Israel was his assassination on October 6, 1981, as he watched a military parade commemorating the 1973 war.

Jordan has also signed a peace treaty with Israel and there was an exchange of territories that satisfied both Israel and Jordan. No other Arab states besides Egypt and Jordan have attempted to make peace treaties with Israel.

Syria and Iran fight a proxy war against Israel through Hizb'allah in Lebanon and Hamas in Gaza. The Palestinians as a whole are committed to a continual low-grade war against Israel while always pleading with the United States, the European Union, and the so-called international community to apply pressure upon Israel in order to force her to make further concessions. Israel has ceded thousands of square kilometers (miles) of territory to the Palestinians and has built hospitals, schools, and universities for them. In return, Israel has received nothing, apart from an upsurge in terror and missile attacks against her civilian population.

It should also be noted here that following Israel's announce-ment of statehood on May 14, 1948, not only did seven Arab armies invade Israel the following day in a bid to destroy the nascent state, but the Arab world drove out some eight hundred and fifty thousand Jews from within its population – after mostly confiscating their houses, lands, and wealth.

On the day Israel declared statehood its population numbered around six hundred thousand persons in total. And Israel not only had to wage a war of self-defense against seven armies – each superior in weapons, troops, and training – but she also had to absorb hundreds of thousands of Jewish refugees that were being driven out from the Arab world.

Amazingly, Israel not only managed to win the war, now known as the War of Independence, but she also doubled the size of the state with the territory captured from the invaders. Israel's population more than doubled, too, owing to the refugees it absorbed from Arab countries and countless other Jews who made their way 'home' to Israel, and who joined their brethren in the fight for the state's survival.

Of the Arabs who either fled their homes or lost them in the Arab-Israeli wars of 1948-49 and 1967, only Jordan ever accorded any of them citizenship. In the West Bank, up until 1988, all Palestinians, including the refugees, held Jordanian citizenship. But this was annulled by King Hussein when he relinquished his claim to that territory. A prominent Palestinian legal expert, Anis F. Kassim, described the abrupt measure in the following terms:

> . . . more than 1.5 million Palestinians went to bed on 31 July 1988 as Jordanian citizens, and woke up on 1 August 1988 as stateless persons.

In 2008 the Jordanian government quietly began canceling the citizenships of Palestinian Arabs living in Jordan in order to preclude them from remaining in Jordan in the advent of a peace treaty being reached between the Palestinians and Israel.

The Hashemite Kingdom of Jordan encompasses seventy-seven percent of the original Promised Land and, while the exact percentile is not known due to no official data existing, it is widely believed that somewhere between seventy and eighty percent of Jordan's population is of Palestinian origin; with a Jordanian population of some six million that makes for a whole lot of stateless persons today. Israel shares the remaining twenty-three percent of the original Promised Land with those who have taken to calling themselves Palestinian Arabs.[2]

At the time of writing the Palestinian leadership in Ram'allah is trying to establish a state of Palestine on two rather small slivers of land – the West Bank and the Gaza Strip. Given the vast area of land that makes up Jordan, together with the huge Palestinian population of Jordan, a more logical state of Palestine would be Jordan itself. This was not lost to the Jordanians and was very apparent to the first monarch of Jordan, King Abdullah.

King Abdullah wanted to call his new country, "The Hashemite Kingdom of Palestine," but gave way to British pressure and called it "Transjordan," which was later changed to "The Hashemite Kingdom of Jordan," now commonly referred to as Jordan. King Abdullah said, in 1948, that "Palestine and Jordan are one . . . ." Abdullah was assassinated in 1951 by a Palestinian on the Temple Mount.

In 1970 the then Crown Prince Hassan, heir to Jordan's throne, told the Jordanian National Assembly:

> Palestine is Jordan and Jordan is Palestine. There is one people and one land, with one history and one destiny.

In 1974, Yasser Arafat, the leader of the terrorist Palestine Liberation Organization (PLO) said: "What you call Jordan is actually Palestine." In 1981, Abdullah's son, King Hussein, said: "The truth is that Jordan is Palestine and Palestine is Jordan." He repeated that in 1984. On October 9, 2012, the former Crown Prince of Jordan, Prince Hassan, was again pushing his "Jordan is Palestine" belief when he told Palestinians in Amman that the West Bank is part of the Hashemite Kingdom of Jordan.

Succinctly commenting on Prince Hassan's October speech in Amman, Mudar Zahran, a Palestinian-Jordanian writer living in London as a political refugee, wrote *inter alia* in an October 22 *Jerusalem Post* op-ed:

> in reality, Jordan is a Hashemite-occupied part of the British Mandate for Palestine, which Jews have given up in exchange for an un-fulfilled promise of peace.

Today, King Abdullah II, Hussein's son, is concerned that the overwhelming number of Palestinians in Jordan – who are "excluded from government jobs, state college education and state healthcare" – will overthrow his monarchy and take power. His fear is growing daily, driven by the so-called "Arab Spring" that is toppling the nations' leaders throughout the Middle East and has begun fomenting anti-monarchy demonstrations in Jordan.

King Abdullah II is quietly and systematically canceling all Jordanian citizenships held by ethnic Palestinians. Abdullah is seeking to complete the divorce between Jordan and the Palestinians which his late father, King Hussein, began in 1988. Reports during the writing of this book said Jordan has decided to revoke the Jordanian citizenship of Palestinian Authority (PA) and Palestine Liberation Organization officials. And Abdullah is even mulling whether to strip Palestinian Authority President Mahmoud Abbas of his citizenship.

As this book neared completion, a surprise June 2012 report from former Jordanian prime minister Ali Abu-Ghareb, and carried by the London-based *Al-Quds Al-Arabi*, a leading Arab daily, said new regulations regarding Palestinians will be issued within days, annulling the practice of citizenship revocation. Abu Ghareb said:

> a clear citizenship law must be drafted in Jordan, limiting the power of bureaucrats to arbitrarily deprive people of their citizenship. We must be clear, a Jordanian citizen is Jordanian and we must stop the practice of citizenship revocation.

The new procedure would allow Palestinians in Jordan – especially the three hundred and fifty thousand registered refugees still living in camps – better employment opportunities.

The report by Abu-Ghareb may well be disinformation meant for local consumption. No official entity of any standing from among the international community has opposed the revocation of citizenships for Jordanians of Palestinian origin. If it proves to be disinformation, it is most likely designed to calm the angry mood among at least four and a half million Jordanians of Palestinian origin whose citizenships are currently slated for revocation. A mass uprising of such magnitude due to vexation with government policy would be bloody and could well overthrow King Abdullah and the whole Hashemite monarchy.

Apart from those in Jordan, not a single Arab refugee has ever been granted citizenship in an Arab state and, as mentioned, Jordan itself has been canceling the citizenships it did extend.

The Arab world's land mass is ten percent of all the livable land on this planet and contains some seventy percent of all known oil reserves. Yet the Arab refugees still languish in filthy, poverty-stricken refugee camps without either sanitation or electricity. At the outset there was far more than double the number of Jewish refugees than Arab refugees, however, while there is not a single Jewish refugee listed anywhere in the world, Integrated Regional Information Networks (IRIN), an affiliate of the United Nations, claims there were seven million, one hundred thousand Palestinian refugees[3] as of June 2010.

It is within the framework of what has been presented above that the reader will recognize the truth contained in the following 1968 article from the *Los Angeles Times* that was mentioned earlier:

ISRAEL'S PECULIAR POSITION
by Eric Hoffer

The Jews are a peculiar people: things permitted to other nations are forbidden to the Jews. Other nations drive out thousands, even millions of people and there is NO refugee problem. Russia did it, Poland and Czechoslovakia did it, Turkey threw out a million Greeks, and Algeria a million French. Indonesia threw out heaven knows how many Chinese - and no one says a word about refugees. But in the case of Israel, the displaced Arabs have become eternal refugees. Everyone insists that Israel must take back every single Arab. Arnold Toynbee calls the displacement of the Arabs an atrocity greater than any committed by the Nazis.

Other nations when victorious on the battlefield dictate peace terms. But when Israel is victorious, it must sue for peace. Other nations, when they are defeated, survive and recover, but should Israel be defeated, it would be destroyed. Had Nasser triumphed last June [1967], he would have wiped Israel off the map, and no one would have lifted a finger to save the Jews. No commitment to the Jews by any government, including our own, is worth the paper it is written on.

There is a cry of outrage all over the world when people die in Vietnam or when two Blacks are executed in Rhodesia. But when Hitler slaughtered Jews, no one remonstrated with him. The Swedes, who are ready to break off diplomatic relations with America because of what we do in Vietnam, did not let out a peep when Hitler was slaughtering Jews. They sent Hitler choice iron ore, and ball bearings, and serviced his troops trains to Norway.

The Jews are alone in the world. If Israel survives, it will be solely because of Jewish efforts. And Jewish resources. Yet at this moment, Israel is our only reliable and unconditional ally. We can rely more on Israel than Israel can rely on us. And one has only to imagine what would have happened last summer [1967] had the Arabs and their Russian backers won the war, to realize how vital the survival of Israel is to America and the West in general.

I have a premonition that will not leave me; as it goes with Israel so will it go with all of us. Should Israel perish the holocaust will be upon us.

Israel has been likened to a clock that determines the time left to this world. The author, along with other Bible academics, believe the hands on the clock are in the last hour and steadily approaching midnight. Upon the midnight stroke the world as we know it will cease to be. The seven plagues of the wrath of God will be poured out upon the earth (Revelation 15:6-16:21). The world's media, in its duplicity, hastens us toward that day as does the inherent antisemitism found in the heart of man.

The above article from the *Los Angeles Times*, remember, was written more than forty-four years ago. A few persons saw the injustices that were being applied to Israel four decades ago and, alas, there are even less that see them today, even though the injustices have increased a thousandfold. Israel is on center stage and the nations and politicians of the world are throwing rotting fruit at her from the balconies simply because she has had the *chutzpah* to survive.

We must never lose sight of God being in complete control. He chose the descendants of Abraham, through the line of Isaac (Genesis 21:12), to be His *"special people"* (Titus 2:14), His own *"inheritance"* (1 Kings 8:53) from among the peoples of the world. God will never spurn His *"inheritance."* In years past He has disciplined Israel, often severely. He has hid His face from her on more than one occasion and even put her aside for a time, but He will never cast off His *"inheritance."* God has not finished with Israel. He knows what she needs and will ensure she gets it and fulfills her destiny. Antisemitism, media and political duplicity play right into His hands.

The Bible is the most quoted, most misunderstood, and most misapplied book in the world. Contemporary man generally dismisses God with a *bon mot* and Christians, especially those in the West, tend to misunderstand, underestimate, and limit Him in their minds. Simply put: God is the first cause of everything. Because God is, we are, and everything else is. He is self-caused, self-contained and self-sufficient.

The promises of God are of no value unless we first understand the nature of God. He is not just mighty, He is *"Almighty"* (Genesis 35:11). God is Sovereign, He is the *"only Potentate"* (1 Timothy 6:16). He is not merely powerful, He is *"Omnipotent"* (Revelation 19:6), which means He has universal, unlimited power, and for this reason He is referred to as *"The Power"* (Matthew 26:24).

Almighty God is also omnipresent: *"God is Spirit"* (John 4:24) and is everywhere – His Spirit fills *"heaven and earth"* (Jeremiah 23:24) – *"in Him we live and move and have our being"* (Acts 17:28). Therefore God is closer than our own breath. A. W. Tozer summed it up thus:

> Wherever we are, God is here. There is no place and can be no place where He is not.

God's own statement differs little in meaning to Tozer's:

> *"Can anyone hide himself in secret places, so I shall not see him?" says the LORD; "Do I not fill heaven and earth?" says the LORD* (Jeremiah 23:24).

The Almighty Creator God has absolute rule over the affairs of man and the events that shape his history:

> *He changes the times and the seasons; He removes kings and raises up kings; He gives wisdom to the wise and knowledge to those who have understanding* (Daniel 2:21).

> *I form the light and create darkness, I make peace and create calamity; I, the LORD, do all these things* (Isaiah 45:7).

The long and the short of this is that God calls the shots in this world, not those with extreme wealth and influence, not the news media, and certainly not the politicians.

The media is the world's mouthpiece. Daily reports concerning Israel are mostly unbalanced and biased against Israel. They are lacking a serious 'other side' and also lacking any real information about the roots of the Middle East conflict.

It is not really surprising that the media's journalists and editors do not report factually on the conflict when they do not first understand the reason for the conflict. Their reporting shows an abysmal ignorance of the facts, which in turn leads to their bias and misrepresentation of the situation.

Major television news networks, leading newspapers and news magazines, control, manipulate and often completely falsify the news for their own ends.[4] Thus they control and manipulate the judgments of their viewers and readers. All this is beneficial to God because it hastens the fulfillment of what was prophesied aeons earlier.

God's nature is diametrically opposed to that of the world's leaders, the politicians. God *"cannot lie"* (Titus 1:2). Further, it *"is impossible for God to lie"* (Hebrews 6:18). Conversely, the great majority of politicians are pathological liars who could pass a polygraph test without the blinking of an eye. The media and politicians firmly believe it is they who are in control of world events when in reality they are little more than puppets dangling on strings above the world's stage. Man has free choice, but man's choices are ultimately God's foreordained decrees. Absurd? Perhaps. But true nevertheless.

It would be reasonable to argue that God is narrow-minded due to His restricted interests. His parochial interests are *"love"* (1 John 4:16), *"righteousness, justice, mercy, truth"* (Psalms 89:14) and *"holiness"* (1 Peter 1:16).

At the same time it would be fair to state that God is a universalist because His heart's desire is that every person of every tribe and tongue *"be saved and to come to the knowledge of the truth"* (1 Timothy 2:4). Pontius Pilate posed the question:

"What is truth?" (John 18:38). The answer is that God is *"truth,"* and He desires that all men come to know Him.

God's big picture includes all the nations of the earth (Isaiah 14:26), therefore God is a globalist.

Ponder some of God's statements and see if it could not be honestly said that God is also a dogmatist? For example:

> *Indeed before the day was, I am He; And there is no one who can deliver out of My hand; I work, and who will reverse it?* (Isaiah 43:13).

> *For I am God, and there is no other; I am God, and there is none like Me, declaring the end from the beginning, and from ancient times things that are not yet done, saying, "My counsel shall stand, and I will do all My pleasure," calling a bird of prey from the east, the man who executes My counsel, from a far country. Indeed I have spoken it; I will also bring it to pass. I have purposed it; I will also do it*
>
> (Isaiah 46:9-11).

As the author's late friend, Derek Prince, once said:

> With God, both the actual and the possible are subject to His command and control — everything is obedient to the voice of God.

Zionism is something the majority of the world's population has come to despise of late; however, it is difficult to escape the indisputable: God Himself is a Zionist:

> *The LORD loves the gates of Zion more than all the dwellings of Jacob* (Psalms 87:2).

> *For the LORD has chosen Zion; He has desired it for His dwelling place* (Psalms 132:13).

> *For Zion's sake I will not hold My peace, and for Jerusalem's sake I will not rest . . .* (Isaiah 62:1).

> *The LORD also will roar from Zion, and utter His voice from Jerusalem; the heavens and earth will shake...* (Joel 3:16).

Thus says the Lord *of hosts: "I am zealous for Zion*
with great zeal; with great fervor I am zealous for
her" (Zechariah 8:2).

God can do (and does) whatever He likes, and no one, nor the aggregate of all this planet's inhabitants, can prevent Him from doing it. Millions scoff at the very idea of an Almighty God, but that in no way negates His existence or involvement in world events: *"Professing to be wise, they became fools"* (Romans 1:22). One man who professes to be wise is Al Gore, the former Vice President of the United States and a Nobel laureate and Oscar winner for his skewed work about global warming. On page 342 of his book *Earth in the Balance* Gore wrote:

> Refusing to accept the earth as our sacred mother, these Christians have become a dangerous threat to the survival of humanity. They are a blight on the environment and to believe in Bible prophecy is unforgivable.

Gore campaigned in 2000 to become president of the United States and he could have been elected; he could have become the most powerful man in the world. George W. Bush owed his narrow victory to the same Christians Gore vilified. Fortunately, America was spared the chagrin of having Gore run for president in the 2004 election.

Israel is vilified daily by the media, politicians, and the nations alike; however, Almighty God says He is *"the Holy One of Israel, and his Maker"* (Isaiah 45:11), and He refers to Himself as *"the* Lord *God of Israel"* one hundred and eight times. This bodes ill for all those who malign His people because He also says regarding His people Israel: *"I will . . . curse the one despising you"* (Genesis 12:3).[5] Therefore it should not come as much of a surprise that many nations and individuals today are in a dreadful mess physically and financially.

It is a given that we are in the last days of the End Times; there are more prophecies to be fulfilled, but not too many. Time, as we understand it, is running out.

Virtually all predictions made by the author in his books *SAGA: Israel and the Demise of the Nations*, *Philistine: The*

Great Deception, and *The Wall: Prophecy, Politics and Middle East "Peace"* have either been fulfilled or are in the process of fulfillment today. The few predictions as yet unfulfilled are for the longer term, possibly requiring several more years before their times arrive. We intend, however, to move on from what the author has previously committed to print except for where a recap of facts or a situation is deemed necessary. We shall look at the current stream of events, both political and physical, and where this is leading Israel.

---

[1] See the book: *Foxbats Over Dimona: The Soviets' Nuclear Gamble in the Six-Day War* by Isabella Ginor and Gideon Remez (Yale University Press, New Haven & London, 2007).

[2] See Chapter 7 of the author's book *Philistine: The Great Deception* for documented details of how the recent term "Palestinian" Arab came into being.

[3] See Chapter 6 of the author's book *Philistine: The Great Deception* for the absurd details of how the United Nations arrive at the number of Palestinian refugees.

[4] See Chapter 9 of the author's book *Philistine: The Great Deception* for an in-depth look at the deceit and duplicity of the media.

[5] Almost all English translations of Genesis 12:3 in the Bible read much the same: *"I will bless those who bless you and curse him who curses you; and in you all the families of the earth shall be blessed."* The first third and the last third of the verse is translated correctly, but the middle section is not. No doubt this is due to tradition, which, along with prejudice, are the two things stronger that fact. There are two Hebrew words used for "curse" in the mid-section of the verse. The first is the word אָרַר (*arar*), the same word God used to curse the serpent in Genesis 3:14; the word means "to curse bitterly." Inside a dissected common snake four atrophied legs can be found – the evidence of the power of the word.

The second Hebrew word used in the verses's mid-section is קָלַל (*kilel*), which means "to make light of," "to despise," "to hold in contempt." What God wishes to communicate to man is that all who despise, hold in contempt, or make light of Abraham – and by extension, all Jews – God will curse with an exceedingly bitter curse.

A few Bible versions do translate the verse correctly, one of these is A Literal Translation of the Holy Bible by Jay P. Green Sr., and his translation reads:

> *And I will bless those who bless you, and curse the one who despises you; and in you shall all the families of the earth be blessed.*

— *three* —

Israel, And Prophecy

Since her rebirth in 1948 Israel has absorbed Jewish immigrants from some one hundred and forty-one countries. And as global antisemitism increases, so it drives more Jews home to Israel. Jews have settled permanently in Israel from every section of the planet. Many of these regional areas are extremely diverse in culture – Arab, Mediterranean, European, North American, South American, Chinese, Russian, African, *et cetera*.

Ashkenazi Jews (eastern European origin) generally consider themselves to be a cut above Sephardi Jews (origins in Spain, Portugal, the Balkans, the Levant, England, the Netherlands and the Americas). Ashkenazis look down their noses at those whom Israelis now openly term Mizrahis – "easterners." Mizrahi Jews were forced out of Arab countries at the founding of the state of Israel. Many thousands came from Morocco and brought a distinctive culture that is closely akin to traditional Arab. According to Matt Rees, a former Jerusalem bureau chief for *Time* magazine, in his book, *Cain's Field: Faith, Fratricide, and Fear in the Middle East*, he quotes David Ben-Gurion, Israel's first prime minister. Apparently, Ben-Gurion needed the Moroccan Jews for the defense of the new state but rejected their culture. Ben-Gurion said:

> The Moroccan Jew took a lot from the Moroccan Arabs. The culture of Morocco I would not like to have here.

Despite it being vehemently denied by the ruling Ashkenazi élite, mizrahis are discriminated against and positions of importance are, more often than not, withheld from them.

Russian immigrants tend to detest the dark-skinned Ethiopians and many fights involving knives have taken place between them. On the flip side, not too many Israelis like the average Russian immigrant who they rightly see as being largely responsible for the manifest jump in Israeli crime statistics, especially involving the burgeoning human trafficking trade – the forcing of women into prostitution.

Apparently it is not only Russian immigrants who despise Ethiopian Jewry. In a December 2007 article in *Yediot Aharonot* it was reported that a Petah Tikva school had separated four Ethiopian girls from their peers. As in the days of South African apartheid the girls were assigned a single teacher responsible to teach all of their subjects; the girls were allotted separate recess hours and were driven to and from school separately.

Israel is divided by ethnicity and racism.

The first large wave of immigrants arrived from Russia in the early 1900s; however, a large number of devoutly religious Jews had lived for centuries in areas that were later included in the modern state of Israel. The influx of godless socialists was diametrically opposed to the beliefs and lifestyle of those clinging to orthodox Judaism. A great divide between secular and religious appeared in Israel the moment the Russian *olim* (new immigrants) set foot in what was then called Palestine. Almost a century later the secular-religious divide has opened into a gaping chasm with genuine hatred between many of the secular humanists and the religious ultra-orthodox.

Secular-humanist Israelis want no truck with religion and deeply resent Israeli governments allocating around one billion United States dollars of their hard-earned, highly-taxed incomes to the ultra-orthodox each year. The money is used to finance the religious schools and social welfare of the ultra-orthodox, most of whom never join the workforce or serve in the Israel Defense Force. The ultra-orthodox, on the other hand, believe the state should support their Torah (first five books of the Bible – the Law of Moses) studies and their large families, and look upon secular Israelis as little more than trash for transgressing the Torah.

One ultra-orthodox Jewish sect, Neturei Karta, rejects outright Israel's right to exist as an independent state. Its members call for the destruction of the "blasphemous Zionist entity" and speak

Yiddish rather than Hebrew, Israel's official language. Neturei Karta, and one or two other groups of ultra-orthodox Jews, consider Hebrew to be a holy language, to be used only in prayer, Torah reading, and Torah instruction.

Four black-clad members of Neturei Karta received accolades from Iranian president Mahmoud Ahmadinejad and attendees at a conference in Iran during October 2005, held under the name, "The world without Zionism." In November 2007, outside the venue of the Annapolis peace summit, two dozen black-clad Neturei Karta anti-Zionists traded insults with a dozen or so black-clad pro-Israel Lubavitcher Hassidim.

In the author's book *When Day And Night Cease*, it was stated that in 1980, the year the author made *aliya* to Israel, there were only about three hundred Israeli Jews believing in Yeshua (Jesus). As the years have passed so that number has greatly increased. From the lowly three hundred in 1980, the Israeli body of Christ had grown beyond twenty thousand persons by the end of the first decade of the new millennium.

Jewish believers in Jesus are known as Messianic Jews, and their *kehilot* (congregations) are to be found everywhere throughout Israel today. To the minds of most Jews, every Christian and every Messianic Jew is a "missionary," and the understanding that Jews hold of the word "missionary" is, "one who is paid to change the religion of another." Therefore, many Israelis despise Messianic Jews and refuse to employ them or rent them a place to live.

There are a few groups devoted entirely to combatting Messianic Jews and messianic Judaism. Harassment of Messianic Jews has often gone well beyond inducing employers to fire them or getting landlords to break rental contracts. Gathering places for Messianic Jews are often vandalized and large rocks have been thrown through windows onto the heads of worshippers. Some years ago a meeting place in Tiberius was set on fire, forcing the congregation to meet in various locations in a forest for two years.

In 2008, a bomb, disguised as an anonymous Purim gift in a basket, was left at the door of a Messianic pastor in Ariel; the bomb exploded when his fifteen-year-old son lifted the cover of the basket, critically injuring him. The bomb damaged the pastor's apartment, destroying much of what they owned, and the son was taken to hospital – blind, covered with blood and burns, and with his body full of screws and nails that were packed around the explosive. Almost two years later an American-born ultra-orthodox Jew was arrested and charged with two counts of attempted murder.

Israel is divided by religious intolerance.

Jewish believers in Jesus do not wish to be called "Christian" due to the Church's persecution of Jews throughout the ages. Hundreds of thousands of Jews, perhaps millions, were murdered by church-going Gentiles, egged-on by historically prominent Christian leaders and preachers.[1] In an obvious allusion to this, Barry Rubin began a September 12, 2011, *Jerusalem Post* op-ed with:

> Most Jews today (or should I merely say many?), even the most secular, have a tremendous fear of Christians – especially fervent believers of the type represented today by Evangelicals and conservatives. There is a material basis for this fear based on past Jewish experience.

Fear and hatred of Christianity are deeply rooted within the Jewish psyche. The Jewish people have suffered terribly under a yoke of Christian antisemitism. Jewish hatred of Christianity often raises its ugly head in attacks against Protestant churches and Catholic convents in Israel, together with overt harassment of Jewish believers in Jesus. Much of the Southern Baptist church in Jerusalem was burnt to the ground in 1982; a few years later its bookstore was firebombed, and in 2007 another serious attempt was made to raze the rebuilt church to the ground. In early 2012 Hebrew graffiti was spray-painted on the exterior stone walls, it read: "Death to Christians."

Several years ago booby-trap grenades were attached to doors of a Catholic convent; fortunately no one was injured. Religious hatred runs deep in Israel.

The Jewish people as a whole must deal with the question of its participation in the crucifixion of Jesus Christ, God's *"only begotten Son"* (John 3:18). The Jews must deal with the issue in order to be healed, both as individuals and also collectively as a people. For too long the Jewish people has denied having any part in Jesus' death, but the mass of historical evidence to the contrary would fill a football stadium.

It is an insult to the Western world's intelligence for the Jewish people to continue with its ridiculous charade concerning the crucifixion of Jesus. It is galling for Gentiles to keep hearing and reading denials by Jews of any Jewish culpability in the death of Jesus.

After the resurrection of Jesus the high priest, the chief priests, the captain of the temple, and the elders of Israel brought the apostles before the Jewish council for having preached the good news of redemption through Jesus. The high priest said:

> *Did we not strictly command you not to teach in this name? And look, you have filled Jerusalem with your doctrine, and **intend to bring this Man's blood on us!*** (Acts 5:28).

The Jews are consistent. They denied their culpability then and they still deny it today. The same lame excuse about the Gentiles being responsible has been trotted out for nigh on two millenniums, and still gets daily airings. That the Jews had a hand in the crucifixion of Jesus is fact, not some reprehensible anti-semitic smear. The Jews say the Gentiles killed Jesus: Gentiles did physically nail Jesus to the cross, certainly, but only after the Jewish leaders of the time had taken Him into custody and later forcibly delivered Him to the Romans. Then they stirred-up the masses and had them call for Pilot to crucify Jesus, and they prevailed.

The Jews had their part in the crucifixion of Jesus as did everyone else. Everyone, Jew and Gentile, had a hand in it – we are all guilty, we are all to blame for the physical death of Jesus, but the greater shame belongs to those who refuse to admit their participation in mankind's ultimate shameful act.

But Jesus had to die. That is what He came for – to take away the sin of the world. And the world includes the Jewish people. Only an imbecile would say the Jews killed Jesus when it is so patently obvious from all historical accounts that Gentiles were involved right up to their necks in it as well. We all killed Jesus. It was the author's sin, the reader's sin, and everybody else's sin that killed him – both Gentile and Jewish.

The conclusion of the matter is as follows: Gentiles need to look to their own hearts and release the Jews from two thousand years of unjust condemnation; Jews need to get real, face reality, and admit what every thinking Western person already knows – that Jewish hands were stirring the boiling pot well before the Gentiles got involved in the crucifixion of Jesus. Continual, pathetic denials tend to make all Jews appear obnoxious in the eyes of millions of Gentiles. To Jewish readers the author says: "Finish with this thing that hangs like a millstone around the neck of the Jewish people and bows it down with its weight. If you refuse to admit Jewish complicity in the crucifixion of Jesus – the paschal lamb of God – the coming wilderness experience will either wring it from you, or bury you in the desert."

The author is a true friend of Israel. He has defended Israel and the Jewish people thousands of times in conferences, seminars, and public meetings on every continent. He has defended Israel and the Jewish people on numerous television and radio programs, and his pro-Israel books are read in multiple languages worldwide. Only a true friend can tell another friend hard truths and still love the friend. The days of Chrysostom, Torquemada, and Luther are past, they will not return. Saddam Hussein has gone, Ahmadinejad and Erdogan will follow them soon enough. What of the Jews? They are eternal. They will never leave center stage – the remnant, that is.

By winning three major wars launched against her by Arab nations, Israel has unintentionally inherited over one million six hundred thousand Arabs along with the land captured in those wars of self defense. These Arabs were granted Israeli citizenship and receive the same medical and welfare benefits as the Jewish population. But there the equality ends. Arab workers receive significantly lower wages and are also discriminated against insofar as their local bodies not receiving equal funding like Jewish local authorities.

As an example of everyday Jewish exploitation of Arabs, the

author's apartment is on the fifth floor of a six-floor 'walk-up' building in downtown Jerusalem. The building has one hundred and eight stone steps from the basement to the top floor. The owner of the building currently pays an Israeli businessman a monthly fee (collected in advance from the tenants) of thousand of sheqels to have all the steps and landings washed four times each week. The Israeli employs Arabs to do the physical work, but allocates only one hour for his Arab worker to clean all the steps from top to bottom, for this the man is paid only twenty-two sheqels (five dollars and sixty cents). This means that each month the Israeli employer receives almost eighty-five percent of all the money paid for cleaning the building while the Arab man only gets fifteen percent (three hundred and fifty-two sheqels – around ninety-two dollars). The Israeli employer has contracts to clean other buildings, including banks. His Arab workers are little more than underpaid slaves. What the Egyptians did to the children of Israel in the days of the Pharaohs, so Israel does to her Palestinian slaves today.

An Association for Civil Rights poll in December 2007 showed that fifty percent of Israel's Jewish population believe Israeli Arabs do not deserve equal rights. This racist discrimination has been a constant source of discontent for the Arab sector that makes up twenty-one percent of Israel's population and it is often a catalyst for violence against Jews.

With regard to her Arab population Israel must truly learn what the LORD meant when He commanded them at Sinai:

> *And if a stranger dwells with you in your land, you shall not mistreat him. The stranger who dwells among you shall be to you as one born among you, and you shall love him as yourself; for you were strangers in the land of Egypt: I am the LORD your God* (Leviticus 19:33-34).

Israel is divided by class discrimination.

The advent of the abortive Israeli-Palestinian peace process, under the guidance of the liberal, secular-humanist Ashkenazi élite, created yet another fracture within Israeli society. As is so often seen with peoples under siege, the besieged take upon themselves the charges and guilt leveled at them by the oppressors. A large percentage of the Israeli population today, especially the liberal, secular-humanist leaders of the ruling élite, have absorbed the charges and guilt of their oppressors and believe that in order to experience peace they must cede huge areas of the Promised Land to those who have little or no valid claim to it. Areas slated to be ceded to the Palestinians today by the liberal left, under the threat of increased terror attacks against Israeli civilians – men, women, children and babes-in-arms – contain tens of thousands of Israeli homes and businesses worth billions of dollars.

Many of the current leaders of Israel have embraced the charges and guilt, not only of the Palestinians, but also of the international community. They have become zealous in efforts to forcefully evacuate thousands of Jews from areas of biblical Israel. In July 2005 they forcefully evicted nine thousand four hundred and eighty Jews from Gaza and northern Samaria. Plans are being made today by left-wing politicians for a coming forced eviction of up to one hundred and eighty thousand Jews living in Judea and Samaria.

Israel's liberal, godless leaders would hand over the areas taken up by the evicted people's homes, community halls, factories, greenhouses, cultivated land, *et cetera*, to the Palestinians, of whom the majority wish to see a continuation of suicide bombings and other violent attacks against Israelis.

Jews are usually credited with having exceptional brain power; however, *"the Holy One of Israel"* is dealing with His *"chosen people."* Given many of the government decisions in recent years, the following scripture is so very applicable today:

> *He deprives of intelligence the chiefs of the earth's*
> *people, and makes them wander in a pathless waste*
> (Job 12:24 NASB).

Israel's godless leaders, being spiritually bankrupt, live under a delusion. They fool themselves into believing that it is they who can and must solve the Arab-Israeli conflict and bring peace to the region. Their misguided efforts, however, spiral the nation further downward into despair and threaten to tear it asunder.

Up until September 2011, the biggest demonstrations ever held in the modern state of Israel had all been antigovernment demonstrations *vis-à-vis* the peace process. (In September 2011, almost half a million Israelis demonstrated against Israel's high cost of living and unaffordable housing. This became the largest demonstration in Israel's history.) The futility of the Oslo Accords signed on September 13, 1993, in the days of Prime Minister Yitzhak Rabin, saw a number of demonstrations in Tel Aviv and Jerusalem each with an excess of one hundred thousand protestors. Millions of Israelis saw the trap laid for Israel in Oslo while the leaders either did not or did not want to see it. Yitzhak Rabin alienated half of Israel's diverse population when he told them they could all "spin around and around like propellers" in their demonstrations – that he would continue on Oslo's path.

Several hundred Israelis were to succumb to terrorist bombings on buses, in cafes, shopping malls, *et cetera*, and tens of thousands were maimed or injured. Rabin told the world that the Israeli victims had been "sacrificed on the altar of peace."

Yitzhak Rabin was hoist by his own petard and was himself "sacrificed on the altar of peace." He was assassinated on November 4, 1995, by a religious Israeli opposed to his "peace" policies. The Oslo process all but collapsed completely in September 2000, exactly seven years following its signing. It is conceivable that this could actually have been the seven-year covenant mentioned in Daniel 9:27.

The Oslo Accords created divisions in Israel between the liberal, secular-humanists who want peace at any price, the conservative, more pragmatic Jews willing to exchange some of the captured territory in return for a real peace, and nationalistic Jews who refuse to give up one square inch or centimeter of the Promised Land.

Prime Minister Ariel Sharon, the former leader of the right-wing Likud party, came to power in 2001. Sharon changed tracks and adopted the left-wing's manifesto in 2004. Elected on solemn promises of security for Israelis and no withdrawing under fire, he launched a plan to forcibly evict nine thousand four hundred and eighty Jews from Gaza and Samaria. The eviction was due to mounting civilian and Israel Defense Force casualties from Palestinian terror groups, thus it was a n actual "withdrawal under fire." Sharon tried to pull the wool over Israeli eyes by saying that his plan was a "Unilateral Disengagement" from the Palestinians, not a withdrawal under fire. His supporters were unimpressed. They rejected his plan. Sharon forged ahead nonetheless.

Sharon's supporters deserted him, and members of his own party in the government voted against him. He fired them all. The Israel Defense Force Chief of General Staff at the time, Moshe Ya'alon, warned of increased terror attacks if Israel proceeded with the forced eviction. Ya'alon's term was cut short and he was replaced by a 'yes man' a few weeks before the eviction began.

Avi Dichter, then head of the *Mossad*, Israel's secret service, briefed the government on intelligence reports warning of increased terror following Sharon's "disengagement." He was immediately removed from his position and replaced by a more 'pliable' person. Israeli democracy is but one small step ahead of a third-world dictatorship.

Sharon's government majority dwindled away until he only had a forty-seat minority behind him in a one hundred and twenty-seat parliament. Sharon managed to hold onto power, however, by bribing parties with taxpayers' money. Finally, he brought the liberal Left and the left of the liberal Left into his government, even bringing in Arab parties that overtly voice heartfelt hatred of Jews and the state of Israel. Sharon wooed anyone and anything that could help him remain in power and force the eviction through.

The nation of Israel was split as never before. Sharon's about turn was even more dramatic than Yitzhak Rabin's, and Sharon could not move without a massive contingent of bodyguards to protect him. Demonstrations reached an heretofore unprecedented one hundred and fifty thousand protesters, and some demonstrations began to turn violent. Sharon forced through his plan to evict all Jews from Gaza and from four towns in northern Samaria, it was completed on July 30, 2005.

Sharon fled the Likud party and formed a new political party, Kadima, on November 21, 2005. Kadima was made up of Sharon's 'yes' men (and women) who also jumped ship from the

Likud party, but four months later the Kadima baton was passed by default to Ehud Olmert.

As of April 2012, more than six years after the eviction, only half of the evicted families had permanent housing; many of the evicted breadwinners still remain unemployed and most are in financial difficulties. Many children are doing poorly in school due to post trauma stress syndrome; the divorce rate among the evicted has mushroomed; and not a few of the evicted Jews – adults and teenagers – have committed suicide since the eviction took place.

And the Olmert government, which succeeded Sharon's, was planning to evict between one hundred and eighty and two hundred and fifty thousand more Jews from homes in Judea and Samaria? Albert Einstein defined insanity as "doing the same thing again and again expecting different results."

Four months following the eviction of the Jews from Gaza and northern Samaria Ariel Sharon suffered a massive cerebral hemorrhage that ended not only his political life, but also his physical life. At the time of writing, seven years later, Sharon remains in a persistent vegetative state under medical care.

There was an unofficial report that indicated Ariel Sharon carried out the eviction of Jews from Gaza and northern Samaria in order to avoid serious charges of corruption against him that were being investigated by the Israel Police. The charges were indeed put on hold in the run-up to the eviction, but Sharon's massive brain hemorrhage and his indefinite comatose condition caused the investigation to be dropped, permanently.

In January 2006, following Sharon's massive stroke, Ehud Olmert succeeded him as the leader of the developing Kadima party and as prime minister of Israel. Olmert is on record time and again in past years vowing that Jerusalem would never be divided again, that Judea and Samaria belong to Israel by divine decree, and that Israel would never relinquish the strategic Golan Heights.

Olmert soon began "negotiating" with the Palestinians and was willing to give them ninety-two percent of all Judea and Samaria – Israel's biblical heartland – and half of Jerusalem, including the Temple Mount, the holiest place in Judaism. Olmert also opened "peace" talks with Syria and was willing to cede the Golan Heights to the Syrians who, for twenty-five consecutive years, had fired artillery shells almost daily from the heights into the fields of Israeli farmers as they were being worked in the Galilee area below.

Olmert was apparently frightened that the minority Arab population in Israel would outgrow the Jewish population and eventually take control of the nation. Therefore he was eager to cede all areas with high Arab population numbers, including the eastern half of the city of Jerusalem, to the Palestinian Authority (PA) and establish indefensible borders around a truncated Jewish state.

In late 2007 Olmert found himself under three simultaneous police investigations on corruption and cronyism charges, with a fourth investigation expected to be opened at any time. According to public opinion polls Olmert was perceived to be both Israel's most corrupt politician and also the most unpopular Israeli prime minister ever, with barely a seventeen percent popularity rating. Many Israelis, including a good few members of the Knesset (Israel's Parliament), accuse Olmert of pushing negotiations with the Palestinian Authority and Syria in an effort to flee from police investigations. National Union MK Zvi Hendel said in December 2007 that Olmert is:

> the most dangerous prime minister Israel has ever had. Today
> he is a wounded animal and there is nothing more dangerous.

Godlessness has been rampant in successive Israeli governments for years and this is the major cause of her present distress. The *"Maker of Israel"* (Isaiah 45:11) has laid down the terms and conditions for Israel's leaders:

> *He who rules over men must be just. Ruling in the*
> *fear of God* (2 Samuel 23:3b).

Apparently, there is no fear of God in the eyes of either Olmert or in those of his slavish minions. The damage done to Israel as a nation by successive godless, corrupt leaders is inestimable. Only time and God will tell what melancholia Olmert would have bequeathed to Israel. For as surely as day follows night, distress for many would have been the consequence of Olmert's desperate attempt to retain his hold on power while dodging criminal indictments for corruption and cronyism.

Yitzhak Rabin ceded thousands of square miles of territory to Yasser Arafat, the godfather of international terrorism, and died from an assassin's bullet just as this author had predicted in his book *Philistine: The Great Deception.* Ariel Sharon evicted nine thousand four hundred and eighty Jews from their homes in Gaza and northern Samaria and by so doing turned Gaza into the Hamastan that it is today. Sharon suffered a massive stroke and lies like a vegetable in a hospital bed. Ehud Olmert was forced to step down as prime minister due to the many investigations he was under. At the time of writing in October 2012, Olmert was still defending himself against corruption charges in court. Apparently, the corruption and cronyism charges prevented Olmert from ceding Judea and Samaria, parts of Jerusalem, and the Golan Heights, which was his plan to do. The corruption charges may well have ruined his political career, but they might also have saved his life.

Following the Gaza eviction the daily bombardment of Israel with missiles and mortars from Gaza was stepped up, primarily from the areas vacated by Israel. In 2008 southern Israel was hit by more than two thousand Palestinian rockets and mortars.

At the time of the eviction almost half of all Israelis believed it was a great mistake to retreat from Gaza. In November 2007 the conscience of National Infrastructure Minister Binyamin Ben Eliezer got the better of him, and he went public:

> I admit and confess I was with those who strongly supported Ariel Sharon, and today I say with my head held high: We erred, we made a very big mistake.

Israel should not have to abide godless leaders who admit, and with "head held high," of having made a "big mistake" that has caused the deaths of Israeli civilians and the destruction of their homes by terrorist rocket fire.

In the waning days of December 2008, following eight years of missiles and mortars raining down upon southern Israeli towns and cities, Israel launched a twenty-two-day Gaza War called "Operation Cast Lead." Of course, Israel was vilified by the international community for attempting to crush Hamas's low-grade war against Israel's civilian population. The anti-Israel brigades accused Israel of war crimes and of having used disproportionate force. Disproportionate force? What use is a nation's military power if it is not allowed to be used in defense of the lives and property of its civilians?

What would the Palestinians and international community have Israel do? Prior to Operation Cast Lead almost twelve thousand missiles had been fired by the Palestinians at population centers in southern Israel. Would Israel's critics have Israel act 'proportionately' by randomly firing missile for missile, mortar for mortar, into Palestinian cities and towns? Imagine what twelve thousand missiles and mortars from Israel would have done to the Palestinian psyche. A taste of their own medicine might well temper their propensity to murder Israelis and create fear by that method.

Today there is a majority among the Jews of Israel against ceding further large areas of territory to the Palestinians who have little valid and no legal or biblical claim to it. And three-quarters of all Jewish Israelis are against any division of Jerusalem. For almost two thousand years Jews faced Jerusalem three times each day and prayed to return to their holy city. Jerusalem is the heart of the Jewish people. There is no way for a body to survive once its heart has been cut out. There has never been a Jewish power in all of Jewish history that willingly contemplated ceding Jerusalem or any part of it to others, especially to sworn enemies who deny thousands of years of Jewish connection to the Holy Land, denigrate the Jewish faith and question Israel's right to even exist.

Ehud Olmert was willing to cede large areas of Jerusalem, including the Temple Mount, the holiest place in Judaism. He had also purposed to cede most of Israel's biblical heartland – Judea and Samaria – *the mountains of Israel* (Ezekiel 37:22). The silent Israeli majority would have become the vocal majority. If a future Israeli government contemplates ceding large areas of land to the Palestinians without a *quid pro quo*, that government will no doubt experience massive anti-government demonstrations, the likes of which will make the September 2011 Social Justice demonstration appear minuscule by comparison.

Israel is divided politically and nationalistically.

Israel today is very much a divided nation. She is divided spiritually, ethnically, culturally, nationalistically, and politically. Almost two thousand years ago the following was spoken by Jesus to address a particular spiritual condition of the time:

> *Every kingdom divided against itself is brought to desolation, and every city or house divided against itself will not stand* (Matthew 12:25).

Those words of Jesus apply equally to the physical, cultural, ethnic, national, and spiritual divisions within Israel today and should be seriously heeded. If Israel does not change voluntarily, God's wrath will fall upon her and she will either change involuntarily or become *"desolate"* – only the remnant *"will stand."*

Israel is treated almost as a pariah state by most of the world's nations. The United Nations spends more time debating issues concerning Israel than it does on any other topic in the world. So great is the detestation of Israel by the vast majority of United Nations member states that one third of all United Nations resolutions concern Israel. Of the one hundred and ninety-three member nations Israel is the only country ever to be the subject of a permanent item on the United Nations Human Rights Council agenda. Israel comes up for discussion at every regular session of the Council, irrespective of crises that might be occurring elsewhere in the world. The United Nations is the most antisemitic organization in the world.

The United Nations' Security Council is made up of five permanent members – America, Russia, China, France and the United Kingdom – and ten non-permanent member countries that are elected by the General Assembly for two-year terms. Israel is the only permanent non-member of the Security Council. That is to say that Israel, in her sixty-four years of statehood, is virtually the only member out of the one hundred and ninety-three members of the United Nations never to have been invited to serve on the Security Council.

Antisemitic attacks and anti-Israel acts are rampant throughout the world and have reached epidemic proportions in a number of countries, including European states.

Israel is divided politically and ethnically from the world.

God Almighty has a plan for both Israel and the nations. This should be apparent to all who read the Bible without preconceived notions concerning doctrine or dogma. If, however, the end of the divine story concerning Israel had not been made known in the Bible it would seem obvious that, left to her own devices, Israel would be a nation without a future.

Israel is in chaos. Jewish immigration to Israel is at its lowest level for nearly two decades. Until the global financial meltdown that began in 2007, the number of Jews leaving Israel had consistently been outweighing the number of immigrants arriving for some years. Now, with Israel's economy forging ahead while other countries implode, many Israeli ex-patriots are being forced to straggle home.

For years, former Supreme Court Justice Moshe Landau had maintained a self-imposed silence – even when involved with investigating some of the most painful episodes in Israel's history. In October 2000, at the age of eighty-eight years, he broke his silence. He felt that the state of Israel was facing an apocalypse:

> I see great external dangers facing us. But the internal dangers are even bigger: the general feeling of bewilderment, the confusion of concepts, the social disintegration. And the weakness of the national will, the lack of readiness to fight for our lives. The illusion that peace will obviate our need to fight and defend ourselves. These things give me no rest. They really keep me awake and are effecting my physical health.

Judge Landau is one who sees the dangers facing Israel. Unlike some elected leaders he is not hiding his head in the sand, but speaking out. The social disintegration is eating the heart out of the nation. Corporate and retail greed has driven Israel's cost of living out of all proportion to other nations. Israel is today one of the most expensive countries in the world in which to live – and it only took a handful of decades to reach that level.

With hatred of Israel everywhere without her borders and rampant corruption and avarice everywhere within, a sense of confusion and bewilderment permeates the land. A good number of Israelis feel in their hearts that Israel indeed has no future, that they will be forced back into the Diaspora again.

Some preachers – the late Art Katz formerly being at the forefront, but replaced today by Dalton Lifsey – are propagating the message around the world that Israel will be destroyed and the people exiled from the land – driven back into the diaspora. Neither is Lifsey content just to have four million Israelis killed in his *"time of Jacob's trouble"* (Jeremiah 30:7), he also believes two thirds (Ezekiel 5:12) of all Jews everywhere, will be killed. There are approximately thirteen million Jews in the world today, therefore, according to Lifsey's math, some eight million six hundred and sixty-six thousand are going to die in his particular time of *"Jacob's trouble."*

Such false teaching is very disheartening and damaging to the psyche of many young Israelis – the spiritually immature Jewish believers in Yeshua (Jesus). Some are actually making inquiries about emigrating elsewhere with their families because of it. When the message is given to the so-called Arab Christians within Israel the majority hoot, holler, whistle, cheer, stamp their feet, and clap.

The author feels the teaching was spawned from an inherent dislike of Jews and of Israel. And surely it would be fair to say that those spreading the belief in a coming destruction of Israel and the exiling of her people would have a desire for their div- inations to come true, perhaps praying for it to happen in order to avoid being labeled false prophets. Jesus issued a warning to those who cause believers to stumble:

> *But whoever causes one of these little ones who believe in Me to stumble, it would be better for him if a millstone were hung around his neck, and he were thrown into the sea* (Mark 9:42).

The author firmly believes that the Bible clearly states in Deuteronomy Chapter 30 that the Jews will only be exiled two times from the Promised Land. The first exile began in 722 B.C.

when Tiglath-Pileser began taking away the inhabitants of the northern kingdom of Israel to Assyria. The northern tribes of Israel were systematically taken into captivity, never to return *en masse*.

Due to the great majority from the northern tribes of Israel not returning back to the land the myth of the ten lost tribes arose and is still with us. The author, however, believes the term "lost tribes" to be a misnomer. Only individuals were lost to Israel, the actual tribes never were:

> *And from all their territories the priests and the Levites who were in all Israel took their stand with him [Rehoboam]. For the **Levites** left their common-lands and their possessions and came to Judah and Jerusalem, for Jeroboam and his sons had rejected them from serving as priests to the LORD. And after the Levites left, those **from all the tribes of Israel**, such as set their heart to seek the LORD God of Israel, came to Jerusalem to sacrifice to the LORD God of their fathers. So **they strengthened the kingdom of Judah**, and made Rehoboam the son of Solomon strong for three years, because they walked in the way of David and Solomon for three years*
> (2 Chronicles 11:13-17).

Later we read that in the days of king Asa many more from those of the northern tribes poured into the southern kingdom of Judah:

> *Then he gathered all Judah and Benjamin, and those who dwelt with them from **Ephraim, Manasseh, and Simeon**, for **they came over to him in great numbers from Israel** when they saw that the LORD his God was with him* (2 Chronicles 15:9).

We should be able to accept with more than a reasonable degree of certainty that in 586 B.C., when king Nebuchadnezzar took the inhabitants of the southern kingdom of Judah to Babylon, that all twelve tribes were then represented.

The length of Judah's exile was decreed to be seventy years

(Jeremiah 29:10) after which Jews from the Babylonian exile returned back to the Promised Land.

In 2 Chronicles 17:14-19 we are informed that in the days of king Jehoshaphat Judah's standing army was well in excess of one million one hundred and sixty thousand mighty men. Compare this number to the comparatively minuscule number of forty-two thousand three hundred and sixty men that returned from the exile (Ezra 2:64.) It is patently obvious that only a tiny percentage of those going into exile came back following God's mandatory seventy-year punishment of Judah. In Ezra 1:5 we read that not all the exiled even wanted to return to Israel. They had made their lives comfortable in Babylon and Persia and were not prepared to make a new life in the Promised Land, much like the vast majority of Jews living in the Diaspora today.

Also, many who did return from the exile:

> *could not identify their father's house or their genealogy, whether they were of Israel* (Ezra 2:59).

Nevertheless, we can still be sure that among those that did return there would have been at least a smattering of Jews from each of the twelve tribes.

The second exile was to be a scattering of Israel to the four corners of the earth. This second exile was to continue until every structure in the Promised Land disintegrated through the passage of time. The Land was destined to lay desolate and empty for aeons (Isaiah 6:11-12). This second exile took place during the Roman occupation of Israel in the late first and early second centuries. The author believes it was the Romans who fulfilled the prophecy concerning *"the time of Jacob's trouble"* (Jeremiah 30:7), when most of existing Jewry was destroyed.

History shows Roman legions all but wiped out the Jewish nation by the end of the second Jewish revolt in A.D. 135. The *Encyclopædia Britannica* informs us that the end of the first Jewish revolt came:

> On the 9th of the month of Av (August 29) in AD 70, Jerusalem fell; the temple was burned, and **the Jewish state collapsed**, although the fortress of Masada was not conquered by the

the Roman general Flavius Silva until April 73. (Authors emphasis.)

The *Encyclopædia Britannica* again informs us that the second Jewish revolt "roused **the last remnants of [Israel's] Jewry**" and "**the rebellion was crushed in 135.**" (Authors emphasis.) We are also informed that the revolt was "**ruthlessly repressed**," that "almost one thousand villages were destroyed" and "In Judea proper the **Jews seem to have been virtually exterminated.**" (Authors emphasis.) The second century historian Josephus also informs us that in the siege of Jerusalem "the number of those that perished was ... **eleven hundred thousand.**" (Authors emphasis.) One million one hundred thousand of "the last remnants of [Israel's] Jewry" died in Jerusalem alone. Josephus also tells us that "ninety-seven thousand were carried captive" to Rome for sport against lions and gladiators in the great arenas. We need to bear in mind that there were only forty-two thousand three hundred and sixty Jews that returned from exile. The descendants of that minuscule number were slaughtered in the millions by their Roman conquerers.

The second exile lasted until Jews began to move back into the Promised Land in the late nineteenth century, and this second ingathering continues today and beyond.

Ezekiel 39:28 informs us that God will bring back the captives from wherever they have been scattered. He will, at a predetermined point in history, completely empty the exile, or Diaspora, as we know it today, and leave not one single Jew in it. Only bones with remain. There will be none in whom can be found the breath of life. Nevertheless, God's great work is hindered by heartless Israeli politicians who do not want to see certain Jewish descendants returning to Israel. In October 2007 Interior Minister Meir Sheetrit, himself a mizrahi, told organizations responsible for bringing Jews back to the land on aliyah:

> Don't go finding me any lost tribes, because I won't let them in anymore. We have enough problems in Israel. Let them go to America.

It was heartening to see that in October 2012, Israel announced the renewal of monthly flights to bring home to Israel the remaining *Falash Mura* (members of Ethiopian Jewry who were forcibly converted to Christianity in the nineteenth and twentieth centuries).

And on November 6, 2012, *The Times of Israel* reported that the Netanyahu government had "quietly approved," after a five-year hiatus, continued immigration of Bnei Menashe, a tribal group based in north-eastern India and in Burma that claims descent from the tribe of Menashe. Some seventeen hundred members of Bnei Menashe are already in Israel while between seven and nine thousand still remain in India and Burma.

It was mentioned earlier that Jews have come back to Israel from every region of the planet. They have historically come from one hundred and forty-one countries and some one hundred and ten languages are spoken in Israel today. There is little doubt that much trouble awaits the modern state of Israel – destruction, death, and heartache a-plenty. Arab nations surrounding Israel gnash their teeth at her. Non-Arab muslim countries – Iran, Pakistan, and Turkey – are today more belligerent than ever toward Israel; the terror militias of Hamas in Gaza and Hizb'allah in Lebanon have been supplied by Iran and Syria with many weapons – in excess of one hundred thousand short and longrange missiles that can strike every part of Israel.

Recent elections resulting from the Arab Spring has brought about the Islamization of Tunisia, Libya, Egypt, Yemen, and Morocco. Consequentially, it will only be a matter of time before a devastating regional war breaks out. Israeli cities and towns will suffer catastrophic destruction from being deluged with thousands of missiles every day. Without doubt, the worst wars depicted in the Bible are yet to come. And Israel is always the aggressors' target. Also, nuclear, chemical, and bacteriological warfare is only around the corner.

However, the author believes there is no biblical evidence indicating a third exile. Zechariah 14:2 does say in regard to Jerusalem:

> *Half of the city will go into captivity, but the remnant of the people shall not be cut off from the city.*

Here the Prophet Zechariah is speaking of only half of one city (presumably it is the half in which the author and his wife live), not millions of people from dozens of cities and towns. We know from the biblical record what Israel's true *"destiny"* is, and we also know the end of the divine plan for Israel. All this we shall soon begin to look at in some detail.

Given the current situation and after reading hundreds of articles, clippings, and pages of data, the author believes that Israel today is beginning to languish in the second chapter of the Book of Hosea. Initially, this will cause Israel a great deal of pain. The pain and distress could be avoided through national repentance; however, the Bible informs us repeatedly that Israel is *stiff-necked* (e.g. Acts 7:51). Israel never repented in the past until after a series of woes had befallen her. The history of the Jewish people is replete with suffering and tears and, unfortunately, history has the habit of repeating itself. Those that ignore history are foolish. The author's present work can, therefore, be likened to the sounding of the trumpet. It is incumbent upon all watchmen to signal the alarm, for it is written:

> *When I bring the sword upon a land, and the people of the land take a man from their territory and make him their watchman, when he sees the sword coming upon the land, if he blows the trumpet and warns the people, then whoever hears the sound of the trumpet and does not take warning, if the sword comes and takes him away, his blood shall be on his own head. He heard the sound of the trumpet, but did not take warning; his blood shall be upon himself. But he who takes warning will save his life. But if the watchman sees the sword coming and does not blow the trumpet, and the people are not warned, and the sword comes and takes any person from among them, he is taken away in his iniquity; but his blood I will require at the watchman's hand* (Ezekiel 33:1-6).

The author has devoted well over thirty years to the defense of the people of Israel and has warned the nation, along with her leaders, of the inevitable consequences of their unrighteousness.

Over the years he has received accolades from the prime minister's office, from prime ministers' advisers, and from other Israelis of note. The plaudits were for the author's defense of the state, but he has yet to see a single influential person take note of his warnings. The author is free from guilt, he has given and continues to give fair warning. And it would be remiss of this author not to remind his readers, particularly his Jewish readers, of what Jude said through the inspiration of the Holy Spirit:

> *But I want to remind you, though you once knew this, that the Lord, having saved the people out of the land of Egypt, afterward destroyed those who did not believe* (Jude 5).

It is beyond the scope of this book to deal with the entire Book of Hosea, so we shall confine ourselves to tackling a few small portions, majoring on verses fourteen and fifteen in Chapter 2:

> *Therefore, behold, I will allure her, will bring her into the wilderness, and speak comfort to her. I will give her her vineyards from there, and the Valley of Achor as a door of hope; she shall sing there, as in the days of her youth, as in the day when she came up from the land of Egypt* (Hosea 2:14-15).

In the author's experience this remarkable passage has been quoted by Christians only in an extremely positive light. Traditional interpretations have it that God is taking Israel into the wilderness to be alone with her in her restoration. The author firmly believes this to be an over-simplification of the facts. On the surface the passage indicates that a glorious restoration of Israel is going to take place. The stated restoration is a complete spiritual, physical and geographical one, and the rest of Hosea's chapter details this. But, just as a storm precedes each calm at sea, so there are troubled waters ahead for Israel before she can experience the more placid waters represented in the scripture. Before going further, however, a few words on biblical prophecy would not be inappropriate here.

Some prophecies have more than one fulfillment. To be more specific, biblical prophecies can have only one literal fulfillment, but a number have one or more 'secondary' fulfillments in addition to its literal fulfillment. In order to understand this better we should look at an actual example.

In the Book of Hosea it is written:

> *When Israel was a child, I loved him, and **out of Egypt I called My son*** (Hosea 11:1).

In the Gospel of Matthew it is written:

> *He took the young Child and His mother by night and departed for Egypt, and was there until the death of Herod, that it might be fulfilled which was spoken by the* Lord *through the prophet, saying, "**Out of Egypt I called My Son**"* (Matthew 2:14,15).

The literal fulfillment of the prophecy is the exodus of the Israelites from Egypt. The reader is sure to remember that Moses was sent to Pharaoh with divine instructions:

> *Then you shall say to Pharaoh, "Thus says the* Lord: ***Israel is My son, My firstborn.** So I say to you, 'let My son go that he may serve Me. But if you refuse to let him go, indeed I will kill your son, your firstborn'"*
> (Exodus 4:22,23).

Through the prophet Hosea the Lord is speaking of Israel being His son and of bringing the Israelite nation out of Egypt. Matthew's gospel, however, provides us with not only an example of Jewish exegesis, but also with an example of a secondary fulfillment. Matthew, a Jew writing to fellow Jews, applied Hosea's prophecy to the return of Mary and Joseph from Egypt where they had fled from Herod with the infant Jesus – God's *"only begotten Son"* (John 3:16).

The Bible is seemingly alive with oddities. It behooves us to be aware of them in order to avoid stumbling spiritually when we come across them.

Before embarking upon our journey into Hosea's prophecy a word concerning biblical context should also be included. During more than four decades of lecturing worldwide in Bible Colleges, churches, Christian conferences, seminars, *et cetera*, on every continent, the author has heard a multitude of Christian complaints against brethren for having taken Scripture out of context. Often the criticism was unjustified. Despite numbers of Bible Colleges teaching otherwise, there really can be no hard and fast rule concerning context. Many Bible students and teachers squeal about context, yet abandon it at will to accord with a tradition.

Without any argument the most authoritative Bible teacher who has ever walked the face of this earth was the Lord Jesus Christ. That being said, let us look at the way He handled the familiar passage from Isaiah in the Nazareth synagogue:

> *The Spirit of the LORD is upon Me, because He has anointed Me to preach the gospel to the poor; He has sent Me to heal the brokenhearted, to proclaim liberty to the captives and recovery of sight to the blind, to set at liberty those who are oppressed; to proclaim the acceptable year of the LORD. Then He closed the book, and gave it back to the attendant and sat down* (Luke 4:18-19, 20).

So, *nu*, what happened to the remainder of Isaiah's prophecy? Here it is:

> **and the day of vengeance of our God**; *to comfort all who mourn, to console those who mourn in Zion, to give them beauty for ashes, the oil of joy for mourning, the garment of praise for the spirit of heaviness; that they may be called trees of righteousness, the planting of the LORD, that He may be glorified*
> (Isaiah 61:2, 3).

Jesus stopped halfway through the passage. In fact He stopped midway through a sentence halfway through the passage. He gave them the good news and omitted the bad bit. Now, where is the Christian who would dare to charge our Lord Jesus with having quoted this passage out of context? The conclusion of the matter is that grace is required of all Christians. We should not be too quick to jump to conclusions and cry foul insofar as context is concerned.

In looking at Hosea 2:14-15 we shall find, specifically in verse fourteen, Hebrew words that require closer examination. And this we shall give them in order to fully understand their importance.

It is easy to miss the real point of a text when reading the Bible in languages other than the original. This should become very apparent to the reader when it is realized that our English translations of the Bible use around six thousand words whereas the Hebrew text uses nearly twelve thousand. Obviously, no translator can render the finer meanings of the Hebrew when given only half the number of tools with which to work. Therefore, we shall make good use of the original Hebrew, but translate, parse, transliterate, and explain it in order that it can be followed with understanding. The Hebrew is shown only in order that the average reader can follow the progression through the text.

------

[1] See Chapter 23, "The Great Hatred," in the author's book, *When Day And Night Cease: A prophetic study of world events and how prophecy concerning Israel affects the nations, the Church, and you,* for documentation of Christian antisemitism through the ages.

An Unwanted God

Having said that it is easy to miss the deeper meanings of the Scriptures when reading them in a language other than the original we are obliged to look at the original Hebrew text of Hosea 2:14. The Hebrew of verse 15 is unnecessary for our purposes and the English translation will not be required until much later.

It is fully expected that the majority of readers will have little or no knowledge of Hebrew. Do be aware that the author understands this. He is also cognizant of the daunting feeling readers may have at seeing a line of what might appear to be an unintelligible jumble of strange characters. Do not despair, this book was written with the non-Hebrew-speaking reader in mind. Everything will be carefully explained as we journey through the prophecy.

Hosea 2:14 is an important prophecy, it provides us with a set of keys that opens the door to Israel's divinely appointed future. These keys also indicate the future of nations. Failure to correctly understand this prophecy will lead to a misunderstanding of what is taking place in our world today, what is about to take place tomorrow, and in the days, months, and years ahead.

Below is the short Hebrew text of Hosea 2:14 (in the Hebrew Bible it is verse 16), together with both its transliteration and the English translation from the New King James Version. Hebrew is read from **right to left**, the transliteration is read from **left to right**, as in English.

First of all, the original Hebrew text:

לכן הנה אנכי מפתיה והלכתיה המדבר ודברתי על-לבה

Second of all, a transliteration of the Hebrew:

la'chen hineh unochi miftihah vehalachtihah hamidbar vedibarti al'livah.

Third of all, the text from the New King James Bible:

Therefore, behold, I will allure her, will bring her into the wilderness, and speak comfort to her.

As we travel through the verse we shall in turn place emphasis on each of the Hebrew and transliterated words that we want to scrabble about in. This will allow the reader to follow with ease.

We begin our study of the verse with the first word in the sentence, which is the first Hebrew word on the right, and the first transliterated word on the left:

לכן הנה אנכי מפתיה והלכתיה המדבר ודברתי על-לבה

la'chen hineh unochi miftihah vehalachtihah hamidbar vedibarti al'livah.

Therefore*, behold, I will allure her, will bring her into the wilderness, and speak comfort to her.*

לכן – *la'chen* – "therefore"

Whenever we come across the word *"therefore"* in the Bible, particularly at the beginning of a verse, we should not proceed further without understanding why that word is used and what the context is. Usually, we will find there are particular aspects in the preceding verses that call for a response, and here, in Hosea 2:14, the word *"therefore"* is a response to the LORD's indictment of Israel's adulterous behavior and the grim promises of divine retribution contained in preceding verses:

And I will destroy her vines and her fig trees, of which she has said, "These are my wages that my lovers have given me." So I will make them a forest, and the beasts of the field shall eat them. I will punish her for the days of the Baals to which she burned incense. She decked herself with her earrings and jewelry, and went after her lovers; but Me she forgot, says the LORD (Hosea 2:12-13).

A little further into Hosea we read more of the LORD's anger toward Israel:

Hear the word of the LORD, you children of Israel, for the LORD brings a charge against the inhabitants of

*the land: "There is no truth or mercy or knowledge
of God in the land. By swearing and lying, killing
and stealing and committing adultery, they break all
restraint, with bloodshed upon bloodshed"*

(Hosea 4:1-2).

Within seven years of Hosea's above prophecy the Prophet
Amos was also recording God's vexation with Israel's behavior:

*Thus says the LORD: "For three transgressions
of Israel, and for four, I will not turn away its
punishment, because they sell the righteous for
silver, and the poor for a pair of sandals. They pant
after the dust of the earth which is on the head of the
poor, and pervert the way of the humble. A man and
his father go in to the same girl, to defile My holy
name. They lie down by every altar on clothes taken
in pledge, and drink the wine of the condemned in
the house of their god"* (Amos 2:6-8).

Israel served the *Ba'als* (pagan gods) and a number of other
deities throughout the days of yore and consequently found
herself in more than a little hot water. The *"Holy One of Israel"*
became so incensed at Israel's perpetual spiritual adultery that
He brought powerful armies against her as punitive punishments;
they ravished the Land and took the people away as captives.
God decreed seven decades of captivity for them the first time.
They were to learn His ways before being allowed back into the
Land.

It did not take long before the returnees were again playing the
harlot with foreign gods. An angry God said:

*The more they increased, the more they sinned
against Me; I will change their glory into shame*

(Hosea 4:7).

But it was another four hundred and fifty years before Israel's
whoredom became too insufferable for the LORD (the Amorite
example in the first chapter showed that God's judgements can
take hundreds of years before they fall) more than at any time
during the preceding sixteen hundred years. The patience of *"the*

Mighty One of Jacob" ran out, again. Losing territory and wealth to neighboring armies had failed to bring a change in Israel's behavior so the LORD brought the might of the Roman Empire against it. The Land and its people were subjected to the cruel occupation of Rome and heavy taxes had to be paid to Caesar.

It was not only *"the Holy One of Israel"* who was exasperated with the Israelites. The Romans found them to be perfidious and vexatious. The Romans became the Almighty's instruments of punitive punishment. A terrible death toll was exacted from the Jews due to their rebellions, insurrections, and wars against the Romans. Over an approximate two-hundred-year period the Roman legions killed several millions of the inhabitants of the land, destroyed the city of Jerusalem, the magnificent temple that King Herod spent forty-six years building (John 2:20), and the mountain fortress at Masada that Herod had also built. The Romans dragged tens of thousands of Jews to Rome and made sport of them for gladiators and lions in their colosseums. Following the slaughter of most of her population, Israel lay in ashes for more than seventeen centuries – broken and almost devoid of people.

At the time of writing the modern state of Israel has been reborn sixty-four years. But it is already filled with abortion (abortion has taken the lives of more Jewish babies in Israel than the total number of Jewish babies and children murdered by the Nazis in WW II) fortune telling, eastern religions, the occult, prostitution, homosexuality, corruption, violence, murder, organized crime, *et cetera*. Within the leadership of Israel itself there is barely a break between one scandal and the next involving government members. Scandals of financial corruption, bribery, sexual assaults upon staff members, vote buying, double voting to ensure the passage of a particular bill, purchasing of false university degrees to obtain higher salaries, grossly and falsely vilifying another member of parliament for personal advancement, *et cetera*.

A lengthy police investigation is underway at the time of writing on a money-laundering scandal involving thousands of millions of dollars. Implicated in this impropriety are some of the richest of the rich of Israel, together with the Israeli ambassador to London.

In January 2007, the Minister of Justice was found guilty of sexually assaulting a young woman. After serving an inadequate sentence of community service he was welcomed back into the Knesset (Israel's Parliament) and appointed to the office of Vice Prime Minister. Also in 2007, the nation's eighth President was forced to leave office in disgrace; he was charged with several accounts of sexual assault upon female staff, which included two charges of rape. Following a long, drawn-out trial he was found guilty in December 2010 and sentenced to seven years in prison.

As was mentioned in Chapter three, in 2007, Prime Minister Ehud Olmert was also subject to police investigations of corruption and cronyism. On July 10, 2012, after a four-year-long trial, Olmert was found not guilty of the two main charges of corruption, due to "lack of evidence" that would prove guilt "conclusively," therefore he was acquitted on grounds of "reasonable doubt." Olmert was found guilty on a third but lesser charge of cronyism and breach of public trust and was given a one-year suspended prison sentence, three years of probation, and a fine of seventy-five thousand three hundred sheqels (nineteen thousand five hundred dollars). Reading from a twenty-seven page verdict presiding Jerusalem District Court judge Musya Arad said: "This was a grave crime, not a procedural error, a crime tainted by official corruption." Arad added that the gravity of the crime ordinarily justified a jail term, but this was "a special case." Olmert's history of corruption apparently 'bought' him some favors within the Israeli justice system. However, on November 6, 2012, the State Prosecution filed appeals against Olmert's acquittals and the leniency of the suspended sentence. The Prosecutor has said that he would like Olmert to serve prison time.

A second trial in which Olmert is implicated is ongoing at the time of writing in 2012. This new bribery trial, involving fourteen defendants, began early in July 2012 and in the first few days enough bombshells were dropped which, if true, expose a brazen and shameless underworld of illegal dealings within governmental offices. Olmert is being tried for acts allegedly committed while he was mayor of Jerusalem from 1993 to 2003.

Another former mayor of Jerusalem, Uri Lupolianski, an ultra-orthodox Jew who reigned from 2003 to 2008, is also implicated along with Olmert in what many consider to be Israel's most serious corruption scandal.

While Olmert's first trial was taking place, another trial, that of Olmert's former bureau chief, Shula Zaken, was also taking place. Zaken was charged with fraud and breach of trust offenses that took place between October 2005 and March 2006. Zaken was convicted of "one of the most serious cases of public-sector corruption in Israeli history." Zaken is also a defendant in Olmert's second corruption trial.

With elections set for January 22, 2013, Olmert, along with another convicted felon, Aryeh Deri, the former leader of the ultra-orthodox Shas party and who served a lengthy prison term for fraud and bribery, is contemplating running again for high political office. However, a November 13, 2012, Smith Research poll conducted by the *Jerusalem Post* showed that sixty-three percent of those polled said it was unacceptable that he should return to politics. Aryeh Deri, on the other hand, was ecstatically welcomed back and given the party's number two slot, "But," Deri says, "I am running Shas."

Israel's Minister of Finance stepped down in 2007 after police charged him with embezzlement and money laundering. And Israel's Foreign Minister and Deputy Prime Minister Avigdor Lieberman resigned on December 16, 2012, just five weeks before the scheduled National Elections. Lieberman stepped down following the announcement by Israel's Attorney General that he intends to charge him with breach of trust and fraud. The justice department has been working on charges against Lieberman for sixteen years! To the author's knowledge this was the third time that the department of justice has announced its intention of indicting Lieberman only weeks prior to scheduled elections, which invariably cause his party to lose seats. One can only wonder who is the more corrupt – Lieberman or the department of justice that obviously wants to harm him in the political arena. The list of corrupt government leaders and government departments is practically endless.

The Bible is replete with heartbreaking examples of what happens when Israel's leaders corrupt themselves through power, greed, women, false gods, *et cetera*. And it is undeniable that a people eventually becomes what its leaders are. In only takes one rotten apple to destroy an entire barrel of fruit.

It should be clearly understood that Israel's leaders do not have a greater propensity for corruption, greed, and godlessness than leaders of most other nations. On a points' scale of between zero and one hundred – zero being highly corrupt and a hundred being the cleanest – Transparency International's 2012 Corruption Perception Index ranked Israel, with a perceived score of sixty points, at number thirty-nine on a list of one hundred and seventy six nations. The United States was placed at number nineteen with seventy-three points, the United Kingdom at number seventeen with seventy-four points, Afghanistan, North Korea, and Somalia all tied for the perception of most corrupt country, each with eight points.

Following news of political events in other nations makes it abundantly clear that the degree of corruption, deception, and sexual fornication committed by national leaders of all political stripes in the Western world is an utter disgrace. If there is a saving grace, it is that Israel will at least incarcerate even the president of the nation. The United States allowed President Bill Clinton to go scott-free after lying before the Grand Jury about having sex with Monica Lewinsky, a White House intern.

Israeli politicians are no worse or no better than the majority of Western politicians, but the LORD rightly expects Israel to march to the beat of a different drum than that of the nations. The LORD chose Israel for Himself and commanded:

> *And **you shall be holy** to Me, for I the LORD am holy, and have separated you from the peoples, that you should by Mine* (Exodus 20:26).

The LORD consistently pointed out that Israel was holy to Him and persistently admonished His people to be holy:

> *For you are **a holy people** to the LORD your God; the LORD your God has chosen you to be a people for*

Himself, a special treasure above all the peoples on the face of the earth (Deuteronomy 7:6).

Israel was to be holy in yesteryear and is commanded to be holy today, for her God is holy:

For I am the LORD *your God. You shall therefore consecrate yourselves, and* ***you shall be holy; for I am holy*** (Leviticus 11:44).

Again and again the LORD admonished Israel to be holy: ***"You shall therefore be holy, for I am holy"*** (Leviticus 11:45) and ***"be holy,*** *for I am the* LORD *your God"* (Leviticus 20:7). Through the Prophet Moses the LORD first commanded Israel to be holy:

Speak to all the congregation of the children of Israel, and say to them: ***"You shall be holy, for I the*** LORD ***your God am holy"*** (Leviticus 19:2).

To be holy means to be set apart to the LORD, consecrated to God; it means to be morally and spiritually excellent. But those in Israel today with a heart for *"the Holy One of Israel"* and His ways are only a small minority. Most modern Israelis are liberal, secular-humanists and want no religious restrictions imposed upon them. A repeat onslaught of punitive punishments stare Israel directly in the face. Apparently, Israel never learns. It was George Santayana who wryly said:

Those who do not learn from history are doomed to repeat it.

Israel, unfortunately, has a proven track record of repeating historical blunders, much to her own chagrin and pain. After each catastrophe there is an official whitewashing of the reasons that brought it upon the nation. For example: the official religious reasoning for the Roman destruction of Jerusalem and the second temple, along with the killing of millions of Jews and their banishment from Jerusalem, is that many Jews in Jerusalem were ill-treating other Jews. That is all. The unpardonable crime of handing Jesus, the *"only begotten Son"* of *"the Most High God"* (Psalms 78:56) over for crucifixion and the terrible curse the people then brought upon themselves when they said: *"His blood be on us and on our children"* (Matthew 27:25) is not up for discussion. In some things Jews are like ostriches who bury their heads in the sand.

The distress looking Israel in the eye will certainly come upon her due to her refusal to humble herself, face the truth, and repent of her apostasy and sins. The stench of religious Jewish pride rises to heaven. In 1998 an American ultra-orthodox Rabbi, who defrauded the author of five hundred dollars, informed the author a week before swindling him:

> We Jews are righteous inside and out. Gentiles are related to pigs that wallow in their own filth.

A ray of hope for a heart-change within Israel came with a December 2011 announcement that Prime Minister Binyamin Netanyahu would emulate the practice of former prime ministers David Ben-Gurion and Menachem Begin and hold a regular Bible study group in his official residence for researchers, public officials and invited guests. Netanyahu said he was establishing the class to perpetuate love of the Bible. In March, 2010, Netanyahu's son, Avner, won Israel's National Bible Quiz, and in July 2010 Netanyahu told Larry King that he likes to study the Bible on Saturday mornings with his son, Avner.

May this fine example of leadership inspire many Israelis to develop a love for the Bible and the *"holy One of Israel."*

We must not, indeed, dare not, overlook the fact that the blessings contained in Hosea 2:14-15 cannot come upon Israel until God first deals with her over her actions specified in the preceding verses.

There are many Israel-loving people today, including several prominent leaders of large Christian ministries, who firmly believe that nothing really bad will ever happen to Israel again. Some even believe that it is unnecessary for Jews to be saved through the atoning blood of Yeshua (Jesus). The author most vociferously begs to differ.

Christians should not be afraid to swim against the current when it comes to what they truly believe. Never mind ruffling a few feathers. The following was penned by Adrian Rodgers:

> It is better to be divided by truth than united in error; it is better to speak truth that hurts and then heals than to speak a

lie; it is better to be hated for telling the truth than to be loved for telling a lie; it is better to stand alone with truth than to be wrong with the multitude.

That said, the author believes Israel faces an extremely difficult and catastrophic time before she gets restored to her *"Creator."* He also believes our Hosea passage will unfold God's plan for the restoration process that has gotten underway.

God is punishing Israel even today. One in every five Israelis has lost a family member or a friend to Palestinian terrorism during the immediate past twelve-year period. Almost thirteen percent of Israelis have had a family member or friend injured during that time, and a similar percentage have witnessed a terror attack or its immediate aftermath. Huge areas of biblical Israel, her divine inheritance, has been ceded to her enemies in a effort to find respite from terror, but peace eludes her. The LORD has again cut off parts of Israel's land and given it over to her enemies just as He gave parts of ancient Israel's inheritance into the hands of her enemies. But the pain Israel is suffering is merely an introduction to what is about to come. Israel must and will learn her lesson. Israel, despite her four thousand-year history, has failed to learn the basic principle demanded of her by her *Maker*:

> *You shall love the LORD your God with all your heart, with all your soul, and with all your strength*
> (Deuteronomy 6:5).

Israel is largely rejecting her *"Creator"* again today. There will be no punitive third exile from the Land; *"the Holy One of Israel"* has other plans.

Several times in yesteryear, when Israel became apostate and had gotten herself in deep trouble, there always came moments when her *"Holy One"* turned blind eyes and deaf ears to her cries. For example:

> *When you spread out your hands, I will hide My eyes from you; even though you make many prayers, I will not hear. Your hands are full of blood* (Isaiah 1:15).

Many Jews and Christians believe that God always answers prayers. This is bad theology. Sincere repentance always guarantees a response from the Almighty; prayer does not always have the same effect and the scripture quoted above is a proof of this. Often, when the Almighty has determined something, all prayer does is bounce, as it were, off bronze heavens. God will not hear.

The author believes Israel is at the point where God is once again shutting His ears to her cries. Israel has brought the situation upon herself. She is again in a virtual apostate condition, and with her abortion record alone her hands are full of blood.

Of necessity, the Almighty must deal harshly with Israel before she arrives at the place where she is cognizant of His involvement in her affairs. Once aware of His presence, Israel will begin to relate to Him and respond to His dealings.

The greater part of world Jewry – the author says this very deliberately – the majority of world Jewry does not believe in God. Those who are not outright atheists merely have a belief about God, not a belief in God. There is a world of difference between believing in God and believing about God; it is like the difference between night and day. It is a staggering statement and some readers may have difficulty accepting it, but "believe" means to "have confidence in," "to be convinced," "to put trust in," and to be committed to that belief.

The overwhelming majority of Jews in America and Israel are liberal, secular-humanists and secular humanism is only a naive form of atheism.

Many of the Israeli secular-humanists could care less about the Land – Israel's divine inheritance. They just want to be left alone – left alone in order to *"sit down to eat and drink, and rise up and play"* (Exodus 32:6). Israel will pay dearly for her actions for thus it is written: *"Their sorrows shall be multiplied who hasten after another god"* (Psalms 16:4).

In the final statement of Hosea 2:13 in God's indictment of Israel, He says: *"but Me she forgot."* And God's opening word in verse 14 is: ***"Therefore,"*** which begins God's reaction to being forgotten. The *"Holy One of Israel"* has set a chain of events in motion in response to Israel forgetting Him and pursuing other

loves. Israel today is rapidly becoming a spiritual and materialistic prostitute.

On the surface, verse 14 in English seems innocent enough:

> *Therefore, behold, I will allure her, will bring her
> into the wilderness, and speak comfort to her*
>
> (Hosea 2:14).

But that verse is not really as innocent as it appears. We shall
better understand this as we go along and break down the verse
into digestible portions. The innocent-looking words cover up
the political, physical, and spiritual hardships that lie ahead. The
word *"therefore"* that follows God's indictment ought to send
tremors of fear down every Jewish spine. Notice in what context
the emphasized word *"therefore"* is used in the following
passage from the Book of Nehemiah:

> *So the people went in and possessed the land; You
> subdued before them the inhabitants of the land, the
> Canaanites, and gave them into their hands, with
> their kings and the people of the land, that they might
> do with them as they wished. And they took strong
> cities and a rich land, and possessed houses full
> of all goods, cisterns already dug, vineyards, olive
> groves, and fruit trees in abundance. So they ate and
> were filled and grew fat, and delighted themselves in
> Your great goodness.*
>
> *Nevertheless they were disobedient and rebelled
> against You, cast Your law behind their backs and
> killed Your prophets, who testified against them
> to turn them to Yourself; and they worked great
> provocations.* **Therefore** *You delivered them into the
> hand of their enemies, who oppressed them; and in
> the time of their trouble, when they cried to You, You
> heard from heaven; and according to Your abundant
> mercies You gave them deliverers who saved them
> from the hand of their enemies.*
>
> *But after they had rest, they again did evil before
> You.* **Therefore** *You left them in the hand of their
> enemies, so that they had dominion over them; yet*

*when they returned and cried out to You, You heard from heaven; and many times You delivered them according to Your mercies, and testified against them, that You might bring them back to Your law. Yet they acted proudly, and did not heed Your commandments, but sinned against Your judgments, which if a man does, he shall live by them. And they shrugged their shoulders, stiffened their necks, and would not hear. Yet for many years You had patience with them, and testified against them by Your Spirit in Your prophets. Yet they would not listen; **therefore** You gave them into the hand of the peoples of the lands. Nevertheless in Your great mercy You did not utterly consume them nor forsake them; for You are God, gracious and merciful* (Nehemiah 9:24-31).

In the above passage, following the word *"therefore,"* came famine, death, exile, and oppression. It was a direct result of "forgetting" Him who had created, loved, and succored Israel. There is little difference between what ancient Israel did and what modern Israel is doing. Therefore the *"therefore"* of Hosea 2:14 will have dire repercussions for today's state of Israel. Only when Israel cries out to the LORD will He hear and turn her fortunes. But she is not crying out. She has forgotten Him, again.

Forgotten, But Not Gone

Having gotten our study of Hosea 2:14 off the ground and flying
in the previous chapter with the word *"therefore,"* we proceed to
the second Hebrew word in the verse:

לכן הנה אנכי מפתיה והלכתיה המדבר ודברתי על-לבה

la'chen **hineh** *unochi miftihah vehalachtihah
hamidbar vedibarti al'livah.*

Therefore, **behold***, I will allure her, will bring her
into the wilderness, and speak comfort to her.*

הנה – *hineh* – "behold"

The word *"behold"* is mostly used in the Bible as a means to
gain the hearer's attention; it is used to introduce something of
import. In English the word would often necessitate an exclamation mark, as it does here – it almost has the equivalent meaning of "certainly," or "surely." *"Behold!,"* therefore, is not only
meant to catch a hearer's awareness, but also urges him to heed
what follows. Used in a context such as we have in Hosea 2:14,
הנה *hineh* (*behold!*) indicates the certainty of that which follows
taking place.

When the LORD GOD speaks, He is not talking for the sake of
talking like many humans do – when He speaks the LORD is only
ever apprising man for man's own good. With that in mind we
may perhaps understand why Jesus is recorded six times in the
Gospels as having said (Matthew 11:15, for example): *"He who
has ears to hear, let him hear."*

In the following chapter of this book we shall see another
example of the word in use as an attention getter, in a threatening
statement to Pharaoh. The second example will unambiguously
show the LORD is often extremely serious, frequently in
uncommonly short speeches.

The word הנה – *hineh* is routinely used in modern Hebrew in response to a question of where someone is. For example, an Israeli mother, wondering where her young son Abraham is, may call out: "Abraham, where are you?" Abraham, like most young children, would doubtless call back with a short, sharp הנה – *hineh!*, meaning, "Here!"

In the Book of Isaiah, the prophet uses a combination of the words הנה – *hineh* (behold) and אני – *ani* (me) in his famous Chapter 6 dialogue with the LORD:

> *Also I heard the voice of the Lord, saying: "Whom shall I send, and who will go for Us?" Then I said, "**Here am I!** Send me!"* (Isaiah 6:8).

Isaiah's Hebrew response to God's call was הנני – *hinehni*, which literally translates as "Behold me!" This is usually translated as "Here am I!," complete with an exclamation mark in the more literal versions of the English Bible. The Israeli idiomatic use of הנה! – *hineh* is, "I'm here!"

Isaiah was responding to the LORD much like a willing schoolboy would to a teacher's request for someone to run an important errand. The teacher might ask of the class: "Who will go for me?" Without a moment's hesitation a schoolboy raises his hand, jumps to his feet, and says loudly, *Here I am!. Send me!*, Isaiah, however, was dismayed by the errand he was given to run for *"the Holy One of Israel."* No doubt he had moments when he rued the day he had been so quick to volunteer. But that is for another time.

In addition to הנה – *hineh* being an attention grabbing "behold!," its use here by *"the Holy One of Israel"* has, at least to the author's mind, an interesting spin. The last segment of His indictment of Israel in Hosea 2:13 was: *"but Me she forgot."* With His use of הנה – *hineh* the LORD says in effect: "Israel forgot Me, but here I am!"

Israel may have forgotten her *"Maker,"* but He has certainly not forgotten Israel. It behooves us to remember that wherever we are God is there also. We may forget Him, but He is still closer to us than the air that we breath. It is only our own sin that prevents us from being conscious of His presence. What holds good for us also held good for the nation of Israel:

> *your iniquities have separated you from your God;*
> *and your sins have hidden His face from you, so that*
> *He will not hear* (Isaiah 59:2).

Modern Israel's sins have separated her from her *"Maker."* And, orthodox Rabbis in Israel are in agreement that Israel is currently in a dispensation in which God is hiding His face from the nation. He may be hiding His face and not hearing prayer on Israel's behalf, but He is not silent. He says: *"Me she forgot. Therefore, behold!...."*

— six —

The Uniqueness Of The LORD

The next word to be considered in our Hebrew text is one that might trouble some Christians. Some will no doubt have problems here due to holding to the belief that there are some things – other than breaking His promises or His word, or lying – that God cannot or would not do. One such example is the hardening of Pharaoh's heart. Time and again God tells us in His word that He hardened Pharaoh's heart. For example:

> *Now the LORD said to Moses, "Go in to Pharaoh; for **I have hardened his heart** and the hearts of his servants, that I may show these signs of Mine before him* (Exodus 10:1).

The LORD explains why He acted thus with Pharaoh:

> *For this purpose I have raised you up, that I may show My power in you, and that My name may be declared in all the earth* (Exodus 9:16).

Several thousand years after the destruction of Egypt myriads of people still speak of the plagues of Egypt and the exodus of the Israelites. Obviously, the LORD's policy was a resounding success. But some cannot accept that the LORD actually hardened the heart of Pharaoh in order to accomplish His purposes.

One such person who apparently could not accept God's absolute sovereignty was Joseph Rotherham, who completed his translation of the *Emphasized Bible* in 1902. Up until the late 1960s, editions of the *Emphasized Bible* continued to carry extensive comments by Rotherham about how God would not, could not, harden the heart of Pharaoh. The author is happy to note that the latest edition of the *Emphasized Bible* no longer includes Rotherham's comments on those passages as footnotes to the text.

Some will no doubt agree with Rotherham. Based on the evidence of the Scriptures most will not. The LORD is absolute sovereign. He has repeatedly shown Himself throughout history to be willing to sacrifice the few for the benefit of the many. Although Rotherham has no notes on the verses immediately below, they must have caused him and others an amount of stress:

> *Thus says the LORD: "About midnight **I will go** out into the midst of Egypt; and all the firstborn in the land of Egypt shall die, from the firstborn of Pharaoh who sits on his throne, even to the firstborn of the female servant who is behind the handmill, and all the firstborn of the animals. Then there shall be a great cry throughout all the land of Egypt, such as was not like it before, nor shall be like it again"*
> (Exodus 11:4-12).

The term *"firstborn"* normally means the oldest son. We do know that the firstborn of all the Egyptians, from Pharaoh down to the lowliest servant, died that night. The LORD unleashed the ultimate despoliation – the death of all the firstborn males in the land of Egypt, from the firstborn of Pharaoh's offspring to the firstborn of everything Egyptian, including servants and animals.

We so often think that the killing of the firstborn was restricted to the sons, like the firstborn son of Pharaoh. But the dead firstborn on that tragic night would also have included many grandfathers, fathers, husbands, and grandsons. It was on that fateful night that God brought the Israelites out of Egypt.

It is equally as foolish to believe that God was not the cause of these deaths as it is to believe that He was not the cause of the hardening of Pharaoh's heart.

In Jeremiah Chapter 18, verses 2-10, we have a parable of a potter molding his clay. The potter represents the LORD. If the pot is not to the potter's satisfaction, he remakes it. In Romans Chapter 9 the Apostle Paul specifically applies Jeremiah's potter parable directly to Pharaoh, and then takes it a step further. In verse 21 Paul says:

Does not the potter have power over the clay, from the same lump to make one vessel for honor and another for dishonor? (Romans 9:21).

In the next verse Paul says:

What if God, wanting to show His wrath and make His power known, endured with much long suffering the vessels of wrath prepared for destruction?

(Romans 9:22)

Pharaoh and the Egyptians were vessels of wrath – people who, due to their obstinate rebellion, were deeply guilty before the Lord – they had fitted themselves for their own destruction; the hardening of their hearts and their ultimate destruction were the consequences of their refusal of God's grace and abuse of His goodness.

Following the seventh catastrophe of rain and hail mixed with fire that decimated the land of Egypt, Pharaoh finally admitted that he had sinned against the Lord and pleaded for a cessation of the rain and hail – the manifestation of God's power:

And Pharaoh sent and called for Moses and Aaron, and said to them, "I have sinned this time. The Lord is righteous, and my people and I are wicked. Entreat the Lord, that there may be no more mighty thundering and hail, for it is enough. I will let you go, and you shall stay no longer" (Exodus 9:27-28).

But as soon as Pharaoh got relief he again returned to his old ways and refused to let the children of Israel go:

And when Pharaoh saw that the rain, the hail, and the thunder had ceased, he sinned yet more; . . .

(Exodus 9:34).

Pharaoh's heart was conditioned to sin and evil and thus he condemned himself and the Egyptian people to divine judgement. And this conditioning to sin and evil also held true for almost the entire population of this planet prior to the great flood. We read:

the Lord saw that the wickedness of man was great in the earth, and that every intent of the thoughts of his heart was only evil continually (Genesis 6:5).

And what was God's response?

> *And behold, I Myself am bringing floodwaters on
> the earth, to destroy from under heaven all flesh in
> which is the breath of life; everything that is on the
> earth shall die* (Genesis 6:17).

It is very important that we recognize and understand Almighty God's absolute sovereignty, both in the heavens and also on earth:

> *He is unique, and who can make Him change? And
> **whatever His soul desires, that He does*** (Job 23:13).

Being unique means God is one of a kind. He is self-existent, self-contained, and self-sufficient. In the beginning God breathed on dust and it became man. God also breathes on man and he becomes dust.

> **Whatever the LORD pleases He does**, *in heaven and
> in earth, in the seas and in all deep places*
> (Psalms 135:6).

> *I form the light and create darkness, I make peace
> and create calamity; I, the LORD, do all these things*
> (Isaiah 45:7).

> *The LORD has made all for Himself, yes, **even the
> wicked for the day of doom*** (Proverbs 16:4).

The latter two verses must also create problems for those who attempt to rationalize God's acts by jumping into the waters of apologetics. As it was mentioned earlier in Chapter two: "both the actual and the possible are subject to the command and control" of God. There is nothing that God cannot or will not do if He wishes to do it. Albert Barnes, the author of the widely respected, *Barnes – Notes on the Bible*, sagaciously wrote: "What God allows, He may be said to do." Those are nine short words that every Christian should take to heart.

Having made an effort to establish the LORD's absolute sovereignty in the minds and hearts of readers, we turn now to our Hebrew text of Hosea 2:14, to the third word:

לכן הנה **אנכי** מפתיה והלכתיה המדבר ודברתי על-לבה

*la'chen hineh **unochi** miftihah vehalachtihah
hadmidbar vedibarti al'livah.*

*Therefore, behold, **I will** allure her, will bring her
into the wilderness, and speak comfort to her.*

אנכי – *unochi* – "I Myself"

A simple *"I will"* in English does not do justice to the Hebrew.
The literal translation of the Hebrew is "I Myself" – it is the
L<small>ORD</small> G<small>OD</small> Almighty, *"the Creator* and *King of Israel"* (Isaiah
43:15) Himself that is going to do the things described in Hosea
2:14-15. Of the hardships that Israel will face and endure, no
one will be able to say that it is their work or the work of Satan,
Hizb'allah, the Palestinian Authority, Hamas, Islamic Jihad, the
news media, America, the European Union, the Gentiles, or a
hundred and one other phantasmal ideas that could be trotted
out. It will alone be the genius of *"the Holy One of Israel."*

There is a verse in the Book of Exodus dealing with Pharaoh
and the killing of the firstborn that exactly illustrates the gravity
of the second and third Hebrew words of our text. We will first
have the English text:

> *And I said to you, "Send My son away, and let him
> serve Me;" and you refused to send him. **Behold, I
> am** about to kill your son, your first-born!*
>
> (Exodus 4:23).

Here now is the Hebrew text of Exodus 4:23 with our
second and third study words emphasized; following that is the
transliteration:

ואמר אליך שלח את-בני ויעבדני ותמאן לשלחו הנה **אנכי**
הרג את-בנך בכרך

*veamar elechah shaluch et beneh veya'avdeni
vetmaen l'shalcho **hineh unochi** horeg et binchah
b'korechah.*

It was shown earlier that the purpose of הנה - *hineh* –
Behold!, is to get the hearer's attention. In this Exodus passage,

it is similarly used and again followed by אנכי – *unochi* – "I Myself."

In the English-speaking world there is the saying: "If you want something done right, do it yourself." When the LORD says *"Behold!,"* and follows that with *"I Myself,"* we can be very sure that what He says will be done, completed to the last *jot* and *tittle* (Matthew 5:18). And we know from the biblical narrative that the the LORD Himself did go out that passover night in Egypt (Exodus 12:27), when all the firstborn were struck down. Thus, in our Hosea passage, we can be one hundred percent certain that what the LORD says He will do will most certainly be done. It is simply a matter of waiting until it comes to pass.

The LORD will, of course, also use others, wittingly and unwittingly, to carry out his purposes. All the tragedy that will come to Israel in the ultimate wilderness will come from the hand of the LORD, just as all the good that ultimately comes to Israel will come from the hand of the LORD. No person, group, Christian ministry, nation or group of nations, will be able to claim responsibility for any of it. It will solely be the work of the LORD – *"the Mighty One of Jacob."*

seven

The Seducer And The Seduced

We have come to our fourth Hebrew word. This new word has more vitality than the previous three; it should wet our curiosity and constrain us to scratch away the superficial in order to reveal the not-so-obvious. The LORD is being more than a little devious in the choice of His words:

לכן הנה אנכי **מפתיה** והלכתיה המדבר ודברתי על-לבה

*la'chen hineh unochi **miftihah** vehalachtihah hadmidbar vedibarti al'livah.*

*Therefore, behold, I **will allure her**, will bring her into the wilderness, and speak comfort to her.*

מפתיה – *miftihah* – "entice her," "beguile her," "seduce her," "deceive her"

Thus far we have gotten literal English translations of our first three Hebrew words: *Therefore, behold!, I myself. . . .* Now we need to add the fourth word.

The New King James Version of the Bible (the author's preferred English version), translates מפתיה – *miftihah* as: *"allure her."* Other popular English translations such as the New International Version, King James Version, New Revised Standard Version, and the New American Standard Bible follow suit and also translate מפתיה – *miftihah* as *"allure her,"* none of which does justice to the Hebrew.

It does not necessarily follow that if a particular version is among the most popular versions of the Bible that it makes them better or more accurate than others. Selecting an English version of the Bible is really a matter of choosing one from the many options available. None are perfect; all remain an option. Some lesser known versions are often more accurate due to being less influenced by tradition and by containing less of the doctrinal coloration of translators. All translations have good and bad points. Bible students should choose one whose good points outweigh its faults.

Some modern translations are certainly easier to read and understand than the more literal versions, modern versions being more idiomatic or virtual paraphrases. But the author feels there is little use in having ease of reading if what is written is not an accurate rendering of the original. The author thinks there are are too many English versions available today; he believes the large number of versions do little more than confuse the English-speaking Church.

The Bible in Basic English has translated מפתיה – *miftihah* as *"make her come,"* which is much better than *"allure her"* as it expresses the intended meaning of there being no choice in it for Israel. Jay P. Green's Literal Translation of the Bible renders מפתיה – *miftihah* as *"lure her,"* which is an even better translation. The word *"lure"* expresses the real meaning of the Hebrew מפתיה – *miftihah*, which really means "to beguile," "to entice," "to deceive," "to seduce."

The word מפתיה – *miftihah* comes from the Hebrew word פתה – *patah* and this word is nowhere else translated in the Bible as *allure* as it does not do justice to the word. פתה - *patah* literally means "to seduce;" "to deceive;" "to entice a simple person."

We need to understand what *"the God of Israel"* is saying here – it is important: Israel has committed spiritual adultery with other gods and has forgotten her *"Creator."* Therefore the LORD Himself will seduce, deceive, beguile, and entice this simple-minded, stiff-necked people into the ultimate wilderness. Initially, Israel will be brought into the wilderness for a time of punitive punishment. Israel will find herself in difficult circumstances; isolated – much like a leper was isolated outside the camp of Israel (Leviticus 13:46). However, modern Israel's isolation will be outside the camp of the international community.

Israel will be seduced by her own desire "to be like other nations." Israel wishes to rid herself of the yoke of her *"King"* and romp in the immorality and materialism of Western nations.

When the late Yitzhak Rabin signed the first "peace" agreement with Yasser Arafat in Cairo in May 1994, he stated, in his official capacity as Israel's prime minister, that "Israel wants to be like other nations." That sentiment has been echoed by several high-ranking Israeli leaders in the years since. But the leaders of Israel need to give heed to what the LORD has to say concerning the matter:

> *For you are a holy people to the LORD your God; the LORD your God has chosen you to be a people for Himself, a special treasure above all the peoples on the face of the earth* (Deuteronomy 7:6).

Israel's calling is to be holy and separate from the nations, not to be like them. Israel is charged with being: *"A people dwelling alone, not reckoning itself among the nations"* (Numbers 23:9). Israel's leaders lead the people astray. And as the author has pointed out earlier: a people will become what its leaders are.

The deceitfulness and pursuit of Western materialism and values is luring Israel into the wilderness; the wilderness is a hard place and Israel is in for a hard time. The LORD is going to bring her into a pressure-cooker wilderness, a place of isolation, harshness, and barrenness, a place where she will be made dependent upon Him for her existence. That is God's plan for her. It will eventually prove to be her salvation. It will be done because of His great love for and His unbreakable commitment to her. The LORD will "lure," "seduce," "deceive," "beguile," and "entice" her in order to get His "stiff-necked" wayward child into the isolation of a cruel wilderness. Israel has already trekked into the initial regions of that wilderness; each day she goes further – enticed by her *"Creator,"* seduced by her own lusts.

Part of the meaning of the Hebrew word מפתיה – *miftihah* is to "entice a simple person." When the history of Israel's distress and sorrow is considered, it is clear Israel has shown very little intelligence. But whatever means God chooses to use to facilitate getting Israel into the wilderness, He will no doubt be appealing to the lusts that have made generous deposits in her heart.

We cannot be lured unless there is first either an open or secret desire – a lust – that is consistent with what is luring us. The

Apostle Peter hints at Israel's lusting when he says *"they allure through the lusts of the flesh"* (2 Peter 2:18). Being enticed, or lured, into the wilderness presupposes a rejection by Israel of her divine calling and inheritance. The wilderness was the Israelites' intervening stage between Egypt and the Promised Land. For modern Israel to be enticed back into the wilderness means she is willing to turn her back on the Promised Land in favor of the three deadly sins:

> *the lust of the flesh, the lust of the eyes, and the pride of life* (1 John 2:16).

That which the Israelites lusted after in the wilderness, while on their forty-year-long journey to the Promised Land, is a type of that which most Israelis lust after today. In yesteryear the Israelites whined:

> *Who will give us meat to eat? We remember the fish which we ate freely in Egypt, the cucumbers, the melons, the leeks, the onions, and the garlic*
> (Numbers 11:4,5).

On their way to the Promised Land the Israelites were miraculously provided for and lacked nothing, yet they lusted after the things of the flesh. After sixty-four continuous years of divine help following her miraculous establishment as a tiny, struggling state in 1948, Israel today has a strong economy, very little unemployment, and a very low inflation rate. Israel has one of the highest standards of living in the Western world and, according to the Giga Information Group (a leading global advisory firm), Western economic development is directly tied to Israel's high-tech industry owing to it being so far advanced. Yet still Israel hankers "to be like other nations."

When her *"Maker"* has lured her into the heart of a soul-destroying wilderness, she may well become like other nations: at the time of writing 2011/2012/2013 saw America, Israel's strongest ally, teetering on a fiscal cliff. Iceland, Greece, Ireland, Portugal, and Spain, are bankrupt. Italy totters financially and its former billionaire premier, Silvio Berlusconi, said in September 2011 that he could not wait to leave Italy—"this shitty country makes me sick." Perhaps the nations mentioned are among those Israel wants to be like?

Israel has again forgotten her *"Maker,"* the One who has wooed her for thousands of years and still reaches out to her today, imploring her to return to Him, saying:

> *I am the LORD, your Holy One, the Creator of Israel,*
> *your King* (Isaiah 43:15).

Israel has apparently not learned anything from the harsh punishments she suffered in the past. She has turned her back upon her God yet again, which is a proven recipe for disaster. Israel does not want her God, she wants "to be like other nations."

Israelis lust after penthouses and luxury villas. They lust after a Mercedes Benz, a BMW, or a Volvo – all of which have long been status symbols in Israel. A synonym of lust is covetousness, and the Bible informs us that covetousness *"is idolatry"* (Colossians 3:5), which the LORD will not countenance. And many Israelis also want to eat what is forbidden to them – swine meat, shrimps, lobster, and shellfish – "like other nations."

Israelis, as a general rule, do not like to get their hands dirty by working in construction and other menial occupations. Israelis employ foreign workers and Arabs for menial work – more often than not at miserably low wages. As an Israeli friend said to the author with a grin some years ago, "We haven't worked since we came out of Egypt!"

The friend's remark cannot be applied as a blanket rule. The *chalutzim* (pioneers) who came from Russia, Germany, and other parts of Europe in the late 1800s and early 1900s, worked exceedingly hard from dawn until dusk, usually in extreme conditions. Those people laid the foundations and built the modern state. But now things have changed.

A materialistic generation has arisen of which much could, generally speaking, care less about the Jewish state. And the greater part of the younger generation is amoral, corrupted by watching MTV and other amoral television channels. Many teens do not want to defend their country by serving in the Israel Defense Force and on May 29, 2012, *The Times of Israel* carried the following headline: "Army planning chief: 'IDF is short thousands of soldiers.'" What an indictment of Israeli youth.

There are Israeli groups dedicated to helping the youth avoid military service, which has been mandatory for all Israelis except ultra-orthodox youth who study Torah in the *yeshivot*. In the latter half of the first decade of the new millennium, and ongoing into the second decade, there has been much discussion in the military hierarchy about the twenty-five percent of the youth who are avoiding serving in the Israel Defense Force, and ideas are being floated on how to combat this. When those in their late teens do serve in the Israel Defense Force, many opt out of going into fighting units, preferring medical or other non-combatant roles. Today, many of Israel's *chalutzim* and Israel Defense Force veterans say, with a depressed sigh:

> For what did we fight? For what did my friends die? We wasted our time building a country for others to slice up and give away to those who hate us and will always hate us.

On June 24, 2012, at least five thousand ultra-orthodox Jews in Jerusalem held a protest against new legislation being formulated to draft *haredim* (ultra-orthodox) into military and national service. On July 16, many thousands of ultra-orthodox men, along with some five thousand children, protested against *haredi* youth being enlisted into national service.

For years the *haredim* have been able to indefinitely exempt themselves from military or national service by studying Torah. At the time of writing there are fifty-four thousand supposed full-time yeshiva students exempted from army service within the framework known as the the Tal Law, which Israel's Supreme Court recently struck down as being unconstitutional. Around ten thousand of the ultra-orthodox exempted from the draft by claiming fulltime Torah studies do not in fact even attend a yeshiva.

For as many years as the Tal Law operated, secular and religiously conservative Jews have felt discriminated against. They constitute the largest part of Israel's workforce and serve in the Israel Defense Force. The vast majority of the ultra-orthodox are not part of the labor force, do not serve in the Israel Defense

Force, or do national service, which includes the police. Among the *haredim* there is a high birthrate and secular taxpayers are forced to pay for many of the benefits that the children receive, including housing benefits and municipal tax breaks, all of which is sufficient to keep the family functioning while the husband studies Torah fulltime.

The Supreme Court ruled for the secular and conservatively religious Jews and struck down the Tal Law. New regulations will force haredim into both the workforce and the Israel Defense Force, and the shortage of soldiers will be overcome. But it will come at a price, the ultra-orthodox can be counted on to be very violent and destructive when faced with a situation perceived as going against their mode of life.

Regulations are also being formulated to remove government benefits, for life, for all youth – Jewish, Christian, or Arab, who evade enlistment into either the Israel Defense Force or national service without just cause.

Today, Israelis generally lust after the materialism of the West. They hunger greedily after the amoral, materialistic life-style of Western nations. And they want to shed the yoke of their *"Maker."* Amorality and greed is diametrically opposed to the will of God:

> *the lust of the flesh, the lust of the eyes, and the pride*
> *of life--is **not of the Father but is of the world***
> (1 John 2:16).

But it is the world that Israel wants, not *"the Father."* As it was in the days of yore so it is today, only the remnant cares – those whom the LORD has reserved for Himself:

> *whose knees have not bowed to Baal, and every*
> *mouth that has not kissed him* (1 Kings 19:18).

Countless numbers in Israel, including her leaders, cry out for Israel "to be like other nations." It matters not whether they desire to throw Israel's *"Maker"* out of His own Land or want "to be like other nations," their *"Creator and King"* will not allow it:

> *What you have in your mind shall never be, when you*
> *say, "We will be like the Gentiles, like the families*

in other countries"… As I live, says the LORD GOD,
surely with a mighty hand, with an outstretched arm,
*and **with fury poured out, I will rule over you***
(Ezekiel 20:32, 33).

With *"fury poured out"* God *"will rule"* over Israel whether she wants Him to or not. And the Bible is well supplied with examples showing that Israel's *"Maker"* has often ruled *"with fury poured out."*

When the author came to live in Jerusalem in 1980 it was possible to hear a pin drop on the sabbath day. Today, a great deal of commercial activity is carried out on *shabbat* (the *"Sabbath"*) in *"the holy city."* Cinemas and other places of entertainment are open, restaurants are open, as are pubs where youth can buy alcoholic drink until 5:00 a.m. The LORD commanded Israel to observe the seventh day, the Sabbath, as a *"holy"* day:

> *Therefore the children of Israel shall keep the*
> *Sabbath, to observe the Sabbath throughout their*
> *generations as a perpetual covenant. It is a sign*
> *between Me and the children of Israel forever*
> (Exodus 31:16-17a).

Other than the religious minority, few in Israel now keep the Sabbath as a holy day of rest. Tel Aviv revels in its reputation as being "the city that never sleeps." The morality of the nation of Israel is rapidly descending to gutter level. Numbers of the youth get drunk and have shouting contests until daybreak. Others get semi-drunk and drive around blasting their car horns or revving up their Harley Davidson motorcycles, also until the light of day.

The *"city of the great King"* is opening up for business and entertainment 24/7 and, except for the religious minority and a mere handful of secular Israelis, most are happy to have it that way. They do not want God's sabbath day in their lives any longer – they crave the flesh pots of Egypt.

Tel Aviv has had a red light district for a good number of years and pornographic movies are shown openly in the city due to many Israelis having a *penchant* for pornography. In Tel Aviv, even some ultra-religious Jews will sell pornographic magazines from their kiosks. When scolded by other religious Jews for selling such trash, they blithely respond, "It's business."

Israelis had illicit prostitution on the nation's streets for years, but the liberal-left Rabin government, which came to power in 1992, legalized it and allowed prostitutes to operate openly from apartment buildings.

Israel also openly boasts of having some of the most liberal homosexual laws in the Western world. And on June 7, 2002, thousands of sodomites and lesbians from all over Israel paraded through Jerusalem on the first of the "Gay Pride" marches to be held in *"the city of the great King."* This sexually and mentally sick, deluded mass, marched under a banner that read in Hebrew: "BLESSED IS HE WHO CREATED US IN HIS IMAGE." Each year this abomination grows bigger and is allowed to parade itself through the streets of Jerusalem, much to the chagrin of many inhabitants.

Official 2007 estimates put the number of homosexual couples living together in Israel at eighteen thousand. And in 2006 Tel Aviv was launched as the "Gay Capital of the World" by Israel's minister of tourism. The city is now being advertised and promoted worldwide as a homosexual "paradise."

In April 2012, the Masorti (the Conservative religious Jewish movement) voted to accept sodomite and lesbian students "for ordination [as rabbis] beginning with the 2012-13 academic year." The chair of the seminary's Board of Trustees said: "its decision highlights its commitment to uphold Jewish law in a changing world."

The *"Holy One of Israel"* is neither blind nor deaf. He will not sanction the pollution of Israel and her cities by homosexuals, especially Jerusalem, *"the city of God."* Israel will ultimately pay a very heavy price for her shameless actions. The LORD has given fair warning:

> *Just as Sodom and Gomorrah and the cities around them, since they in the same way as these indulged in gross immorality and went after strange flesh, are exhibited as an example, in undergoing the punishment of eternal fire* (Jude 7).

The 1992 Rabin government also promoted abortions, which are widespread among the secular majority in Israel. As mentioned in Chapter four, Israelis have murdered more of their own unborn Jewish children than Hitler's Nazis did live ones.

All single Israeli girls must serve for two years in the Israel Defense Force and, due to the number of abortions performed on these girls during their years of service, religious Jews deprecate the Israel Defense Force and refer to it as "the national brothel." Each female soldier is allowed three abortions courtesy of the Jewish state. Those requiring more than three abortions are obliged to pay for the excess procedures themselves.

It was in Tel Aviv where the largest demonstrations in favor of "peace" with Yasser Arafat were always held. Anything that smacks of interfering with their pleasure, such as the ongoing conflict with the Palestinians, is considered worthy of a demonstration by tens of thousands of those that make up the city's predominantly liberal, secular-humanist population.

Conversely, it is in Jerusalem, where there is at least some semblance of the fear of God and adherence to His commands, that huge "anti-peace" demonstrations take place.

The late Abba Eban, one of the most eloquent and best known of Israel's liberal statesmen, wrote of the different Israeli religious and secular views concerning Israel's stunning military victory in the 1967 Six-Day War. In that war the Israel Defense Force smashed five logistically superior Arab armies in six days. Eban personally scoffed at the idea of "belief in a higher power," but being a diplomat, he wrote concerning Israel's astonishing victory:

> Those who thought in religious terms saw a divine hand in the outcome of the war. A more secular view attributed our triumph to our efficient military performance and planning.[1]

A sad situation exists in Israel today between the godless and the religious. The liberal, secular-humanists fight tooth and nail against the religious at every turn. But it was the religious Jews who refused to assimilate and thus kept the Jewish nation alive during the almost two thousand years of exile from the Land. And it is the religious Jews who are still the real heroes today.

The religious Jews are the ones who have settled in the territories captured from the Arabs after they repeatedly launched their armies against Israel and lost their wars of aggression. These Jews are being continuously attacked with roadside bombs, rockets and mortars, and shot at in their homes and cars by hate-filled Arabs. In March 2011, a husband and his wife, and three of their children were murdered in their beds by two knife-wielding Palestinians. Two sons, aged eleven and four were the first to die, the parents were next in their room. Each had been stabbed repeatedly and had their throats slit. As the murderers were leaving through a window there came a baby's whimper from an adjoining room. One of the Arabs returned and slit the throat of a three-month-old baby daughter. Fortunately, the Arabs never knew of two other sons, aged eight and two, sleeping in another room – five members of a single Jewish family were sent into the next world in a matter of minutes.

Following an intensive weeks-long search for the murderers by Israeli forces they were finally apprehended in a nearby Arab village. Neither showed a hint of remorse; one said he was sorry he had missed the surviving children.

Instead of leaving for safer areas within the Green Line,[2] the numbers of Jews going to live in the disputed territories are increasing daily. They believe the *"God of Israel"* has brought them back to the Land, and the Land back to them. The godless Jews, on the other hand, are willing to cede large portions of the Land to the Arabs for a make-believe "peace" that will last only until the next war, which will likely start before the ink has dried on the latest of the "peace" agreements.

Several million Israelis have turned their backs on their divine inheritance today and are content to see it ceded to Israel's worst enemies through "peace" agreements. The minority that constitutes the remnant, and which seeks after God, mourns the loss of its divine inheritance and laments the nation's moral decline. And the religious-liberal divide in Israel is increasing apace with the absorption of more than a million godless immigrants from the former Soviet Union, now the Commonwealth of Independent States (CIS). Half of those who came from the Commonwealth of Independent States have not a single drop of Jewish blood in their veins – they purchased their emigration papers with cash or sex from the communist authorities. The Russians have so greatly contributed to organized crime and prostitution in Israel that it was necessary for a special crime force to be set up that deals solely with Russian crime. And tens of thousands of liberal Jews are coming each year from other countries. The liberal, secular-humanist avalanche is smothering the righteous remnant in the Land. *"Therefore, behold, I, Myself, will lure her ...."*

---

[1] Abba Eban, *Personal Witness: Israel Through My Eyes* (New York: Putnam, 1992), p. 442).

[2] The Green Line refers to the demarcation lines set out in the 1949 Armistice Agreements between Israel and her neighbors. The name derives from the green ink used to draw the line on the map while the talks were in progress.

Lured By Her Creator

We have arrived at our fifth Hebrew word in Hosea 2:14:

לכן הנה אנכי מפתיה והלכתיה המדבר ודברתי על-לבה

*la'chen hineh unochi miftihah **vehalachtihah** hadmidbar vedibarti al'livah.*

*Therefore, behold, I will allure her, **will bring her** into the wilderness, and speak comfort to her.*

והלכתיה – *vehalachtihah* – "**and** bring her"

The Hebrew here is more succinct, crisper than the idiomatic English translation. God's *"I Myself will lure and bring"* is assertive and commanding. The translation's *"I will allure, will bring"* is too tender for the context.

The Jewish people have been virtually universal in their blaming of the Gentiles for all the woes that have befallen them throughout the ages. Few and far between within the Jewish world are those who have sufficient courage to acknowledge that it was the multiplied sins of the people that brought the LORD's judgments upon Israel. Almost as universal as the blanket blaming of the Gentiles for all Jewish woes is the total rejection of the hypothesis that Israel's God was the cause of them.

In his book *The Wall: Prophecy, Politics and Middle East "Peace"* the author included a chapter entitled "The Indictment of Israel" which listed all the kings of Israel who have been recorded in the Bible as doing evil in the sight of their *"Maker,"* and also the kings who were written down as walking righteously in His eyes. Only six kings: David, Asa, Jehoshaphat, Jotham, Hezekiah, and Josiah – all from Israel's southern kingdom of Judah – did what was right in the eyes of *"the Holy One of Israel"* All other kings throughout ancient Israel's long history did evil in the sight of the LORD. Those dozens of kings led the people of Israel deeper and deeper into sin, they:

> *had encouraged moral decline in [Israel] and had*
> *been continually unfaithful to the LORD*
> (2 Chronicles 28:19).

Consequently, these rulers led the nation further and further away from the LORD. The end result of their repeated sin was repeated death, destruction and, ultimately, the exile of the people from the Land.

The Wall was written primarily for Christian readers, but the author has also received correspondence from ultra-orthodox Jews, both in Israel and from America, thanking him for penning the truth. Those Jews looked truth squarely in the face and acknowledged the veracity of it. Every Jew will ultimately be brought face to face with the truth of their own history and, for the majority of them, it will take place in the wilderness where Israel's *"Maker"* is bringing them.

God often uses humans as the instruments of His punishments. And when He chooses to use human agencies to punish the Jews what option does He have but to use Gentiles? There are after all, only Jews and Gentiles in this world. (Some, due to the way they read the New Testament, will no doubt argue that there is a third group – Christians – but the discussion of that doctrinal belief is not within the scope of this book). Of course God used the Gentile nations as instruments of His punishment. When God determined to punish His *"chosen people"* He had to choose between using Gentiles or 'natural' catastrophes. Not much of a choice.

God foresaw questions arising as to why the Jewish people has traversed the valley of tears so often throughout its long history. When the inevitable questions arose Israel's God had already decreed the response:

> *Then they will answer, "Because they forsook the LORD*
> *God of their fathers, who brought them out of the land*
> *of Egypt, and embraced other gods, and worshiped*
> *them and served them; therefore He has brought all*
> *this calamity on them"* (2 Chronicles 7:21b-22).

Antisemites are schadenfreude, which means to say they take pleasure in the misfortune of Jews. However, antisemites must face the wrath of Israel's God and Hebrews 10:31 reminds us that *"It is a fearful thing to fall into the hands of the living God."* Neither the Gentiles nor Mother Nature can be blamed for the suffering of the Jewish people throughout the ages. The LORD gave warning time and again through His prophets:

> *The LORD is with you while you are with Him. If you seek Him, He will be found by you; but if you forsake Him, He will forsake you* (2 Chronicles 15:2).

The blame for Jewish suffering lies wholly within the heart of the Jewish people:

> *Now with whom was He angry forty years? Was it not with **those who sinned**, whose corpses fell in the wilderness? And to whom did He swear that they would not enter His rest, but to **those who did not obey**? So we see that **they could not enter in because of unbelief*** (Hebrews 3:17-19).

The Bible informs us that: *"Foolishness is bound up in the heart of a child; the rod of correction will drive it far from him"* (Proverbs 22:15). Sin is bound up in the heart of man, but God's *"rod of correction"* drives it far from him. It has been necessary for the *"rod of correction"* to strike Israel's rear-end countless times, but Israel has yet to grasp the fact that it is sin that forms the conduit through which suffering flows: *"The soul who sins shall die"* (Ezekiel 18:4, 20).

Antisemitism has its place as a means of accomplishing God's will. Antisemitism is Jew-hatred. And an antisemite has been defined as "someone who dislikes Jews more than is absolutely necessary."[1] Classic antisemitism is that the Jew is the poisoner of the wells. Today's new international antisemitism has Israel and the Jewish people as the poisoners of the international wells. In December 2001, the French Ambassador to Britain, Daniel Bernard, made the comment:

> All the troubles in the world are because of that shitty little country Israel.[2]

Israel is excluded from international forums in the United Nations, and Israel has never once been asked onto the United Nations Security Council in sixty-four years while practically every other nation has been. Arabs often have two member states on the Security Council, including Syria, which is a leading sponsor of international terror.

Israel is discriminated against and condemned by most governments of the world, by the United Nations, the world's news media, and by many giant business corporations that refuse to sell their products to Israel. The *"God of Israel"* has determined to bring Israel into the ultimate wilderness; this will, of necessity, include near total political, diplomatic, and international isolation.

"The Holy One of Israel" has said that he would *"lure"* Israel and *"bring her into the wilderness."* As has already been mentioned, God declared in the days of yore that Israel would be taken into captivity, and Israel underwent two exiles from the Land, the second of which scattered her people to the four corners of the globe. There being only two exiles for Israel decreed in God's Word she will not be going out of the land again. Instead she will now to be taken into *"the wilderness,"* which could be equally as devastating as being physically exiled from the land.

A whole generation perished in the wilderness that followed the exodus from Egypt. In like manner will unbelieving, godless Jews from a multiple of generations perish in the wilderness into which Israel is being lured.

Israel's *"Creator"* says He Himself will *"bring"* Israel into the wilderness. It will be a personal involvement like the Lord's personal involvement with Noah and the Ark: God said to Noah, *"**Come** into the ark, you and all your household"* (Genesis 7:1), which presupposes the Lord was actively in the Ark at the time.

When the Israelites were slaves in Egypt God said sixteen times that He would *"bring"* them out of Egypt and into the Promised Land. He did *"bring"* them out of Egypt and into the Promised Land according to His word. And it was no fault of God's that the Israelites had a forty-year delay before entering the Promised Land – unbelief was responsible for that. However, it is interesting to find eighty-three verses in the Bible where God uses the phrase *"I brought them out of the land of Egypt."* It was a hugely personal involvement. God personally led the Israelites on their journey. He went before them in a pillar of cloud by day and a pillar of fire by night. He was also their rearguard in times of trouble – He would move behind the stragglers and shield the congregation from the enemy (e.g. Exodus 14:19).

When we look at prophecies containing God's words, *"I will bring."* we find there are ninety-eight such prophecies in the Old Testament. For example:

> *I will bring you into the land which I swore to give to Abraham, Isaac, and Jacob* (Exodus 6:8).

> *I will bring a nation against you from afar, O house of Israel* (Jeremiah 5:15).

> *I will bring them back into their land which I gave to their fathers* (Jeremiah 16:15).

Having the benefit of hindsight we know that each of the ninety-eight prophecies were fulfilled to the letter. When we understand the personal involvement of Israel's *"Maker"* lying beneath the surface of the words, *"I will bring,"* and the absolute certainty of the prophecy's fulfillment, we can better appreciate the weight of the words in our Hosea passage: *"Behold, I Myself will lure her and bring her...."*

---

[1] *Antisemitism in America Today: Outspoken Experts Explodes the Myths*, Jerome A. Chanes, New York: Carol, 1995, p. 5.

[2] "The return of 'respectable' English anti-semitism." *Jerusalem Post*, December 21, 2001.

— *nine* —

The Wilderness
(Multifaceted)

The wilderness into which Israel is being lulled is a literal wilderness in a figurative sense; however, both literal and figurative wildernesses can have many facets. We shall look at some of those facets here and in subsequent chapters.

Israel's moral condition today is nothing less than a moral wilderness. Godlessness among Israelis is disturbingly on the march upward; homosexuality and pornography are both increasing at an alarming rate; crime is on the rise as is prostitution, abortion, divorce, murder, rape, greed, and corruption. The nation's youth generally appears to be lacking in purpose; it is wild and lawless, given to alcohol and drug abuse. Many youths carry knives – even school-age children – for what they cynically call "self-defense," and they have a ready propensity to use their weapons in deadly fights with their peers. In May 2012, a Jerusalem teen was arrested for holding a knife to his teacher's throat and threatening to kill him. Also in that month, following a national crime wave involving lethal stabbings by youths, northern district police officers held a weekend operation against youth violence, arresting no fewer than seventy-five youths. A police officer said: "Alcohol and knives are an explosive mix." He added: "Kiosk owners who sell alcohol to minors are 'blinded' by money." On August 12, 2012, paramedics reportedly treated knife injuries from six brawls in the Haifa district alone.

Currently, some twenty-five percent of the youth is evading conscription into the Israel Defense Force and this figure is projected to rise to around forty percent within ten years.

At the time of writing there is a crisis of violence before, during, and after soccer matches, and it is becoming ugly. In March 2012, following a soccer match in Jerusalem, fans ran amok in a nearby shopping mall. They screamed racial epithets and targeted Arab workers and cleaning staff and generally disrupted the mall. The following month, in April, a fight erupted in Haifa involving players and trainers; another brawl broke out in April, on Friday afternoon, on the field in Tel Aviv between opposing players and club officials. All Saturday matches were cancelled as a result.

Some have opined that the repulsive behavior is essentially a reflection of the violent nature of Israeli society.

In just half a decade, between 2005 and 2010, Israel changed. Israel's prevailing mindset today is eat or be eaten. The population has generally became self-centered and the country has become one of the most expensive countries of the world in which to live. It is now a country where most everything, except fruit and vegetables, costs two to three times that of identical items overseas. Wages have not kept pace with the cost of living and the high housing costs have accelerated to well beyond the point of being ludicrous. Israeli capitalism has made its business moguls aggressive and egoistic, driven by unadulterated greed.

The reason for the change for the worse in Israel only came to light in the first report of Israel's new State Comptroller, Yosef Shapira, in September 2012. Shapira's report was published just before *Rosh Hashanah* (Jewish New Year) and on the heels of recent hikes in bread and fuel prices and tax increases that went into effect on September 1.

According to the Comptroller's report:

> government offices abandoned supervision of food costs in Israel between 2005 and 2011, allowing companies in a non-competitive market to set the prices. This brought about increased profits for manufacturers and importers, while contributing to the economic hardships faced by the average Israeli.

On November 1, 2012, Israel's Interior Minister Eli Yishai called on the public to boycott supermarket chains, especially Super-Sol, Israel's largest chain, due to announced plans to bump up the prices of thousands of products. Yishai picked on Super-Sol specifically because it planned to raise the prices of thousands of its products by an average of four percent, and this following its disclosure that its millions in profits had doubled in the fiscal third quarter of 2012.

Instead of being ashamed of being morally perverse Israelis make jokes about their evil ways. And the only reason the government stepped in and began to regulate the cost of basic, staple foods again is because Israelis began taking to the streets in 2011 in protest at the high cost of living. As mentioned in Chapter three, September 2011 saw half a million Israelis demonstrating against Israel's high cost of living and unaffordable housing. It was the largest demonstration of protest in Israel's history; it galvanized the government into taking some action – politicians jobs were on the line. Thus the Interior Minister has now called for the public boycotting of food chains in order to help bring food prices down. The food chains' executives are, in reality, little less than fagins tutoring in the art of greed.

Not only Israeli food chains salivate over financial profits. On December 2, 2012, it was widely reported that Israel's two major banks, Leumi and Hapoalim, had announced that between them they were going to fire some sixteen hundred workers. The job cuts are intended to streamline the banks' services following a government ruling requiring banks to reduce commission costs and extra fees in 2013. Bank Leumi reported its net profit had tripled in the third quarter of 2012, and Hapoalim's net profit rose thirty-two percent in the same period – Israel's modern oligarchs care not that their avarice is shylocking thousands of struggling Israeli families.

Throughout the ages Israelis have been betrayed by their leaders and teachers. Nothing has changed between old yesteryear and the new today. As the author said earlier: people become what their leaders are.

Other facets of a wilderness experience has spiritual dimensions – Israel today is in a spiritual wilderness.

John the Baptist was *"the voice of one crying in the wilderness"* (Matthew 3:3). John's wilderness was both moral and spiritual. John addressed the prevailing conditions of the time. Both John and Jesus denounced the spiritual hypocrisy of the religious establishment. John called the religious leaders a *"Brood of vipers!"* (Matthew 3:7). In like manner Jesus called them *"Serpents, brood of vipers!"* (Matthew 23:33). The stranglehold that the religious leaders of today have over daily life in Israel is choking many Israelis with their religious rules, regulations, and hypocrisy.

It was shown in Chapter three that thousands upon thousands of predominantly young Israelis have embraced Yeshua (Jesus) and are holding firm to their faith despite persecution from the ultra-religious community. The ultra-religious do all that is in its power to hinder the propagation of the gospel in Israel. Again, little has changed since yesteryear when Jesus walked this earth. But, as in the days of the apostles when the gospel was preached through much tribulation and the Jewish Church grew rapidly, so today the gospel is preached through tribulation and the Jewish Church is growing rapidly – much to the chagrin of the ultra-religious community.

In many ways, Jewish ultra-orthodoxy equates with the Muslim Taliban. It demands gender-separate buses where women must sit at the back of the bus and it instituted gender-separate streets in *Mea She'arim*, a predominantly ultra-orthodox neighborhood of Jerusalem. Two-meter (six-feet six-inches) high barriers covered with cloth were erected to divide the men from the women, while private stewards directed genders to the appropriate part of the street. Israel's Supreme Court ruled the segregation illegal and that there must be no segregated streets from 2012 onwards.

In past years young girls have been severely beaten in *Mea She'arim* and thrown into the road for not conforming to ultra-orthodox ideas of 'modesty' that mandates a covering of arms and legs and the wearing of skirts or dresses to the ankles.

In a July 2012 landmark ruling, a Beit Shemesh judge awarded a fifteen-year-old schoolgirl the equivalent of three thousand two hundred dollars for being made to sit at the back of bus by two ultra-orthodox men. The men demanded Ariella Marsden and two friends sit at the back of the bus, when Marsden refused the bus driver asked her to move in order to allow the two haredi men to sit down in the front of the bus. The judge ordered the bus company to pay the fine.

On August 13, 2012, the *Times of Israel* reported that an out-of-uniform teenage soldier suffered a torrent of abuse from ultra-orthodox passengers and was reduced to standing at the back of the bus, in tears. Her ordeal began before she entered the bus when an ultra-orthodox man on the bus denied her entry through the front doors. the *Times* reported:

> the driver of the bus, who was well aware of the unfolding events, did not intervene or come to her aid and only told her to stop crying.

Eventually, the soldier chose to disembark from the bus before completing her journey to avoid further abuse. A spokesman for the bus company – which in the past had run completely segregated bus lines through *Mea She'arim* until a Jerusalem court ruled that it was illegal – told *Israel Radio* that the matter is being investigated.

An August 10, 2012, *Globes* report tells of an American Jewish woman, Debra Ryder, who is suing El Al Israel Airlines for fifty-thousand sheqels (twelve thousand five hundred dollars) because she was forced to switch seats and go to the back of the plane away from ultra-orthodox Jewish men. Ryder was seeking compensation for emotional distress and gender discrimination.

The Apostle Paul wrote of the irreconcilable difference between those who believed and those who did not:

> *What then? Israel has not obtained what it seeks; but the elect have obtained it, and the rest were blinded. Just as it is written: "God has given them a spirit of stupor, eyes that they should not see and ears that they should not hear, to this very day"*
> (Romans 11:7-8).

Once more we are led into the argumentation regarding the LORD's absolute sovereignty: the elected remnant obtains salvation, all others are blinded – by the decree of God Almighty. Now let us inquire into this as we did with Pharaoh and the Egyptians.

The author made the case in Chapter six that Pharaoh and the Egyptians were vessels of wrath – people who, due to their obstinate rebellion, had fitted themselves for their own destruction. It was pointed out that the hardening of their hearts and their ultimate destruction were the consequences of their persistent refusal of God's grace and their abuse of His goodness. And so it is with the Jewish nation.

God sent His *"only begotten Son"* – God incarnate – into the world (John 1:14) with the express purpose of being the paschal lamb who would take away *"the sin of the world"* (John 1:29). Jesus was the *"express image"* of God (Hebrews 1:3) and whoever saw Jesus also saw God Almighty (John 14:9), and Jesus only ever did and said what God Almighty Himself would have done and said (John 5:19-23, 8:28).

The great majority of the Jewish nation and its religious leaders not only ignored the words and teachings of Jesus, but they also ignored the miracles He performed: Jesus made the maimed whole (Matthew 12:10-13); turned water into wine (John 4:46); gave sight to the blind (Matthew 15:30); hearing to the deaf (Matthew 11:5); cleansed the lepers (Matthew 15:30); gave speech to mutes (Matthew 11:5): the ability to walk to the lame (Matthew 11:5); gave life to the dead (John 12:1); fed multi-thousands from no more than a small boy's lunch (Matthew 14:19 - 20), *et cetera*. Not content with turning blind eyes and deaf ears to the words and miracles of Jesus, they insulted and dishonored God (John 8:49) by repeatedly accusing Jesus of having a demon and even of being mad (John 7:20, 8:52, 10:20).

The great majority of the Jewish nation had willfully closed its eyes against the light that Jesus brought, the very light that would have awakened the Jewish conscience and brought life. They rejected the gospel – the good news of God; they were insensible to its claims and truths and blasphemed the Holy Spirit through which Jesus performed the miracles. The Bible makes it very clear that blasphemy of the Holy Spirit is an unpardonable sin (Matthew 12:31). God gave the Jews over to the insensibility of their own making, just as He has given mankind over to its own *"uncleanness"* (Romans 1:24) and to its *"vile passions"* (Romans 1:26). It is as though the LORD has said, "You made your bed, now lie in it!"

That is not to say that all unbelieving Jews and Gentiles today are doomed to destruction tomorrow. The first recorded word of Jesus' earthly ministry was *"Repent"* (Matthew 4:17). That is God's one and only condition for acceptance into His kingdom, and those that repent of their perversity and turn from their obstinate ways will find the LORD waiting for them with open arms and a full salvation:

> *"I have no pleasure in the death of one who dies,"*
> *says the Lord GOD. "Therefore turn and live!"*
> (Ezekiel 18:32)

> *The LORD is not slack concerning His promise, as*
> *some count slackness, but is longsuffering toward*
> *us, not willing that any should perish but that all*
> *should come to repentance* (2 Peter 3:9).

Indeed, our LORD is the one true living God:

> *who desires all men to be saved and to come to the*
> *knowledge of the truth* (1 Timothy 2:4).

Israelis today see themselves in one light while God sees them in their true light:

> *There is a generation that is pure in its own eyes,*
> *yet is not washed from its filthiness*
> (Proverbs 30:12).

Jesus disturbed Israel morally and spiritually almost two thousand years ago; Israel's *"Maker"* will greatly disturb her – morally, spiritually, and physically – in the very near future.

Another of the wilderness's facets is one that the Christian Church has formulated against Israel. This facet is known as Replacement Theology.[1] Replacement Theology has been called the "Goliath of theology in the Protestant church" and appropriates all of God's good promises given to the nation of Israel to the Church; it teaches that the Church is the new Israel, that God has cast off physical Israel, which is not only scripturally wrong, it is blasphemy.

In Mark Chapter 12, Sadducees, who did not believe in the

resurrection, tried to ensnare Jesus with a witless question concerning the resurrection. Jesus responded to them and would give the selfsame answer today to those who hold to Replacement Theology, to fatuous questions concerning God's eternal commitment to the Jews as His special people. In verse 24 Jesus answered and said to the Sadducees:

> *Are you not therefore **mistaken**, because **you do not know the Scriptures nor the power of God**?*
> (Mark 12:24).

Jesus pushed home the point about not knowing the Scriptures when He says in Mark 12:26: *"have you not read?"* And in verse 27 Jesus admonishes those supposedly learned in the Scriptures that they were *"greatly mistaken."*

Reading and meditating on the Scriptures are the keys to understanding them. Many folk underline passages in their Bible, but it is the passages that do not get underlined that usually require the reader's attention.

In Replacement Theology only God's good promises to Israel are appropriated by the Church; it leaves all the promises of judgement unappropriated – they are left to the Jewish nation. Those that hold to Replacement Theology and believe the Church to be the new Israel – the Church having replaced the nation of Israel as God's chosen people – must, by implication, have inherent antisemitic, anti-Jew feelings buried within their hearts.

Replacement Theology banishes Israel to a spiritual wilderness.

Returning now to our Hebrew text in Hosea, the sixth word:

לכן הנה אנכי מפתיה והלכתיה המדבר ודברתי על-לבה

*la'chen hineh unochi miftihah vehalachtihah **hadmidbar** vedibarti al'livah.*

*Therefore, behold, I will allure her, will bring her into **the wilderness**, and speak comfort to her.*

המדבר – *hamidbar* – "the wilderness"

The Hebrew word מדבר – *midbar* literally means "a desert wasteland;" "a barren wilderness" that supports little life. It is an isolated, sandy, parched, intense environment, an uncultivated, uninhabited, inhospitable, and torrid region with negligible rainfall.

The word wilderness derives from the notion of "wildness" – in other words, that which humans do not control and have not developed. A biblical wilderness is personified by its lack of moisture:

> *And they went **three days** in the wilderness **and found no water*** (Exodus 15:22).

> *. . . there was **no water** for the people to drink*
> (Exodus 17:1).

> *And now she is planted in the wilderness, in **a dry and thirsty land*** (Ezekiel 19:13).

> *I knew you in the wilderness, in **the land of great drought*** (Hosea 13:5).

> *. . . that **great and terrible wilderness**, in which were **fiery serpents** and **scorpions** and **thirsty land where there was no water*** (Deuteronomy 8:15).

> *He found him in **a desert land** and in the **wasteland**, a **howling wilderness*** (Deuteronomy 32:10).

Many people are prone to think of a wilderness as being a rather flat, sandy or scrubby area. However, the desert wildernesses of and around Israel are anything but flat – they are rocky, rugged, mountainous terrains, often precipitous in nature and where thorns and briers flourish freely in the dry conditions.

The characteristics of a wilderness is disorderly confusion; a barren dusty wasteland where very little grows and almost nothing matures. If there is fruit it is scrubby. If there is grain it has no food value due to its parched world. A wilderness is a disconcerting environment:

> *They are **bewildered by the land**; the wilderness has closed them in* (Exodus 14:3).

Some modern nature writers believe wilderness areas are vital for the human spirit; obviously the LORD believes this to be true. Of Jesus it is written:

*So He Himself often **withdrew into the wilderness
and prayed*** (Luke 5:16).

It is in deserts and on mountains that God has so often chosen
to meet with His people. We have examples in both Old and New
Testaments:

*Then the LORD came down upon Mount Sinai, **on the
top of the mountain**. And the LORD called Moses to
the top of the mountain, and Moses went up*
(Exodus 19:20).

David, the man after God's *own heart* (Acts 13:22), worshipped God on a mountain's top:

*. . . David had come to **the top of the mountain**,
where he worshiped God* (2 Samuel 15:32).

Elijah was commanded to meet with God on a mountain:

*Go out, and **stand on the mountain** before the LORD*
(1 Kings 19:11).

God met with Jesus, Moses and Elijah on a high mountain:

*Jesus took Peter, James, and John his brother, led
them up on **a high mountain** by themselves; and He
was transfigured before them. His face shone like the
sun, and His clothes became as white as the light.
And behold, Moses and Elijah appeared to them,
talking with Him* (Matthew 17:1-3).

The post resurrection meeting between the risen Christ and
the disciples was also on a mountain:

*Then the eleven disciples went away into Galilee, to
the mountain which Jesus had appointed for them*
(Matthew 28:16).

God likes to meet with His people on mountains for a number
of reasons, not the least being that –

a)   A person who climbs a mountain in order to meet with God
is serious about being in His presence.

b)   When a man meets with God on a higher level he is more
able to see things from God's perspective.

There will be numerous high mountains for Israel to climb in the desert wilderness where God is bringing her. The LORD's ultimate objective for Israel in the wilderness is that she meet with Him – on His terms.

Israel's journey through her ultimate wilderness will be a time of judgement that precedes reconciliation.

In the Book of Ezekiel the LORD says:

*I will bring you into **the wilderness of the peoples***
(Ezekiel 20:35).

From the above scripture we see that there is another type of wilderness that the LORD is wont to use. The Ezekiel passage no doubt refers to the scattering of the Jews among the Gentile nations. In *"the wilderness of the peoples"* the Jews were subjected to unimaginable hardships and persecution – it was a time of judgement.

In our Hosea passage we have a different *"wilderness of the peoples;"* it is a **wilderness** of the **peoples'** own making – brought about by Israel's stiff-necked rebellion against the LORD.

There are interesting parallels with the wilderness experiences following the Exodus from Egypt and that of *"the wilderness of the peoples,"* and later we shall see parallels with the ultimate wilderness. Here is a *"wilderness of the peoples"* parallel:

*And I will bring you into the wilderness of the peoples, and there I will plead My case with you **face to face**. Just **as I pleaded My case with your fathers in the wilderness of the land of Egypt**, so I will plead My case with you,"* says the Lord GOD
(Ezekiel 20:35-36)

Despite the LORD pleading His case *"face to face"* with Israel in the first wilderness, an entire unbelieving generation doomed itself to perishing in the desert and was buried there. In *"the wilderness of the peoples"* the LORD also pled His case with the Jewish nation – millions suffered and died among the nations in that two-thousand-year-long wandering. Later we shall see the LORD again speaking with Israel *"face to face"* – in the ultimate wilderness where He is taking her.

We should remember that the ultimate wilderness, into which the LORD is luring Israel, is first a wilderness of judgement and punitive punishment, only later will it become a place of reconciliation. The LORD will become *"King"* over all Israel and it will take another desert experience for her to accept this. The ultimate wilderness will be a purging for the nation of Israel – the bleached bones of the unclean and unbelieving will never leave it.

Some of today's believing body will doubtlessly drop out due to hardships and *"the cares of this world"* (Matthew 13:22), but multitudes who do not currently believe will be added to the congregation of the LORD.

God will humble His people like He humbled them in the days of yore – by want and distress. But He will also deliver her in her hour of need like He did in the days of Moses. God provided the Israelites with water from the rock and bread from heaven, their clothing and sandals never so much as wore out after forty consecutive years of use, plus the LORD delivered Israel from all her enemies.

The wilderness is a dry and dusty, harsh and lonely local. It is in these conditions that God will prepare modern Israel's soul for her salvation. In the depths of her despair she will cry out to the depths of her *"Creator's"* compassion – *"deep shall call unto deep"* (Psalms 42:7).

It is God's unflagging love for His covenant people that forces Him to use heavy hands upon her. The promises that God made in turn to Abraham, Isaac and Jacob shall be honored. The promises spoken through the prophets shall be fulfilled. God's credibility in a disbelieving world is at stake. As grapes are crushed in order to release the sweet juice within, so God must crush Israel until the old whine becomes new wine.

Our look into Hosea 2:14 has thus far shown us that the LORD will personally bring Israel into a multifaceted wilderness. She will be enticed, seduced and deceived by her own inherent lusts. Going into the wilderness bodes ill for Israel in the near term.

As the Israelites in days long ago saw the miracles and wonders that God performed, so also has modern Israel witnessed many miracles from the hand of God, these latter miracles have been no less wondrous than those performed in Egypt and Canaan.

More prophecies have been fulfilled in the past sixty-four years than in the preceding two thousand years. Our Hosea prophecy is in the process of fulfillment.

It is an undeniable fact that the greater part of evangelical Christianity today believes that we are in the last days of the End Times. That being so we should expect the momentum of events concerning Israel to accelerate in the immediate days, months, and years ahead.

---

[1] See Chapter 4 of the author's book *When Day And Night Cease: A prophetic study of world events and how prophecy concerning Israel affects the nations, the Church and you* for a full exposition and refutation of Replacement Theology.

— *ten* —

The Wilderness
(Geographical)

When we take a map of the Middle East and are conversant with the demographics of the countries on the map, we see that all states making up this area are exclusively Islamic apart from one – Israel. The Jews' National Homeland is the exception to the Islamic rule in the entire Middle Eastern-North African area.

When we look more closely at our map we can note the position of this non-Islamic state. This tiny country of Israel stands out like a sore thumb. Israel is centrally located – positioned in the very center of the Islamic heartland – the birthplace of Islam. Israel is like a bullseye on a target. She stands alone in an Islamic sea, a very hostile Islamic sea. Israel is in a literal, uncongenial, geographical wilderness.

It was the LORD who set the boundaries of every nation, and He specifically set boundaries with Israel in mind:

> *He set the boundaries of the peoples **according to the number of the children of Israel***
> (Deuteronomy 32:8).

Some might argue that Israel existed long before Islam was a glint in the eye of Mohammed. This is true, but we must never forget that God is omniscient, which means He is all-knowing. God knows everything there is to know – past, present, and future:

> *I am God, and there is none like Me, **declaring the end from the beginning, and from ancient times things that are not yet done**, saying, "My counsel shall stand, and I will do all My pleasure'*
> (Isaiah 46:9-10).

Obviously, the LORD took Islam into consideration when He set Israel's boundaries, Islam did not catch Him napping because the Bible assures us that He who *"keeps Israel neither slumbers nor sleeps"* Psalms 121:4).

The land of Israel is a special land in a singularly distinctive location, it is:

> *a land for which the* LORD *your God cares;* **the eyes**
> **of the** LORD **your God are always on it**, *from the*
> *beginning of the year to the very end of the year*
>   (Deuteronomy 11:12).

Being the omniscient all-knowing God, the LORD knew that Mohammed and his followers would gnash their teeth at Israel and try to destroy her. Mohammed tried in vain to turn the Jews away from Judaism and have them follow him. They refused.

Mohammed and his followers used to keep Saturday, the Jewish Sabbath day, as their holy day, and they prayed five times each day facing Jerusalem. The Jews, however, made Mohammed irate because they would not follow him and he changed the Muslim holy day to Friday and altered the direction of prayer so that Muslims faced Mecca, in Arabia. And Mohammed began to fill the Qur'an (Koran) with diatribes against the Jews.

In the Qur'an Mohammed calls for the destruction of all Jews. The *Hadith*, the sayings attributed to Mohammed and handed down through the centuries, also calls for the death of all Jews. The *Hadith* goes as far as saying that it is a Muslim obligation to liquidate the Jews, that the Muslim messiah cannot come "unless there is first a great slaughter of the Jews."

One of Mohammed's most oft quoted texts – made on his deathbed – is: "Never do two religions exist in Arabia." Although the Arabian peninsular of today includes the nine Arab countries of Jordan, Iraq, Kuwait, Bahrain, Qatar, the United Arab Emirates, Oman, Yemen, and Saudi Arabia, Mohammed would most certainly have considered ancient Israel's enclave as part of his geographical Arabia. Most Arabs today look upon the entire Middle East as constituting Arabia, even though much of it is merely Muslim, not Arab, and they apply Mohammed's edict to the whole area.

Arabs, under the Kurdish-Muslim warrior Salah ad-Din (Saladin) defeated the Crusaders in the eighth century and drove them from the Holy Land. The Arabs held and ruled the land only briefly – a fleeting twenty-two years – but Muslims believe that what was once under Muslim control forever belongs to Islam. No other religion can be tolerated. Judaism especially, and Christianity generally, must be eradicated. After Jordanian troops captured the eastern section of Jerusalem in the 1948-49 war with Israel, all the ancient Jewish synagogues were destroyed – fifty-seven synagogues, dating back to the thirteenth century – ancient Jewish gravestones were uprooted and used for Muslim urinals, and Jews were forbidden access to the Western (Wailing) Wall, Judaism's holiest shrine, to pray.

Most of the early Christians, dating back almost two thousand years, have fled the region due to centuries of brutal Muslim oppression and persecution. In the immediate past few years alone, hundreds of churches, Christian homes, and Christian businesses have been burnt to the ground in the Middle East. On March 12, 2012, Grand Mufti Sheikh Abdul Aziz Al-Asheikh – Saudi Arabia's foremost religious leader – was quoted in Arabic media reports as telling a visiting Kuwaiti delegation that in line with Mohammed's injunction, it was "necessary to destroy all the churches of the region."

Israel exists in an ocean of bitter enemies – enemies who must fight the Jews and keep fighting and killing them because their Qur'an and other holy writings demand it of them. The Qur'an says that Israel is finished and that the Jews are "sons of pigs and monkeys." The Bible, on the other hand, says hundreds of times that the Jews will return to their ancient land and rebuild their cities, and they have done so. The fulfillment of these biblical prophecies proves the Bible to be true and the Qur'an untrue. This, for a Muslim, is unthinkable. Israel must be destroyed in order to vindicate both Mohammed and the Qur'an.

It is the constant wars waged against Israel by her aggressive, numerically superior Arab neighbors that has caused the Israel Defense Force to become one of the world's most powerful militaries. Israel must remain alert and strong enough to defeat all of her enemies at once. Israel was not alert in 1973 when the Arabs launched the Yom Kippur War that sent the Israel Defense

Force reeling along the Suez Canal. Israel learnt her lesson the hard way.

The Arab nations fight for a religious cause, Israel fights for her survival. Attacking Arab armies have been defeated by Israel time and time again. They will continue to attack her and continue to be defeated by her. If Israel were to lose only one war she would cease to exist.

Following the Yom Kippur War an Israeli officer spoke to an Egyptian officer he had captured. He said to the Egyptian: "We have fought five times now, and five times you have been defeated. Why do you keep fighting us?" The Egyptian replied:

> You may have defeated us five times, and you may defeat us fifteen times. But the sixteenth time we win.

There is no peace in the Middle East, there will be no peace and can be no peace until Jesus, the *"Prince of Peace"* (Isaiah 9:6), returns to rule and to reign from Jerusalem. Israel dwells in a geographical wilderness – an Islamic wilderness, a turbulent sea of Muslim hatred.

eleven

The Wilderness
(Diplomatic)

The term "diplomatic wilderness" in its true context means that a person, a body, or an entity, is in a position of disfavor. Israel is in a position of political disfavor. Israel is purposely being isolated by the nations, but the upside of this antisemitism is that it drives many Jews out of the diaspora into their divine inheritance – the land of Israel, thus fulfilling a number of biblical prophecies.

From the inception date of the modern state of Israel in 1948 until the late 1970s Israel could do little wrong in the eyes of the developed world. Her battling of enemies and winning against overwhelming odds in a succession of wars launched against her by Arab neighbors brought her accolades and admiration from around the world. Israel's lightening defeat over five powerful Arab armies in just six days in June 1967 stunned the world. Israel rode high in the estimation and respect of much of the world and her brilliant tactics in that war are still being taught in Western military academies.

In October 1973, a surprise attack was launched against Israel by a multiple of Arab armies on the holiest day of the Jewish year – Yom Kippur, *"the Day of Atonement"* (Leviticus 23:27) – a day when almost everything stops in Israel. Yom Kippur is a day when there is no public transportation, no newspapers, no television, and no radio. On this most holy day virtually only ambulances move on the roads and most Israelis will not answer the telephone if it rings. Everything except essential services cease on Yom Kippur. On *"the Day of Atonement"* much of the Israeli populace dresses in white clothing and walks to synagogues for hours-long services.

It was on this most holy of days that two armies, Egypt and Syria, with a vast number of men, machines, and weaponry,[1] launched the first wave of attacks that swamped the unsuspecting, bare-minimum of Israeli troops who had been left on duty. The Egyptian and Syrian armies were quickly joined by ten other Arab armies. And North Vietnam sent pilots to help Egypt; North Korea sent pilots to help Syria.

There being no means of communication on the holy day Israel could not mobilize her troops and few even knew that a war had been launched. Sirens were sounding, but Israelis thought they were malfunctioning. Nobody was listening when the Israel Defense Force radio network went on the air and no one answered the telephone when calls were made for troops to deploy. It took Israel three days to mobilize her troops by which time there had been a high loss of Israeli soldiers' lives – some units literally fought to the last man.

On the tenth day of the war Israel had already driven all the invading armies from her soil, and in twenty days her fighting men were at the gates of Cairo and Damascus. The Soviet Union was airlifting weapons to Egypt and Syria and threatened to "nuke" Israel if she did not withdraw her troops from Syrian and Egyptian soil.

In one of the most dramatic face-offs of the 1973 Yom Kippur War, the Soviet Mediterranean Squadron and the United States Sixth Fleet circled each other hundreds of miles out to sea in a bizarre dance in the confined waters of the Mediterranean. Over one hundred and fifty vessels, including three carrier task forces and more than thirty submarines, some with nuclear warheads, maneuvered around each other, their commanders' fingers on the button. It was the largest naval confrontation of the Cold War, but with the world's attention focused on Israel's fierce, two-front land war, the United States-Soviet Union encounter virtually went unnoticed. Only this seaborne intervention by the United States prevented a nuclear war.

However, after deploying the largest fighting force in Arab history – estimated to have been in excess of one million two hundred thousand men – and having launched the war with a surprise attack on Israel's holiest of religious days when she was preoccupied with religious activity, the Arabs were again defeated. Israel lost almost two thousand seven hundred of her finest young men, but the Arab world had suffered losses many times that number. For the Arabs it was a time for a new strategy. War had become too costly, too humiliating.

The new Arab strategy at that time was to use the oil weapon. They used it against the world to turn the nations against Israel. It has proven to be an effective weapon. In the immediate aftermath of the Yom Kippur War thirteen nations broke all diplomatic ties with Israel. It was the beginning of the downward slide of Israel's popularity. The nations' kowtowing to the oil producing nations continues to this day. And Israel's oil-lubricated plunge into an oil-induced diplomatic wilderness continues also.

There is a growing worldwide attempt to make Israel illegitimate. This is a danger to the existence of the Jewish State. Israel is the most isolated, lonely country in the world. Today, Israel is on the defense against a brand new form of weaponry. The Arab world did not succeed in any of the military wars it launched against Israel and its economic boycott also failed. And its terrorism has failed; now it is delegitimization – (dealt with in detail in the next chapter).

Among a profusion of vitriolic rants, Iran's President Mahmoud Ahmadinejad has said that Israel "must be wiped off the page of time." But the danger of Iran's potential to become a nuclear power is eclipsed by the new anti-Israel culture that was launched by the Arab and Muslim worlds, and which has since been adopted by the agencies of the United Nations and many Western nations, especially those of Europe.

In August 2012, Iran hosted a conference of the Non-Aligned Movement in Teheran. Representatives of one hundred and forty nations were in attendance, including two kings, twenty-seven presidents, numerous foreign ministers and the United Nations Secretary General. In Iran's Supreme Leader Ali Khamenei's speech he labeled Israel "a state of bloodthirsty wolves" and Palestinian Authority Foreign Minister Riad Maliki disgorged such vitriol upon Israel that Israel's then Foreign Minister Avigdor Lieberman said Maliki's speech was "something that Joseph Goebbels [Hitler's propaganda chief] could have written." Both Khamenei and Maliki found receptive audiences – nobody walked out, nobody heckled, nobody protested.

Israel is more isolated today than she has ever been. Her prospects of breaking out of this isolation are bleak, to say the least – there are so many individuals, groups, organizations, and governments working hard at demonizing and discrediting Israel.

Hamas rules Gaza. Hizb'allah rules Lebanon. Turkey has turned hostile. The Palestinian Authority has given up on America and demands a sovereign state from the United Nations General Assembly and the United Nations Security Council. Thanks to President Barack Obama, Hosni Mubarak, Israel's partner in Egypt, is gone and the Israeli embassy in Cairo has been sacked. Mobs in Amman, Jordan, have tried to do the same to Israel's embassy there.

The gas pipeline that carried Egyptian natural gas to Israel was blown up fourteen times in the first fifteen months following the fall of Hosni Mubarak in January 2011. In April 2012, Egypt's new Islamic government illegally cancelled the gas agreement contract with Israel in its entirety. The agreement was negotiated with the Mubarak regime and the economic loss to Israel has been greater than all the boycotts, embargoes, sanctions, and disinvestments combined.

On June 24, 2012, Mohammed Morsi of the Muslim Brotherhood became the new president of Egypt. Morsi has shown himself to be virulently anti-Israel in the past and has promised to "renegotiate" the peace treaty with Israel and forge closer ties with Iran. Morsi has also reportedly said he wants "to conquer Jerusalem."

When Hosni Mubarak was still holding power he told Israeli government officials that "Israel had made peace with the Egyptian government, not with the people of Egypt." Like the cancellation of the gas contract with Israel, official Egyptian actions since Mubarak's ousting make this all too obvious. On June 6, 2012, Egypt's *Al-Ahram* daily reported that production of an Egyptian film, *Regheef Aish* (Loaf of Bread), was stopped by the nation's censor due to allegations that it promoted normalization of relations with Israel.

Apparently, the peace treaty Israel signed with Jordan was also only with the Jordanian government and not with the Jordanian people. The independent Jordanian daily *Al-Arab Al-Yawm* reported on June 5, 2012, that Israeli tourists were assaulted in a southern Jordan market and that one witness said:

> Those who talk about peace between Israelis and Jordanians are delusional. The signed agreements are nothing but ink on paper. They are meaningless.

The "Arab Spring" that brought down Egypt's Hosni Mubarak and other Middle East autocratic leaders and dictators unleashed the demons of ethnic nationalism and Islamic fundamentalism that are virulently anti-Israel.

Next to the oil weapon in effectiveness the greatest onslaught against Israel has come from the United Nations (UN) organization. The United Nations, being an institution of surpassing cynicism and mendacity, is the most antisemitic organization in the world. With fifty-seven Islamic states and a roomful of the most corrupt, repressive, tin-pot regimes on earth among the one hundred and ninety-three member states of the United Nations that kowtow to the Arab oil producers and Iran, negative votes against Israel in the General Assembly are axiomatic. In the Security Council the United States has wielded its veto power against anti-Israel resolutions and has saved the day for Israel many a time.

Ask almost any Israeli politician, university lecturer, or taxi driver their opinion of the United Nations and the odds are that the response will be *"Oom Shmoom,"* the pejorative Hebrew slang term for "United Nothing." This contemptuous term has come to epitomize the Israeli mentality toward the United Nations ever since it was coined by David Ben-Gurion sixty years ago.

It was said earlier in Chapter three that Israel is treated as a pariah state by most of the world's nations. The Lord holds Israel to the highest moral code and, as in ancient days, modern Israel will pay heavily for turning her back on God's laws. However, the nations also hold Israel to a different standard of ethics and morality – a standard far higher than what they themselves operate under. This is utter hypocrisy.

Europe and Scandinavia are becoming increasingly belligerent toward Israel, and being anti-Israel is merely a metaphor for being antisemitic. Antisemitism is embedded in the DNA (deoxyribonucleic acid) of the majority of Europeans and Scandinavians. In general, their politicians lack the cojones needed to deal with the Muslim invasion of their countries and Islamists need only demonstrate against Israel in European and Scandinavian capitals, threatening violence, and the nations capitulate and take an even stronger stand against Israel.

The United Nations spends more time debating issues concerning Israel than it does on anything else in the world. The singling out of Israel for condemnation in the United Nations is an overt example of an international campaign to quietly destroy the Jewish State. One third of all United Nations' resolutions concern Israel. If the number of resolutions against Israel were to be used as a meter it would show the utter contempt the international community of nations has for Israel. Of all the member nations Israel is the only country ever to be the subject of a mechanism known as "item 7" – a permanent agenda item on the United Nations Human Rights Council. Israel is up for discussion at every session of the Council no matter what inhumanity toward man is going on elsewhere in the world.

Israel is experiencing a forced isolation from among the nations, but aeons ago her *"Creator"* said to her: *"I am the LORD your God, who has separated you from the peoples"* (Exodus 20:24) and decreed that Israel should be a nation that dwelt alone. It was evident to the spiritually perceptive:

> *And [Balaam] took up his oracle and said: "Balak the king of Moab has brought me from Aram, from the mountains of the east. 'Come, curse Jacob for me, and come, denounce Israel!'*
>
> *"How shall I curse whom God has not cursed? And how shall I denounce whom the LORD has not denounced? For from the top of the rocks I see him, and from the hills I behold him; there! **A people dwelling alone, not reckoning itself among the nations**"* (Numbers 23:7-9).

The contempt the nations show for Israel and the diplomatic isolation they force upon Israel plays right into the LORD's hands.

At the time of writing the United States is floundering in a severe recession with house market values having dropped to the lowest rate since the Great Depression. As of November 2012, more than forty-seven million Americans are receiving food stamps, untold millions are out of work – the author uses "untold millions" due to the official figures released being light years away from reality. The Obama administration calculates the number of unemployed by the number drawing unemployment benefits; however, unemployment benefits are only good for a limited number of months and many millions are now no longer eligible for benefits. Therefore, those millions are not counted in the published percentile of unemployed, which would triple the administration's official unemployment rate if they were. On September 9, 2012, *CNSNews* reported that the number of Americans whom the United States Department of Labor counted as eligible but "not in the civilian labor force" in August hit a record high of eighty-eight million nine hundred and twenty-one thousand, which means that America's real unemployment is around twice the official unemployment figure published monthly.

By early September 2012, the United States government had run up a national debt in excess of sixteen trillion dollars, the interest of which is far greater than the entire cost of the nation's annual defense budget. A September 11, 2012, report by the federal Bureau of Economic Analysis, the United States Gross Domestic Product (GDP) for 2012 will be almost half a trillion dollars less than the federal debt as at the close of business on September 10, 2012, which means America's debt was one hundred and three percent of the Gross Domestic Product on that date.

The United Kingdom is in recession, Greece, Spain, Portugal, Italy, and Ireland are all either bankrupt or teetering on the brink of bankruptcy and the Eurozone could break up due to the fiscal ineptitude of many members. Israel's economy however, continues to advance and the effect of the Global financial meltdown has been minimal for Israelis. Perhaps the nations and their leaders will one day understand that their prosperity hinges on their relationship and dealings with the nation of Israel.

Israel's economic expansion in the midst of a severe global recession may well be a reason for the current increase in the venom being spewed at Israel by European countries – nothing succeeds like success, and nothing infuriates another like someone else's success.

Thousands of years ago the LORD God Almighty, Israel's *"Creator,"* drew a line in the sand and declared that whoever blessed the Jewish people – and by extension the nation of Israel – would be blessed and whoever despises, reviles, humiliates, or ridicules them would be cursed. The truth of this has, largely due to tradition, all but been lost to us because almost all English Bibles incorrectly render the Genesis 12:1-3 promise. Here is how the majority of translations render it:

> *Now the LORD had said to Abram: "Get out of your country, from your family and from your father's house, to a land that I will show you.*
>
> *I will make you **a great nation**; I will bless you and make your name great; and you shall be a blessing.*
>
> *I will **bless** those who **bless** you, and I will **curse** him who **curses** you; and in you all the families of the earth shall be blessed"* (Genesis 12:1 - 3).

To the author's knowledge only Jay P. Green's A Literal Translation of the Bible renders the Hebrew of verse three correctly, and for this the author salutes him. In contrast to the traditional rendering of verse 3 Green correctly translates it thus:

> *"I will bless those who bless you, and **curse** the one who **despises** you; and in you shall all families of the earth be blessed"* (Genesis 12:3 Jay P. Green's A Literal Translation of the Bible).

The difference in the translation of verse three may appear to be slight, but it is not. The verse holds the physical, spiritual, and financial welfare of countless millions of people – Christian and non-believer alike – in those two words: *"bless"* and *"curse."* The Hebrew word translated as *"bless"* is ברך *(baruch)* which means "bless," "praise," "honor," and is the same word correctly used in each of the four usages in this passage. However, there are two distinctly different Hebrew words in verse three that are both translated as *"curse"* in the majority of English versions. Apparently, the editors and publishers of those translations are motivated more by tradition and profit than they are by truth and fact – they do not wish to rock the boat.

The first Hebrew word translated *"curse"* is אָרַר (*arar*) and it has truly terrible consequences. It is the word the LORD used when He cursed the serpent in Genesis 3:14 and said that henceforth it would travel on its belly and eat dust all its life. Most people are unaware that when a snake is dissected there are four atrophied legs tucked up inside. It was an animal that walked on all fours until God humbled it, permanently. The word is used against humans in several other instances, all with equally tragic results.

The second Hebrew word rendered *"curse"* in the popular translations is קָלַל (*killel*) which does not mean curse at all, it means "despise," "contempt," "revile," "humiliate," "ridicule," *et al.* And here lies the rub: all those who bless, praise, or honor Israel will be blessed, praised, or honored by God Almighty in return. All those who despise, ridicule, humiliate, revile, or hold Israel in contempt will be cursed (אָרַר – *arar*) in return by her *"Creator,"* and the outworking of that terrible curse upon individuals and entire nations is too awful to contemplate.[2] Nations, you have been warned! And the United Nations as a body needs to learn an important lesson from the oracle of Balaam:

> *Come . . . denounce Israel! "How shall I curse whom God has not cursed? And how shall I denounce whom the LORD has not denounced?"*
> (Numbers 23:7b-8).

Israel's relationship with the United Nations is tempestuous at best. The League of Nations, the forerunner of the United Nations, was instrumental in delivering Israel into the world of nations. However, the United Nations today unfairly opposes and condemns Israel at every turn and on every level.

The United Nations has a special rapporteur on human rights in the Palestinian territories, Richard Falk, an American Jew.

For readers to gain perspective on Richard Falk it is only fair to include here that he is a champion 9/11 "truther," which means to say that he firmly believes and postulates that the September 11, 2001, terrorist attacks were perpetrated and then covered up by the United States government and media.

Falk is an outspoken, strident, biased critic of Israeli actions in the West Bank and the Gaza Strip. He has compared Israeli policies toward the Palestinians with the actions of Nazis toward the Jews.

The world of diplomacy and organizations learned long ago that in order to have someone appear eminently qualified to wield a big stick over Israel, that person needs to be a Jew. Falk, a professor emeritus in international law at Princeton University is a self-hating Court Jew. A self-hating Jew is a Jew who wishes he were not a Jew, and a Court Jew is a Jew who rises to a position of power in the Gentile world. Proof of loyalty to the position of Court Jew, especially in an anti-Israel organization, are repeated condemnations of Israel – it adds "believability" to the condemnations. For Falk, Israel can do nothing right; the Palestinians can do nothing wrong. Thus, Israel's government refuses to cooperate with Falk and refuses him entry into Israel and the West Bank.

The practice of embedding Jews into organizations and groups hostile to Israel has been coined as "Jew Washing," and "Jew Washing" is widely practiced by non-governmental organizations (NGOs) in order to give "believability" to their biased reports, thereby increasing their funding.

In an August 2011 posting, Richard Falk posted a cartoon of a dog with "USA" written on his midriff and wearing a *kippa* (Jewish skull cap) urinating on a depiction of justice while devouring the bloody bones of a skeleton. The United Nations Watch monitoring organization wrote a letter to Navi Pillay, the High Commissioner for Human Rights calling for a condemnation of Falk for posting the "manifestly anti-Semitic" cartoon, adding that it incites "hatred against Jews as well as against Americans." The response from the Office of the High Commissioner for Human Rights (OHCHR) was:

It is not the place of the Office of the High Commissioner for
Human Rights to comment on a special rapporteur who was
appointed by the Human Rights Council.

Such is the farcical impartiality of both Falk and the Office of
the High Commissioner for Human Rights.

On July 1st, 2012, Richard Falk delivered a sixteen-page
report on Israel to the United Nations Human Rights Council.
In his multi-page diatribe, Falk had the shameless gall to say:
"Israel's military retaliation against Palestinian rocket fire from Gaza is not
justified." No doubt he would opine and apply the same degree
of fairness if Iran were to launch nuclear missiles at Israel and
Israel were to respond.

On October 25, 2012, Falk was back making headlines
with another assault upon Israel at the United Nations General
Assembly human rights group and submitted the report to the
United Nations General Assembly. Falk's latest report calls for:

an international campaign of legal attacks and economic
warfare (boycotts) on a wide group of companies that do
business in Israel.

Among the companies highlighted by Falk in his report were:
Caterpillar Inc. (United States); Veolia Environnement (France);
G4S (United Kingdom); Dexia Group (Belgium); Ahava
(Israel); the Volvo Group (Sweden); the Riwal Holding Group
(Netherlands); Elbit Systems (Israel); Hewlett Packard (United
States); Mehadrin (Israel); Motorola (United States); Assa Abloy
(Sweden); and Cemex (Mexico). The report warns American
employees of targeted companies that they face legal risks:

Employees of companies can face investigation and prosecution
for human rights violations committed irrespective of where the
violation was committed.

The United States Ambassador to the United Nations, Susan
Rice, condemned Falk's report and said his boycott call was
"irresponsible and unacceptable and poisoned the environment for peace."

Canadian Foreign Affairs Minister John Baird said Falk's
report was "offensive and unhelpful." A spokesman for the Foreign
Affairs Minister wrote in an email:

Canada calls on Mr. Falk to either withdraw this biased and disgraceful report, or resign from his position at the United Nations.

Israel and the United States joined Canada in calling for Falk's resignation and replacement.

A 2012 *BBC* (British Broadcasting Corporation) poll taken in twenty-two countries and involving more than twenty-four thousand respondents showed that only Pakistan and Iran were ranked negatively lower than Israel, which tied with North Korea for third place as the most negatively viewed state. Only majorities of respondents in the United States (fifty percent positive to thirty-five percent negative), Nigeria (fifty-four percent positive to twenty-nine percent negative), and Kenya (forty-five percent positive to thirty-one percent negative) felt Israel had a more positive effect upon the world than their countrymen who held opposing views.

Countries such as the United Kingdom and Germany – while often critical of Israeli policies – are still considered to be broadly supportive of the Jewish state. Yet the United Kingdom showed negative polling of (sixty-eight percent negative to sixteen percent positive) and Germany (sixty-nine percent negative to sixteen percent positive).

Canada is considered to be Israel's best friend in the world at this time of writing, even more so than the United States. Yet fifty-nine percent of Canadians surveyed in the *BBC* poll hold negative opinions of Israel while only twenty-five percent viewed Israel positively. Evidently it is not the Canadian government that is affecting the Canadian public's perceptions toward Israel.

If it is not governments that influence public opinion on Israel, then the most obvious cause is the news media's continual flow of biased and often completely fraudulent[3] coverage of Israel. Leading Western anti-Israel media titles include a clutch of British ones that contain the *Guardian*, the *Independent*, and the *BBC*; following close upon the British heels are America's *New York Times*, *Time Magazine*, *Newsweek*, and *CNN* (Cable News Network).

One of the basic tenets of journalism is to ensure the credibility of the information gathered is unquestionable. Today, by and large, that tenet has been discarded. Facts do not sell newspapers, magazines, or television advertising slots; news does – and news is only what the media makes it to be. Attitudes are now inserted by many reporters, which colors or embellishes the story according to the dictates of the reporter's worldview, and Israel invariably gets the shorter end of the stick. A reporter is entitled to his or her own opinion, but not to his or her own facts. The media conditions people to be anti-Israel.

The next greatest cause of negative public opinion concerning Israel is the overt antisemitic actions and policies of the United Nations. And the predominantly liberal left-wing news media is only too happy to give United Nations' antisemitic resolutions premium space and time, often with fanfares and banner headlines.

Israel's enemies, including terrorist organizations, recognized long ago that the modern battlefield is not only dependent on guns, tanks, or aircraft, but also on cameras and the written word. The constant, resolute feed of stories about the Arab-Israeli conflict is impossible to ignore. At some point Israel will become such a political hot potato that no politician will dare express support for her at the risk of alienating voters.

The United Nations' Durban I, II, and III Conferences were perhaps the most regrettable and damaging events of the first decade of the third millennium. They showed the total failure of the international community in general, and the United Nations in particular, to deal with the evils of racism and antisemitism.

More regrettable is the fact that the one attempt by the international community to deal with racism at the 2001 Durban Conference was that it was allowed to be hijacked – to be usurped, politicized, and manipulated into becoming a bitter, racist, antisemitic, and anti-Israel hate-fest.

No less immoral was the endorsement given at the Durban event to a global campaign to delegitimize the State of Israel within the international community of nations. The damage was and is immeasurable. Its effects continual.

The 2001 Durban I Conference, the forum that might have

originally been intended to deal with the above issues in a serious manner, became a by-word for razor-edged racism, intolerance, hatred, antisemitism, and Israel-bashing.

The initial conference documents, developed through a series of regional conferences, expert seminars, and a formal preparatory committee, and placed before the conference delegates at the opening of the conference, contained a series of bracketed paragraphs. These bracketed paragraphs dealt with: "Zionist racist practices against Semitism;" describing Israel as a "racist, apartheid state;" accusing Israel of "ethnic cleansing of the Arab population in historic Palestine;" calling for revoking legislation in Israel based on racial or religious discrimination, such as Israel's Law of Return; and the downgrading of the term "Holocaust" by multiple references to "holocausts" suffered by other peoples, including the Palestinians, which was a clear insult to the memory of the six million Jews murdered in the Nazi Holocaust.

Similarly, the Draft Program of Action called for an end to the "foreign occupation of Jerusalem by Israel, together with all its racist practices" and called upon all nations to refrain from recognizing Jerusalem as the capital of Israel. The United States and Israel walked out of the Durban I conference on the fourth day.

In an attempt to "re-legitimize" the Durban process the General Assembly of the United Nations decided to convene a Durban Review Conference in 2009 in Geneva, generally termed "Durban II." True to form, the United Nations Human Rights Council chose to elect Libya to chair the Preparatory Committee, assisted by Iran and Cuba.

In early 2008 it was evident that several countries intended to boycott the review conference on the strength of the reputation Durban I had built. In January 2008, Canada announced its decision to boycott Durban II:

> We withdrew from a process that sees Iran sitting on the organizing committee, a country whose president has repeatedly engaged in inciting genocide against the Jewish nation, a conference in which Libya plays a central role on the organizing committee, a conference where many of the key organizing meetings were set, no doubt coincidentally, on

Jewish high holidays to diminish the participation of Israeli and Jewish delegates, a process which re-invited to participate all of the NGOs that turned the original Durban conference into the notorious hate-fest, including those responsible for circulating copies of the "Protocols of the Elders of Zion" and organizations which outside the conference venue held up portraits of Adolf Hitler, and a conference which as well re-invited those NGOs made it difficult or impossible for Jewish NGOs to come as observers.

In May 2008, the United Kingdom's Minister for Europe said:

I wish to be clear that the UK government will play no part in a gathering that displays such behavior. We will continue to work to make sure that the conference is a success, but we will play no part in an international conference that exhibits the degree of anti-Semitism that was disgracefully on view on the previous occasion.

Following Canada and the United Kingdom, Israel, the United States, Australia, Poland, New Zealand, the Czech Republic, Germany, and Italy also boycotted the Durban II conference.

Unable to shed the negative reputation that had been built up in Durban I, the Durban II conference rapidly descended into a mode of total hostility regarding Israel and anti-Zionism, with the formal opening address by none other than Iranian President Mahmoud Ahmadinejad who, true to form, made a call for the eradication of Zionism, attributing all the ills of the world to Zionism and Israel:

"The word Zionism personifies racism that falsely resorts to religion and abuses religious sentiments to hide their ugly faces."

That vile statement prompted many delegations to leave the room.

Resolutions adopted at the 2009 and 2010 sessions of the United Nations General Assembly called for a one-day plenary event at heads of state and government level to be convened in September 2011. It was to be a follow-up to and a commemoration of the tenth anniversary of the 2001 Durban Conference. It became known as Durban III, and that antisemitic, anti-Israel hatefest was held in the United Nations building in New York.

The Canadian Minister for Citizenship, Immigration and Multiculturalism, Jason Kenney, called upon the United Nations High Commissioner for Human Rights, Navi Pillay, a native of Durban, South Africa (whom an August 2010 op-ed in the *New York Daily News* referred to as "the United Nations' anti-Israel czar"), to "stop the process and realize that the poison at Durban I has placed the entire process under a permanent cloud." The official Canadian government announcement dated November 25, 2010 stated:

> Our government has lost faith in the Durban process. We will not be part of this event, which commemorates an agenda that promotes racism rather than combats it.

In June 2011, the United States informed the United Nations of its decision to boycott the session, saying:

> The United States will not participate in the Durban Commemoration. In December, we voted against the resolution establishing this event because the Durban process included ugly displays of intolerance and anti-Semitism, and we did not want to see that commemorated.

In a similar vein, the Czech Foreign Ministry announced on 21 July 2011 that it will not attend the session:

> Prague is dissatisfied with the Durban process as it has been often abused for a number of unacceptable statements with anti-Jewish connotations.

A further eleven nations boycotted the event, including major democracies. Durban III, the tenth anniversary commemoration session, was scheduled to take place at the same time as the Palestinian unilateral action that sought formal recognition by the United Nations of a sovereign Palestinian state "within the 1967 borders" It is very doubtful that the double scheduling was coincidental, and it was only the threat of veto by the United States that prevented the United Nations Security Council from passing the resolution and admitting "Palestine" to the United Nations.

The United Nations Relief and Works Agency (UNRWA) was founded in December 1949 to help the thousands of Arabs (the term "Palestinian Arab" did not exist at that time[4]) uprooted during Israel's War of Independence. Today it runs clinics, schools, and social services for a reputed seven million[5] refugees and their descendants in camps in the West Bank (biblical Judea and Samaria), the Gaza Strip, Jordan, Jerusalem, Lebanon, and Syria.

Palestinians are the first people to come to mind when the word "refugee" is uttered, and they have paid dearly to reinforce this misconception. Palestinians have been largely dispossessed by their own fellow Arabs and have lived as second-class citizens in the Middle East for over six decades.

Thousands of young, pro-Palestinian persons around the world annually protest the *nakba* (Arabic for "catastrophe") of Israel's birth and the supposed creation of hundreds of thousands of Arab refugees. "Palestine" is one of the great global, radical chic causes of today. But none of these indignant protestors give a single thought for the other *nakba* – the Jewish one.

Joan Peters, in her monumental work, *From Time Immemorial*, documents from the myriads of records in the British Archives, to which she had unfettered access, that "a maximum of 340,000 Arab refugees" fled in one direction, from Palestine, while more than eight hundred and fifty thousand Jewish refugees fled in the other direction – from Arab countries.

Israel was heartened to learn that on November 8, 2012, Canadian Member of Parliament and former Minister of Justice, Irwin Cotler, tabled a motion in the Canadian Parliament for formal recognition of eight hundred and fifty thousand Jews "forcibly displaced and exiled from Arab countries since the declaration of the State of Israel in 1948." Cotler said:

> The Arab countries rejected the United Nations Partition Resolution of 1947-1948, and launched their double aggression of a war against the nascent Jewish state and assaults on their own Jewish nationals, resulting in two refugee populations, Palestinian refugees and Jewish refugees from Arab countries.

> The time has come to restore the pain and plight of Jewish
> refugees from Arab countries to the international peace and
> justice narrative from which it has been eclipsed these past
> sixty years.

The cause of the flight of the Arabs in 1948 was war – a war which seven Arab nations launched against the fledgeling state of Israel the day following her historic declaration. In the Arab countries the cause of the Jewish flight was ethnic cleansing and dispossession. Israel has never had a deliberate policy of driving out her Arab population. Had she had instituted such a policy Arabs would not constitute twenty-one percent of her population today, nor would Arabs be occupying prominent positions in the Israeli government and the judiciary.

By contrast, in Arab countries that together occupy ten percent of all the world's livable land, the Jewish population has dropped from above one million to less than four thousand. The Arab Spring that began in late 2010 in Tunisia is taking a further toll on the Jewish remnants in Tunisia, Yemen, Egypt, and Morocco. A reduction of over ninety-nine percent in the Jewish populations within the Arab world cannot be explained away as "Jews leaving their homes of their own free will." They were driven out.

Widespread riots, executions, internment and abuse of Jews in the Arab world were looked upon as justifiable retaliation for the birth of the Jewish state in the heart of "Muslim Arabia."

All those exercised by the destruction of Arab villages in Israel during the war should spare a thought for the Jewish life, culture and civilization erased from almost every city and town in the Middle East and North Africa. According to the World Organization of Jews from Arab Countries, Jews lost not only homes, schools, shops, markets, synagogues, and cemeteries, but also "deeded land and property equivalent to five times the size of Israel itself."

Israel, in the 1948-49 War of Independence, was fighting for her life, yet she absorbed the refugees being driven out by the Arab states. In what must surely be recognized as a modern miracle, Israel actually absorbed a greater number of refugees than the number of her entire population at that time – around six hundred thousand persons. It is an official fact that in 2012 some fifty percent of Israel's population are refugees or descendants of refugees from Arab lands.

Israel absorbed all the refugees from Arab lands, yet twenty-one Arab nations, with all their huge amount of territory and vast oil deposits that place them among the richest nations on the planet, have not absorbed a single Arab refugee. Only Jordan ever accorded her refugees any form of citizenship, but since 1988, as was stated in Chapter two, Jordan has stripped multitudes of refugees of their Jordanian citizenship, rendering them stateless, and plans to cancel the citizenships of every Arab refugee.

The 1948-49 war created an irrevocable de facto exchange of population that took place to the overwhelming benefit of the Arab countries. The Arab attack upon Israel created two concurrent refugee problems, but due to the Western news media everyone in the world knows only about Arab refugees. The refugees flowed in two directions, but justice is demanded only for the Arabs.

Concerning the treatment of refugees, one is again constantly subjected to television film clips and newspaper and magazine photographs (some genuine and others not) of the squalid living conditions of the Arab refugees. Many refugees living in camps do indeed live in squalid rat-infested conditions, but that is not the fault of Israel. First of all, many Middle Eastern Arabs have little concept of health or sanitation and open or no sewerage has been a way of life for generations. Second of all, Israel did not build the refugee camps – the Arabs did. Third of all, Israel has tried repeatedly to rehouse Arab refugees into better conditions.

Israel has been engaged in consistent efforts to improve the living conditions in refugee camps in her territory. Beginning in 1970, plans were drawn up and steps were taken to improve the situation of the refugees, and provide them with proper housing and an infrastructure of services. Residential projects were built, housing some ten thousand families who chose to leave the camps. Each family was given a plot of land, and more than seventy percent of the families built their own homes according to their needs and preferences. The new neighborhoods were built on State land within Municipal areas near the camps, and each was provided with its own network of electricity, water, sanitation, roads, paved sidewalks and developed surroundings. In each neighborhood, public buildings – schools, health clinics, shopping centers and mosques – were built.

The policy continues today. A refugee who wishes to leave the camp is given a plot of land, chooses his own type of dwelling and construction plan, receives a building permit from the Municipal authorities who are responsible for supervising construction, and becomes the full property owner once the building is completed, his property being registered in the Land Register. Israel seeks to show that a solution to the problem is feasible.

However, since 1971, a little-noticed United Nations Resolution on the Gaza Strip has been annually adopted. The resolution states *inter alia*:

> The General Assembly reiterates strongly its demand that Israel desist from the removal and resettlement of Palestine refugees in the Gaza Strip.

A similar annual Resolution on the West Bank, states *inter alia*:

> The General Assembly is alarmed by Israel's plans to remove and resettle the Palestine refugees of the West Bank and to destroy their camps. The General Assembly calls once again upon Israel to abandon those plans and to refrain from any action that leads to the removal and resettlement of Palestine refugees in the West Bank.

It is ironic that most of those who preach about the need to overcome the plight of the refugees in the camps repeatedly lend their hands to United Nations Resolutions that perpetuate the problem.

The United Nations does not want the refugees to leave the camps, it wants Israel out of her land. The Arab refugee problem is political. It is a weapon used against Israel and the suffering of refugees is of no concern to those who use that weapon.

Jewish refugees from Arab countries were all absorbed into Israel, but a grossly exaggerated seven million[5] refugees and descendants from the 1948 war continue to languish in fifty-nine United Nations Relief and Works Agency "temporary" refugee camps.

Born in December 1949, the United Nations Relief and Works Agency is now funded to the tune of one point two billion dollars annually by thirty-eight Western democracies, with the American government donating twenty-five percent of the annual budget.

The United Nations Relief and Works Agency makes no effort to seek any long term solutions for descendants of Arab refugees who have wallowed in the indignity of refugee life for more than sixty-three years. It could adopt the principles of the United Nations High Commission For Refugees which successfully relocated thousands of Arab refugees from Iraq, placing them in a number nations around the world, beginning with Chile.

Conversely, the United Nations Relief and Works Agency instills millions of Arab refugee descendants with the false hope that they will be repatriated to their 1948 villages, even though these villages no longer exist. It makes no effort to even encourage Arab refugee descendants to plan for a future Palestinian state that may be established in the West Bank and Gaza Strip. Instead, the United Nations Relief and Works Agency embraces the "right of return" curricula of the Palestinian Authority, Syria, Lebanon, and Jordan. United Nations Relief and Works Agency facilities boast maps of "Palestine" which replace Israel, where all Israeli cities are described as Arab cities.

The United Nations Relief and Works Agency school system's call to join the armed struggle to realize the "right of return" has transformed the camps into a breeding ground for terrorists, complete with military-style training and provision for weapons storage. In March 2012, the Hamas terror group won its fifth consecutive election to take charge of the United Nations Relief and Works Agency trade union and the United Nations Relief and Works Agency teachers' union in Gaza.

Some two million Palestinian refugees are registered with the United Nations Relief and Works Agency's Jordan offices. In 2011 the association of United Nations Relief and Works Agency employees endorsed a decision to ban the introduction of Holocaust studies in the Agency's schools:

> Teaching UNRWA students about the so-called "Holocaust" as part of human rights harms the Palestinian cause and changes

the students' views regarding their main enemy, namely the Israelis.

Since 2009, Hamas in Gaza has actively opposed the United Nations Relief and Works Agency's attempts to introduce the Holocaust into the school curriculum in Gaza. Hamas claims it "contradicts Palestinian culture."

The United Nations Relief and Works Agency purposely perpetuates the Arab refugee problem by resuscitation; it is an anachronistic institution that should have died decades ago.

A recent development that could throw a wrench into the United Nations Relief and Works Agency's works is the June 2012 amendment to a bill, recently approved by the United States Senate Appropriations Committee, mandating that the secretary of state must report how many of the Palestinians serviced by the United Nations Relief and Works Agency fled or left homes in Israel during the War of Independence and how many are only their descendants.

In 1950, the United Nations Relief and Works Agency defined a refugee as someone who had "lost his home and his means of livelihood" during the war launched by Arab countries in response to Israel's declaration of independent statehood. In 1965 the United Nations Relief and Works Agency decided – against objections from the United States – to include as refugees the children, grandchildren, and great-grandchildren of those who left Israel. And in 1982 the United Nations Relief and Works Agency further extended eligibility to all subsequent generations of descendants – forever.

Under the United Nations Relief and Works Agency rules, even if the descendant of a Arab refugee has become a citizen of another state, he's still a refugee. For example: of the two million refugees registered in Jordan, all but one hundred and sixty-seven thousand hold Jordanian citizenship. By adopting this policy, the United Nations Relief and Works Agency flagrantly violates the 1951 Convention Relating to the Status of Refugees, which clearly states that a person shall cease to be considered a refugee if he has "acquired a new nationality, and enjoys the protection of the country of his new nationality."

Jonathan Schanzer, who researches the Palestinians for the Foundation for Defense of Democracies, estimated that the number of living refugees who were displaced during the War of Independence is about thirty thousand people, in contrast to the seven million counted by the United Nations Relief and Works Agency.

Schanzer said the bill's passage by the Senate Appropriations Committee at least has a symbolic impact:

> The Palestinians have had an extended position on the right of return for years. No one's questioned it. This shifts the center of gravity on the debate.

The Palestinian Authority's reaction to the Senate refugee amendment was laughable. It said the amendment may further delay a peace deal with Israel. Who is kidding whom? The Palestinians have been using every tactic in its big tome of tricks to avoid peace. The Palestinians should wake up to the fact that the longer they take to get back to the negotiating table the less they will end up with – less land for their state, and perhaps a lesser count in their political "refugee" weapon.

The United Nations Human Rights Council (UNHRC) has been described as being "Orwellian." Novelist Eric Blair, better known by his pseudonym George Orwell, is responsible for the above adjective that is derived from his adopted name and which has become commonplace in the English language. "Orwellian" denotes a bizarre reality and the United Nations Human Rights Council is truly a bizarre reality.

The United Nations Human Rights Council was established in 2006 after Secretary-General Kofi Annan acknowledged that its forerunner, the Human Rights Commission, was mired in partisan agendas, allowed countries with appalling records to join and had lost direction. Annan assured the world that the Human Rights Council was in dire need of reformation.

The old disease has proven itself better than Annan's cure. Nations such as Iran, Sudan, Zimbabwe and North Korea – all of which violate human rights as official policy – have been voted onto the Human Rights Council. Libya, where abuse is commonplace, was elected to chair the organization even while being investigated for corruption.

On November 8, 2012, the United Nations General Assembly, in another Orwellian move, elected Sudan, led by warlord Omar al-Bashir, to a seat on the United Nations Human Rights Council starting in 2013 – al-Bashir's Islamist regime received more votes than the did the United States.

Sudan's President Omar al-Bashir has been wanted by the International Criminal Court since early 2009 on charges of war crimes and crimes against humanity stemming from the conflict in Darfur. Genocide charges were added in 2010.

United States Representative Ileana Ros-Lehtinen said:

> Allowing this genocidal dictatorship, which has killed thousands of its citizens, to serve on such a body is beyond hypocrisy, it is callous, dangerous, and tragic – it's just gone too far.

Ros-Lehtinen added: "It is beyond apparent that the United Nations is broken."

On December 10, 2012, the United Nations Human Rights Council marked Human Right Day by electing Mauritania to the Council. Mauritania is a North African Islamic state where conversion to another faith carries the death penalty. Slavery of black Africans has been rooted in Mauritanian society for centuries and it is estimated that up to eighteen percent of the population is in slavery today. A word more bizarre than "Orwellian" need be found to describe the outlandish actions of the United Nations Human Rights Council.

The loser in this shameful state of affairs? Human rights and human beings. The Iranian girls who can be forcibly married from the age of nine. Saudi women, who cannot vote, drive, walk outdoors without a male guardian or claim sexual abuse without four witnesses. The innocents of Darfur, Harare, and Beijing who suffer indignities with negligible hope of the perpetrators being held to account. People who suffer genital mutilation, child slavery.

In March 2012, Mohammed Merah murdered a rabbi, three Jewish children, and three French paratroopers in Toulouse, southern France. Merah cited allegiance to al-Qaeda ideology as his motivation. The viciousness of his actions – particularly the chilling cruelty with which he pursued eight-year-old Myriam Monsonego and grabbed her by the hair before shooting her three times – brought France to a standstill and its presidential campaign to a halt. Merah's sister, Souad, was recorded saying: "I am proud of my brother – proud, proud, proud!"

And the United Nations Human Rights Council – the world bastion of human rights? Did it find it within itself to denounce this barbaric violation of the most fundamental of human rights – the right to life? Or to pause, even fleetingly, to offer solace to the grieving families which had been destroyed in an act so callous as to cry out for condemnation? It didn't happen. What did happen, hours later, was that the Human Rights Council mustered all due gravity to pass five resolutions condemning Israel, establishing a mission to investigate the:

implications of settlements on the civil, political, economic, social and cultural rights of the Palestinian people.

The unashamedly one-sided resolution failed to mention terrorism, ongoing incitement by naming schools after suicide bombers, or rockets targeting civilians. Passed thirty-six to one, its sponsors included Iran and Syria – the latter having slaughtered almost eighty thousand of its own citizens in less than two years. As with the Goldstone Report on the Gaza war – also a Human Rights Council "inquiry" – Israel was deemed guilty at the outset by virtue of its terms of reference.

It is tragic that the world's putative parliament of nations is unable to mount even a semblance of protecting, let alone advancing, human rights. Membership of the Human Rights Council is determined by distributing seats among five regional groups, the Africans and Asians compromising the majority. Members of the Organization of the Islamic Conference (OIC) are the majority within the African and Asian groups, giving them the balance of power, with Israel the only one of the one hundred and ninety-three United Nations members excluded from a group.

Given these numbers, it is no coincidence that the United Nations Human Rights Council has passed more resolutions against Israel than against all other one hundred and ninety-two members combined, has a permanent agenda item which criticizes Israel and has commissioned thirty reports condemning it, compared with five on Syria, three on Iran and none on Saudi Arabia, China or the genocidal charter of Hamas – whose envoy, Ismail al-Ashqar, addressed the Human Rights Council in Geneva in March 2012.

On June 2012, Sameh Habeeb, media head of the "Palestinian Return Centre" spoke at a United Nations Human Rights Council meeting. The "Palestinian Return Centre" is one of the central institutions through which Hamas operates in Britain. Habeeb said, *inter alia*, in a United Nations room, using a United Nations microphone, at a United Nations-advertised event associated with the United Nations top human rights body:

> In 1947, 1948, and 1949 the Palestinian refugees were ethnically cleansed by the Israeli gangs. Some Arab armies came to Palestine to fight the Zionist project, which came from all over Europe to take over Palestine and to make it as a national home for the Jews, although it was always the national home for the Palestinians for thousands and thousands of years.

This Arab propaganda – nothing but lies from beginning to end[6] – is of the worst kind. It further delegitimizes Israel before an already biased body that is antagonistic toward Israel – and the lies are swallowed whole by the credulous listeners.

It is a sorry commentary on the international community of nations – that it welcomes and allows vested interests to get in the way of righting moral inversions.

Tensions have also grown between the United Nations Office for the Coordination of Humanitarian Affairs and the Israeli government, particularly after a United Nations Office for the Coordination of Humanitarian Affairs information officer, Kuhlood Badawi, tweeted a picture in March 2012 of a Palestinian father carrying a blood-soaked young daughter and Badawi's tweet claimed that she was killed by an Israel Defense Force strike. Badawi's photograph was accompanied by the comment:

> "Palestine is bleeding. Another child killed by Israel. Another father carrying a child into a grave in Gaza.

The photograph went viral on the internet.

Israel denied Badawi's report. It subsequently emerged that the picture was from an archived *Reuters* report published in 2006. *Reuters* verified that the photograph was of a Palestinian girl who died in an accident totally unrelated to Israel. Kuhlood Badawi has been involved in several other incidents dating back to 2008 where she uses Twitter to incite local disturbances. Israel's Ambassador to the United Nations, Ron Prosor, has become frustrated with Valerie Amos, a British national and head of the United Nations Office for the Coordination of Humanitarian Affairs, because she has refused to terminate Badawi's employment at the United Nations even though she has a history of incidents that have violated the organization's ethics.

But lies, deceit, and inaction are an integral part of the United Nations policy of delegitimizing Israel in the eyes of the world.

Despite lobbying by the United States and last-minute appeals, the United Nations Educational, Scientific, and Cultural Organization (UNESCO) voted at the end of October 2012 to admit "Palestine" as its one hundred and ninety-fifth member. The United States responded within hours by discontinuing funding for the agency, and a sixty million dollar payment due the following month went unpaid.

A United States' law from the 1990s bars Washington from funding any United Nations' agency that recognizes a Palestinian state without there being a negotiated peace agreement with Israel. Palestinian Authority President, Mahmoud Abbas, has refused to return to the negotiating table until Israel meets his demands. Abbas demands that Israel freeze all construction in the disputed territories; accept a sovereign Palestinian state within the 1967 borders – with only minor adjustments; and release all of the thousands of Palestinian prisoners who are incarcerated in Israeli jails for involvement in terrorist activities against Israel.

The first two of Abbas's demands are a direct result of President Barack Obama's political ineptitude. Almost three years ago Obama told the world that "Israel should stop building settlements in the West Bank [biblical Judea and Samaria]." Obama's statement became Abbas's mantra. Since that time Abbas has insisted that Israel freeze all settlement activity before talks can restart.

One year ago Obama said that "the basis for an Israel-Palestinian peace agreement should be the 1967 borders," which Abbas pounced upon and this became his second demand. On May 14, 2012, Abbas said that he himself "cannot be less Palestinian than Obama." Apparently, Obama only removes one foot from his mouth in order to replace it with the other.

A September 12, 2012, *Jerusalem Post* editorial titled "**The Palestinian Authority's sorry state**" began with:

> No headlines were generated when Palestinian Authority President Mahmoud Abbas recently insisted that there would be no peace unless Jews were "evacuated from Jerusalem, our holy city and the eternal capital of our state.

Certainly no headlines were generated in Israel or, apparently, even in the mainstream media. Israel tends to dismiss Abbas's propensity for ludicrous, often racist demands, because of the supposed "peace negotiations" having been on and off due to Palestinian intransigence for some eighteen years at the time of writing. With the settlements, Israelis cannot be expected to wait forever for a new home, a new bathroom, or an additional bedroom, therefore construction continues and will continue until a negotiated agreement brings change.

One of many myths that distort the international perception of the Arab-Israeli conflict is that there were actual pre-1967 "borders" between Israel and the west bank of the Jordan River. The 1967 Six-Day War was the result of the renewed Arab effort to "wipe Israel off the map" – a renewal of the 1948 War of Independence that had ended only in a temporary cease-fire, with no interest among most Arab leaders for a long-term peace treaty with Israel. This is the reason that there were never any pre-1967 borders between Israel and the west bank of the Jordan River.

The 1949 cease-fire lines are exactly that – cease-fire lines. Those armistice lines are not and never have been legally recognized as Israel's borders, they are merely the lines the Israel Defense Force was holding when the fighting stopped in 1949 and from which they defended the nation at the outbreak of the 1967 war.

Another myth is the belief that in the 1967 war Israel occupied "Palestinian east Jerusalem and the West Bank." In fact this territory had been occupied by Jordan in the 1948 war and from there Israel was repeatedly attacked. Sacred and historic Jewish Jerusalem was systematically closed off and desecrated during this period. In 1967 the Jewish presence was restored when the Israel Defense Force defeated the Jordanian forces. Jordan had annexed Judea and Samaria in 1950 and renamed it the West Bank, but this annexation was recognized only by two countries – Britain, a country that harbors anti-Israel sentiments, and Pakistan, a stridently anti-Israel country.

And while the Israeli government adopted a policy of trading land for a long-awaited peace, the Arab League, meeting in Khartoum, slammed the door in the face of any negotiations or agreements forever with the now famous three No's – "No peace with Israel, no recognition of Israel, no negotiations with Israel." This was the unplanned and impromptu beginning of the settlements – they were built on the foundation of Arab rejectionism.

In the decade that followed the 1967 war only a handful of settlements had been constructed on the captured territory. After 1977, continuing Arab belligerence provided the impetus for the expansion of the settlement movement. At the time of writing there are some three hundred thousand Israelis living in one hundred and twenty-one settlements in the West Bank (biblical Judea and Samaria). These settlements today constitute less than two percent of the land in the West Bank. Obviously, the small amount of land these settlements occupy do not and would not prevent a Palestinian state from being established in the West Bank and Gaza Strip, where Israel has no presence. Only Mahmoud Abbas's set-in-stone demands prevent peace negotiations from beginning again. Albeit they would likely collapse again as soon as the Palestinians could think of another reason to disrupt them.

Agreeing to the 1967 lines for a Palestinian state is a non-starter. Those lines are indefensible for Israel and have been described as "Auschwitz lines" – a reference to the Auschwitz extermination camp in Poland where the Nazis murdered more than one million one hundred thousand Jews in World War II. Israel must have secure, defensive borders in any negotiated agreement with the Palestinians.

Mahmoud Abbas's third demand, that Israel release all Palestinian prisoners before he will restart talks with Israel, is another non-starter. Releasing around six thousand Palestinians from Israeli prisons – thousands of whom are dedicated terrorists with Israeli blood on their hands – is tantamount to signing death warrants for hundreds or thousands of Israeli civilians.

Palestinian Authority President Mahmoud Abbas knows full well that Israel will never capitulate to his latest set of demands, and that suits the Palestinian leadership well because it can continue to blame Israel for the lack of progress in restarting the talks. Abbas, who was Yasser Arafat's deputy, no more wants a state for his people than Arafat himself did. Prime Minister Ehud Barak offered Arafat ninety-eight percent of the West Bank and all of east Jerusalem, including the Temple Mount, the holiest place in Judaism, but Arafat turned it down and started a low-grade war known as the second *intifada*, in which thousands of Palestinian and Israeli civilians lost their lives.

Prime Minister Ehud Olmert was prepared to destroy tens of settlements and evict upwards of one hundred and eighty thousand Israelis. Olmert offered Abbas ninety-two percent of the West Bank and all of east Jerusalem, including the Temple Mount, but Abbas turned the offer down. Let the author make the following point crystal clear: the Palestinian leadership does not want a state that has been negotiated between themselves and Israel, they want Israel destroyed. They now believe they have found the way to bring that about. And that way is via the latent antisemitism that resides in the DNA of European and Scandinavian peoples.

Mahmoud Abbas is hotly pursuing the recognition of a sovereign state of "Palestine" through the United Nations, which, as stated previously, is the most antisemitic organization on planet Earth. If it was up to the General Assembly to admit "Palestine" to the organization, it would be a shoo-in for the Palestinians. But the Security Council alone has the power to admit or reject an application for full membership, even if the General Assembly approves it. Mainly through the efforts of the United States, the Palestinians could not muster a majority among the fifteen members of the Security Council in September 2011 to force the United States to use its veto. But many of the members of the Security Council only have two-year terms. Abbas will wait until new members of the Security Council (elected by the General Assembly) make up a more favorable grouping, forcing the United States to use its veto to prevent "Palestine" from being admitted. Legally it would be a loss for the Palestinians, but it would be a moral victory and portray to the world that the United States is prejudiced against the Palestinians.

The United Nations Educational, Scientific, and Cultural Organization's vote to admit "Palestine" as a full member was a significant victory for the Palestinians. It conducted the vote knowing full well that the United States had threatened to cut its funding, which is twenty-two percent of the United Nations Educational, Scientific, and Cultural Organization's entire budget. Yet it went ahead and one hundred and seventy-three countries voted: one hundred and seven were in favor, fourteen were opposed, and fifty-two abstained.

Mahmoud Abbas's office let it be known that it was preparing to apply for membership in eighteen United Nations' agencies. But with the United Nations Educational, Scientific, and Cultural Organization having lost in excess of ninety million dollars per annum, and the American promise to cut funding to every agency that followed suit, United Nations Secretary-General Ban Ki-noon lost no time is summoning Abbas to persuade him not to apply for further memberships in United Nations' agencies. The United Nations stood to annually lose several hundred million dollars, which it can ill-afford to do.

At the time of writing Abbas has been successful in his unilateral bid for the United Nations to recognize "Palestine" as a "non-member state," a status enjoyed today only by the Vatican. Abbas garnered the support of United Nations geopolitical regional groups to this end. The Palestine Liberation Organization has been defined as a "permanent observer" since 1974.

Chief Palestinian negotiator Saeb Erekat told the London-based daily *Al-Quds Al-Arabi* that the status upgrade turns "Palestine" into "a state on the 1967 lines, with east Jerusalem as its capital," adding that the Palestinian state would then "be recognized as a state under occupation."

The status of "non-member state" will not allow the Palestine Liberation Organization voting power in the United Nations General Assembly, but will enable it to join international institutions such as the International Court of Justice and the International Criminal Court and sign international conventions. Abbas may well have been reading George Orwell who said:

> "He who controls the present, controls the past. He who controls the past, controls the the future."

Nowhere is this more true than in the explosive Middle East.

The Palestinian leadership only wants a state in order to gain access to the International Criminal Court and the International Court of Justice. With the United Nations recognition the Palestinians will be able to file a plethora of legal actions against Israel – for war crimes, crimes against humanity, state terrorism, occupation of a neighboring state, *et cetera* – actions that will require an army of Israeli lawyers to defend against (the subject of "legal warfare" is dealt with in greater detail in Chapter thirteen).

Abbas is attempting to bypass negotiations and rig the process in his favor. The United States has reiterated the importance of direct negotiations in achieving a "two-state" settlement of the Palestinian-Israeli dispute, and by wielding its financial clout Washington officials believe – although it is doubtful – that they can stop Abbas in his tracks. The United States warned Abbas that success in pushing "Palestine" through the United Nations, will cause America to cut all aid to the Palestinians. As one Obama administration official said: "There are consequences for short-cutting the process." Abbas brushes this aside, calling the American promise "a mere threat that will not prevent us from achieving a just solution for Palestinians."

Some United Nations Educational, Scientific, and Cultural Organization member states have already used the agency to take sides in disputes between the Palestinians and Israel, notably over sites with historical and religious significance.

Early in 2011, the Israeli government included the burial site of the biblical patriarchs Abraham, Isaac and Jacob on a list of one hundred and fifty national heritage sites and triggered and uproar. Although the Cave of the Patriarchs has an almost four thousand year-old link to the Jewish people, its location in Hebron places it within the area claimed by Palestinians as part of a future state. Muslims, brainwashed by Islamic teaching, also revere the biblical patriarchs as "Islamic prophets," and the Organization of Islamic Cooperation demanded that the United Nations act against "this Israeli unilateral aggression."

Eight months later the board of the United Nations Educational, Scientific, and Cultural Organization passed a resolution, by forty-four votes to one (the United States) reaffirming that the site in Hebron was:

> an integral part of the occupied Palestinian territories and that any unilateral action by the Israeli authorities is to be considered a violation of international law, the United Nations Educational, Scientific, and Cultural Organization Conventions and the United Nations and Security Council resolutions.

Four other resolutions passed on the same day by overwhelming majorities sided with Palestinian and other Arab positions against Israel. Mahmoud Abbas wants to submit the Cave of the Patriarchs site, as well as others including Jesus' traditional birthplace in Bethlehem, for the United Nations Educational, Scientific, and Cultural Organization world heritage status. (In June 2012, the United Nations Educational, Scientific, and Cultural Organization's World Heritage Committee shortcut the traditional eighteen-month long process and quickly approved the Palestinian bid to place the Church of the Nativity in Bethlehem on its list of sites of world heritage in danger).

Palestinian Prime Minister Salem Fayad welcomed the decision as a victory for justice and "Palestine." Palestinian spokesperson Hanan Ashwari said the vote was an affirmation of Palestinian sovereignty over the site which marks the place where Christians believe Jesus was born.

The drive to get the Nativity Church quickly recognized as a

World Heritage site is viewed as part of the Palestinians' bid to win international recognition.

The Israeli prime minister's office said, in reaction to the Organization's decision, that:

> the international body has proven again that it is driven by political and not cultural considerations.

It should be noted that the Church of the Nativity was desecrated in 2002 by dozens of Palestinian terrorists who fortified themselves inside the church for thirty-nine days – holding several hundred monks and pilgrims hostage – damaging the church and also defecating and urinating in it for that length of time).

CNSNews reported at the end of May 2012 that the United Nations Educational, Scientific, and Cultural Organization held three days of meetings in Paris. Speakers charged Israel with "systematic terrorism," "throttling the people" of Gaza, pursuing "criminal" policies and a "policy of racist violence." They also accused Israel of "operating a torture machine" and spreading propaganda to downplay the Palestinians' plight.

As was mentioned above, last November the United States government cut funding to the United Nations Educational, Scientific, and Cultural Organization after it became the first United Nations agency to grant full membership to "Palestine." President Barack Obama wants to restore the funding and at the time of writing is looking for support in Congress for a waiver, the passing of a new law, that would make it possible. Obama is inherently, but covertly anti-Israel, but has mouthed pro-Israel platitudes to keep the Jewish vote in his favor. He was reelected for a second term and received sixty-nine percent of the American Jewish vote. In contrast, Jewish absentee voters in Israel cast eighty-five percent of their votes for Mitt Romney.

Of the three-day Israel-bashing fest in Paris, Representative Ileana Ros-Lehtinen, chairwoman of the House Foreign Affairs Committee, said:

> This reminds us that UNESCO's admission of "Palestine" was not a fluke, and that UNESCO is reverting to anti-Israel bias and is unworthy of U.S. funding.

Ros-Lehtinen went on to say:

> Rather than trying to defend the indefensible, the Obama administration must stop spinning for UNESCO, condemn that body's anti-Israel behavior, and withdraw its request for Congress to amend U.S. law to restore funding to UNESCO.

The United Nations Educational, Scientific, and Cultural Organization will prove to be even more of a thorn in Israel's side following its admission of "Palestine." But the greatest damage will be the acceleration of negative public opinion toward Israel, deepening her isolation in the world.

The most recent "Orwellian" move by the United Nations (at the time of writing) was when it appointed Iran as deputy leader of a fifteen-member committee of the United Nations Arms Trade Treaty conference on July 7, 2012. Iran's appointment came at the same time as the United Nations Security Council slammed Teheran's illegal arms shipments to other rogue states and terror groups. As Hillel Neuer, UN Watch's executive director said: "This is like choosing Bernie Madoff to police fraud on the stock market."

Britain's news media has long been a leader in biased reporting against Israel, and Britain has some extremely active, anti-Israel politicians that cause Israel inestimable damage by focusing public attention on their high-profile, pro-Palestinian statements and activities – always at Israel's expense.

Sadly, in May 2012, Prime Minister David Cameron apparently succumbed to pro-Palestinian pressure and removed his name from the list of Jewish National Fund patrons. Since 1901, the sitting British prime minister has always been the patron of the Jewish National Fund. Cameron became the first British prime minister not to be patron in the one hundred and ten years of its existence.

Presumably, Cameron's name was removed at Downing Street's request; however, pro-Palestinian activists have taken credit for the move and Downing Street declined to comment on the fact that the Stop the JNF Campaign actively lobbied Cameron to withdraw as patron of the charity.

Cameron's removal of his name from being a patron of the Jewish National Fund – a charity that has planted over two hundred and forty million trees in Israel, built one hundred and eighty dams and reservoirs, developed two hundred and fifty thousand acres of land and established more than one thousand parks – received wide media attention, adding to Israel's diplomatic isolation.

The European Union was lambasted in May 2012 by a Jerusalem-based organization, NGO Monitor, for spreading inaccurate information about Israel and the Middle East conflict.

Between 2010 and early 2012, six documents from the offices of European Union representatives in Israel and the West Bank have been leaked, and all of them were critical of Israel. Now, NGO Monitor, Israel's watchdog of human rights bodies, said it has identified dozens of factual inaccuracies in the reports.

One of the reports stated that in 2009 the Palestinian population of the Jordan Valley was fifty-six thousand. The report claims that before Israel seized the area in 1967 the population "was estimated at between two hundred thousand and three hundred and twenty thousand." NGO Monitor wrote in response:

> Israel's 1967 West Bank census showed nine thousand and seventy-eight residents in the Jericho district, which encompasses Jericho - the only city in the Jordan Valley - and its outlying areas.

Another report contains misrepresentations of Israeli law. The report holds that "Only citizens of Israel or Jews can buy property built on state-owned land." However, the vast majority of all Israeli homes are built on state-owned land, and Israeli law allows for every citizen or permanent resident to buy property built on state land, regardless of religion, race, or nationality.

The European Union's reliance on false information to frame its foreign policy adds to the existing and ever increasing friction between Europe and Israel and is counterproductive to establishing a peaceful region. The European Union blindly accepts assertions made by not-for-profit non-governmental organizations (NGOs) without verifying them and this is a failure to exercise due diligence.

NGO Monitor's Chief Executive Officer, Professor Gerald Steinberg, says:

> These leaked documents, which violated the most basic tenets of due process and diplomacy, further inflame the highly complex issues they address, such as Jerusalem and Arab-Israeli citizens.

According to Professor Steinberg, the fact that in this rare leaking of documents it is alarming that there is such a clear line between the Israeli and Palestinian human rights lobby and European Union report-writing teams. The European Union's Israel Delegation declined to comment on the reports. Further European Union involvement in the delegitimization of Israel can be found in Chapters twelve and thirteen.

Europe is a virtual hotbed of antisemitism and anti-Israelism. This sad state of affairs has been a part of Europe's psyche for at least a thousand years. In the twelfth century (1189) Britain's King Richard led the third Crusade against the Holy Land. Upon reaching Jerusalem his troops rounded up the entire Jewish population – all the men, women, children, and babes at the breast – and herded them into Jerusalem's great synagogue before setting fire to it, incinerating everyone within. In the twentieth century Nazi Germany, with some collusion with many French, Hungarian, Romanian and Croatian officials, murdered six million Jews by gassing them before burning the bodies in specially-built crematoriums.

Today, European antisemitism is once again reaching epic levels, partially due, no doubt, to the ever increasing number of Muslim immigrants entering into the European countries. Many Jews now fear for their lives in parts of Britain, Germany, Austria, France, Holland, Hungary, and Sweden, and others living in Norway and Denmark feel the hatred on the streets also. On December 13, 2012, Israel's ambassador to Denmark warned Jews to avoid being identified as such; he advised them not to wear skull caps on the streets or openly display Star of David jewelry. In November 2012, anti-Israel protestors vandalized the Israeli Embassy in Copenhagen, a city where thirty-nine antisemitic attacks took place within the past year.

On October 18, 2012, a Romanian member of the European Parliament, Corneliu Vadim Tudor, denied the Holocaust on a television talk show. In every niche of Europe Jews and Israel are subject to derisiveness and harassment.

In Oslo, Norway, in June 2012, a sixteen-year-old Jewish student at a school barbecue was branded on his neck with a red-hot coin. It was an ethnic Norwegian, not a Muslim, that pressed the red-hot coin into the back of the student's neck. School officials did not contact the family after the branding. The student had been the target of repeated antisemitic bullying and violence because his father is Israeli. The student's mother had complained in 2010 in a radio interview about the antisemitic atmosphere in the school and said the schools administration had not intervened. The student was transferred to a new school and was warned not to associate with ethnic Norwegians or Muslims.

But the hostility toward Israel is not restricted to the streets and schools. Trine Lilleng, a Norwegian diplomat to Saudi Arabia, emailed dozens of pictures to friends – the pictures portrayed Jews as Nazis; they were Holocaust pictures juxtaposed with images from Israel's twenty-two day war with Hamas in December 2008.

In October 2010, Norway's Foreign Ministry announced that it would not permit the German shipbuilder HDW to test its Dolphin class submarine, built for the Israeli navy, in Norwegian territorial waters. This despite the fact that HDW leases a base from Norway to test its submarines in deep water.

At a heated panel discussion in Jerusalem organized by the Jerusalem Center for Public Affairs (JCPA), on November 5, 2012, prominent historian, best selling author, and senior Norwegian diplomat, Hanne Nabintu Herland, slammed Norway for being "the most antisemitic country in the West." Herland said:

> The degree of anti-Israelism in Norway today on the state level, in the media, in the trade unions and at the universities, colleges, and schools is unprecedented in modern Norwegian history. The powerful individuals that have pushed for these negative and biased attitudes in Norway are today responsible for creating a politically-correct hatred towards Israel that today portrays my country internationally as the most antisemitic country in the West.

Herland went on to say that Oslo's stance toward Israel and Norwegian antisemitism were closely related: "Anti-Israelism is antisemitism's new face in Europe," and she showed from surveys and antisemitism reports that "Jew" is the most often used curse word in Oslo's schools.

Representing the Norwegian Embassy in Tel Aviv, Vebjørn Dysvik, the mission's deputy head, rejected Herland's claims but admitted that his "government had work to do regarding anti-Jewish sentiment within Norwegian society."

On August 15, 2012, during a soccer match between Israel and Hungary in Budapest, groups of Hungarian fans shouted antisemitic slurs throughout the match and waved Palestinian and Iranian flags. On a video of the match supporters of the Hungarian team can be heard shouting "filthy Jews" and "Buchenwald" (the name of a Nazi death camp) and jeered throughout the playing of Israel's national anthem, *Hatikva*. The antisemitic hooliganism was a reflection of the growing antisemitism in Hungary.

Until the 1967 Six-Day War, France was the main supplier of Israel's weapons. In 1967 Charles de Gaulle made a one-sided disconnection with Israel. The reason was that de Gaulle supported Egypt, Syria, and Jordan, Israel's Arab neighbors, and as a result instituted an arms embargo against Israel.

In 1969 de Gaulle retired from the presidency of France and Israel hoped that new president Georges Pompidou would bring about better relations between Israel and France, but Pompidou continued the weapons embargo.

Francois Hollande, the new French president who took office in May 2012, said he wanted to deepen ties with Israel although he was worried that his election would embolden the anti-Israel left.

Nicolas Sarkozy, defeated by Hollande in the May elections, was seen as among the most pro-Israel leaders in Europe, yet he let the arms embargo remain.

The United Kingdom revoked a number of arms export licenses to Israel following the twenty-two-day Gaza war, but insisted that the move did not constitute a partial embargo, which is diplospeak for an embargo that the British refer to as "sanctions."

Britain did indeed slap a partial arms embargo on Israel, refusing to supply replacement parts and other equipment for Sa'ar 4.5 gunships because they participated in the Gaza war called "Operation Cast Lead."

On December 27, 2008, after enduring an eight-year-long barrage of over twelve thousand rockets and mortars launched at civilian population centers in the south of Israel, and having exhausted every other option, Israel launched the twenty-two day military operation against Hamas in Gaza. Because Israel had the *chutzpah* to defend her people, she was lambasted by Europe and the United Nations.

In a November 27, 2012, *Jerusalem Post* article entitled "**How the British responded to Palestinian terrorists**," Rafael Medoff quotes from recently-released British government documents describing atrocities the British metered out to Palestinian Arab terrorists in the 1930s. Medoff prefaced his article by writing:

> the British have no right to preach morals to Israel considering British army atrocities against the Arabs in Palestine during those years.

The documents recounted several anti-terror tactics employed by the British against the Palestinian Arabs in the 1930s that included:

> shooting handcuffed prisoners, blowing up civilians' homes and forcing Arabs to drive mine-sweeping taxis in front of British soldiers searching areas where they suspected mines were planted.

Also, Naomi Shepherd, in her book *Ploughing Sand* (about British rule in Palestine) describes how:

> eight Palestinian Arabs in Halhul died of heat exposure when, on a scorching day, British soldiers rounded up a group of men during a search for arms and kept them standing without water for hours.
>
> After an attack on a British patrol in the village of Kawkab Abu Haija, the British army destroyed the entire village.
>
> When a British army vehicle ran over a mine near Kafr Yasif, soldiers burned down seventy houses and machine-gunned nine villagers.

In any war, civilians get killed. The "brave fighters" of Hamas, Islamic Jihad, and Hizb'allah operate from within civilian apartment buildings, schools, hospitals, and next to and sometimes even from within United Nations' facilities. This is known a "perfidy" and is a serious violation of the law of war as laid down in the Geneva Conventions.

In a *Jerusalem Post* op-ed on June 20, 2012, Louis René Beres, a professor of international law at Purdue University in West Lafayette, Indiana, and an author of many books and articles dealing with terrorism, international law and the law of war, wrote:

> Under international law, deception can be acceptable in armed conflict, but the Hague Regulations do not permit the placement of military assets or military personnel in populated civilian areas. Prohibition of perfidy can be found at Protocol I of 1977, additional to the Geneva Conventions of 1949.

Some eight hundred of the twelve hundred Palestinians killed in Operation Cast Lead were positively identified as combatants. But, if civilians willingly provide cover for gunmen and their weapons, can anyone justifiably call them non-combatants? Many civilians were forced against their wills to be used as human shields, but most were not coerced – they were voluntarily and actively helping the terrorists.

Israel is constantly accused of using disproportionate force because she uses her military power to defeat her enemies. In his *Post* op-ed Beres writes:

> The law of war requires that every use of force by an army or insurgent group meet the test of "proportionality." Proportionality stipulates that every resort to armed force must be limited to what is absolutely necessary for meeting essential military objectives. This principle applies to all calculations of military advantage, and to all reprisals.
>
> Proportionality does not mean that the defending state must limit its use of force to the precise "amount" being used by the other side. Here, the conventional wisdom is flat-out wrong.

Like the United Nations special rapporteur on human rights in the Palestinian territories, Richard Falk, who was mentioned earlier, the antisemitic, no-nothing talking-heads in Europe's capitals would also rather Israel not retaliate against Palestinian and Hizb'allah missiles raining down on her cities and towns. But perhaps Israel should launch her own rockets and mortars – one-for-one – willy-nilly onto Palestinian and Lebanese civilian areas in direct proportionality to what is being fired at her? One Israeli missile for each of the thousands of Palestinian missiles launched against Israeli cities and towns? It would certainly be "proportional" force and would no doubt end the propensity of the Arab terror groups to indiscriminately fire rockets and mortars into Israel's population centers.

Europe's time will come. The London and Madrid bombings were but a taste of what lies ahead for it. Europe will soon enough sing a different tune. The perpetrators of the London and Madrid bombings were referred to in the European media as "terrorists," but Palestinians who blow up buses and murder Israeli women and children – like slitting the throats of five members of a single family, including a toddler for instance– are still merely called "attackers." Such hypocrisy.

Five European nations, Britain, Spain, Italy, Portugal, and Germany have informed Israel's largest airline that *El Al* flights carrying heavy munitions cargo to Israel will no longer be allowed to stop for refueling at their airports. All five nations have diplomatic relations with Israel and have been involved in the effort to expand the United Nations Interim Force In Lebanon (UNIFIL), the peacekeeping force in Lebanon. Nonetheless, they now refuse to allow Israel's national carrier to make stopover landings for refueling when carrying heavy military cargo from the United States.

In a letter to Israel's prime minister, Itai Regev, chairman of *El Al*'s pilots union, complained that the new rules severely restrict deliveries to Israel from the United States. Regev wrote:

> Cargo planes are taking off from the United States with much lighter weight, and are reaching Israel with significantly fewer munitions than needed."

A full-fledged crisis between Israel and Turkey shows little sign of becoming less intense. On the contrary, it is heating up. Turkey and Israel were firm allies until May 2010. Trade between the countries had built up to be worth billions of dollars annually. Seventy percent of Israeli travelers either passed through or vacationed in Turkey, which was a popular holiday destination for Israelis. And then came the flotilla raid in which nine hardcore Turkish Islamic activists were killed by Israeli commandos in self-defense.

The Gaza flotilla raid was a military operation by Israel against six ships of the "Gaza Freedom Flotilla" on May 31, 2010, in the Mediterranean Sea. The flotilla, organized by the Free Gaza Movement and the Turkish Foundation for Human Rights and Freedoms and Humanitarian Relief (IHH), was carrying aid for Gaza and its intention was to break the Israeli-Egyptian blockade of the Gaza Strip.

On May 31, 2010, Israeli naval commandos boarded the ships from speedboats and helicopters in order to force the ships to the Israeli port of Ashdod for inspection. On the Turkish ship MV Mavi Marmara, the boarding commandos faced deadly resistance from some forty IHH activists – later described in a United Nations report as a "separate hardcore group" – who were armed with iron bars, chains, and knives. The Mavi Marmara was not on a peaceful mission. It's cargo was made up of weapons and construction materials that would have been used for building reinforced bunkers.

In the ensuing struggle nine activists were shot and killed by the commandos, and numbers were wounded. Ten commandos were wounded, one of them seriously. The five other ships in the flotilla employed only passive resistance, which the commandos dealt with without any major incidents. The ships were then towed to Ashdod where all the passengers were detained before being deported.

The name Turkish Foundation for Human Rights and Freedoms and Humanitarian Relief is deceptive. It is a radical Islamic organization and is defined by Israel, the United States, and Germany as a terrorist organization. The Turkish government was directly involved in working with this terrorist group and was therefore complicit in mounting what was a deliberate provocation. Videos taken of the boardings by Israeli naval personnel on accompanying naval vessels show the ferocity of the attacks against the commandos as they rappelled down ropes dropped from their helicopters. The commandos were equipped with paintball guns, but some were forced to use their personal sidearms with fatal consequences.

Even the United Nations has upheld the legitimacy of Israel's blockade of Gaza, which was imposed in order to prevent weapons being brought into Gaza for Hamas and Islamic Jihad to use against Israel. Several "flotillas" had previously and since been stopped by Israel, the boats towed to Ashdod for cargo inspection before it is loaded onto trucks and taken into Gaza in a convoy.

In June 2012, the Office of Prime Minister Binyamin Netanyahu was quoted in the State Comptroller's report as saying that Turkish Prime Minister Recep Tayyip Erdogan had given Israel the impression, through third parties, that he would keep the Mavi Marmara from setting sail in May 2010. The state comptroller's report quoted the Prime Minister's Office as saying:

> Prime Minister Netanyahu worked intensively through diplomatic channels, principally with the Turkish Prime Minister Erdogan, to stop the flotilla. The efforts led to a high feasibility that the Turkish flotilla would be prevented.

The Turkish prime minister has demanded an official apology from the government of Israel; compensation packages for the families and dependents of the dead activists; and the lifting of the Gaza blockade. Israel did compromise and offered a statement of regret over the killings and a six million dollar compensation package, but refused to apologize for having her commandos viciously attacked by Islamic activists and will not end the blockade of Gaza until Hamas, Islamic Jihad, *et cetera*, renounce their terror campaigns against Israel. Erdogan dismissed Israel's offer out of hand.

Following the flotilla incident, Turkish Prime Minister Recep Tayyip Erdogan expelled the Israeli ambassador and cancelled all military cooperation. Israel is a world leader in the design, manufacture, and export of unmanned aircraft (UAVs), but

Erdogan, attended by considerable publicity and citing "poor performance," has returned three Aerostar drones and is demanding a full refund plus compensation.

Erdogan has also banned Israeli military aircraft from entering Turkish airspace, prohibited Israel from exporting previously ordered weapons, ordnance, and unmanned aircraft (drones) to Turkey, threatened to send warships into the Mediterranean Sea to escort further flotillas and to attack any Israeli naval vessel that exits Israel's territorial waters and enters international waters. Especially hard hit have been the military ties that once underpinned the "special relationship."

Prime Minister Recep Tayyip Erdogan has taken to working against Israel at every opportunity. Israel is shocked afresh by each of Erdogan's premeditated and steadily escalating assaults on what were highly symbiotic relations between the two countries. Israel issued a travel warning against visiting Turkey, but Israeli tourists dropped plans for Turkish vacations on their own volition and tour companies reported mass cancellations. Israeli visitors to Turkey today can be counted just in the tens instead of the former tens of thousands.

Turkey was more than just a country with airspace and waters in which the Israel Defense Force could train. There was an active intelligence sharing on terror threats. There was also the Israeli strike in September 2007 against the nuclear reactor President Bashar Assad was building in northeast Syria. After the bombing and as they lit their boosters to evade Syrian air defense missiles, the Israel Air Force fighter jets dropped their supplemental fuel tanks over Turkish territory. The Turks, who were accused of allowing Israel to use its airspace, made a fuss and asked Israel for clarifications, the event was quickly shelved in the interest of both countries.

Israel could be losing not only a diplomatic and military ally, but also a partner in the war on terror, which could mean that the Turks might no longer have a strong interest in intercepting weapons shipments passing through their country on their way to Iran's terror proxies in Gaza and Lebanon. However, important as "special relationships" may be, none is indispensable.

Reliable information has come to light since the flotilla

fracas that has proven the flotilla to be the opportunity Erdogan had been waiting for. Turkish-Israel ties were very strong until Erdogan, the leader of the Islamist Justice and Development Party – also called the AK Party – came to power in 2003. Turkey was founded by Mustafa Kemal Atatürk as a secular Muslim country and the Turkish military prevented Islamists from taking power. However, since Erdogan, the leader of an Islamic movement, rose to a position of great power he has challenged the nation's secular élite and pushed the military out of its longstanding role of guardian of the country's secular governing tradition.

Without doubt, Erdogan's nine years as premier has brought Turkey into the twenty-first century and restored both the country and its currency to its former vitality. Erdogan's party is the ruling party, but Erdogan himself is the undisputed ruler. Erdogan is ambitious and driven, and his every wish and thought are deferred to by every official. Turkey, like the United States at the time of writing, is now ruled by the leader of a personality cult.

Slowly, slowly, Erdogan has introduced more and more Islamic laws. He is is Islamizing the country. For instance, there is the new law requiring every shopping mall, movie theater and every public facility in the country to have a Muslim prayer room. There is no burning need for such things, the laws come because the government is determined to Islamize the once secular nation.

In June 2011, there was a mass resignation from the top military echelon – Erdogan purged himself of the military, his biggest rival. And as of early 2012 there were almost one hundred journalists, editors, and publishers in jail for having dared to be critical of his policies.

Erdogan does not disguise his aspirations to return his country to the glorious days of the Ottoman Empire and to become the regional and Islamic pivotal power, with himself as the sultan. To reach his objective Erdogan must demonstrate his leadership by striking out at the Arab and Muslim worlds' adversary – Israel.

Erdogan's regime is so unrelentingly hostile towards Israel that the leader of the Turkish opposition asked whether Erdogan intended to go to war against Israel. Turkey also decided to file criminal charges against the high-ranking Israeli officials involved in the attempt to stop the Mavi Marmara from running the blockade on the Gaza Strip. On May 28, 2012, the Turkish newspaper *Today's Zaman* reported that Istanbul's Seventh Criminal Court was seeking nine counts of aggravated life imprisonment for the Chief of General Staff, OC (Officer Commanding) the Israeli Navy, OC the Israeli Air Force, and the head of Air Force Intelligence. Turkey may well turn to the International Criminal Court in the hope of redress against Israel.

As mentioned above, reliable information came to light well after the flotilla fracas that proved the flotilla was Erdogan's opportunity. The flotilla to Gaza was not the cause of a new Turkish strategy, but rather an opportunity Erdogan had long been waiting for.

In February 2012, Wikileaks, the online organization that publishes submissions of private, secret, and classified media from anonymous sources, posted online emails leaked from the United States-based global security analysis company, Stratfor, that showed Turkish Prime Minister Recep Tayyip Erdogan had planned to downgrade relations with Israel and "burn its bridges" with her long before the flotilla.

A leaked email from George Friedman, the head of Stratfor, reveals that Erdogan told former United States Secretary of State Henry Kissinger that "at some point he would burn bridges with Israel in favor of a closer relationship with the Islamic world." According to the Turkish newspaper *Sunday Zaman*, Friedman also wrote in the same email:

> Turkey does not get along with Israel and the United States. An attack by Israel on Iran would provide a good opportunity for Erdogan to finally cut Turkey's ties with Israel and the United States and to expand Turkey's power.

Erdogan has become another Middle East bully. Israel and Cyprus are threatened militarily. Greece, Bulgaria, and Armenia are wary, due to realistic suspicions, and the list goes on. Erdogan's biggest fans are Gaza's warlords. The more pugnacious Erdogan appears toward Israel the more he secures his credentials as an Islamic stalwart. In the Middle East, a state which responds to perceived threats with mere rhetoric and condemnation cannot claim regional leadership.

In early June 2012, Erdogan said that Turkey is not looking to repair its relations with Israel. "We do not need Israeli tourists. We have succeeded to fill their places" he told the Israeli *Ma'ariv* daily during the regional World Economic Forum summit. Erdogan added:

> The crisis over the matter of the occupation and relations with
> Israel is not harming the Turkish economy.

On November 5, 2012, a court in Istanbul began the afore-mentioned trial in absentia of four ex-Israeli military commanders whom Turkey considers responsible for the deaths of the nine Islamic activists on board the Mavi Marmara. The ludicrous mock, or show trial, which Israel called "political theater," will call some four hundred and fifty witnesses to testify on a long list of trumped-up charges topped by **"incitement to kill monstrously and by torture."** The aim is to convict, amid great fanfare, Israel's former top military brass including the Chief of General Staff, OC (Officer Commanding) the Israeli Navy, OC the Israeli Air Force, and the head of Air Force Intelligence, and to absurdly sentence them to **individual** prison terms of **more than eighteen thousand years**. It is a foregone conclusion that the Israelis will all be found guilty as charged and international arrest warrants will be sought for them. If such warrants are issued by the International Court of Justice none of these fine men will ever be able to leave Israel without the risk of arrest. Turkish Prime Minister Recep Tayyip Erdogan wishes to humiliate Israel expeditiously, which will strengthen his bid for leadership of the Islamic world.

Unfortunately, Turkish Prime Minister Recep Tayyip Erdogan has become United States President Barack Obama's bosom pal and they have had several private *tête-à-tête* meetings in the White House, resulting in Obama showing definite preference for Turkey over Israel.

The leaked Stratfor email shows that Erdogan has no love for the United States. A Pew Global Attitudes Project survey, released in mid-June 2012, found that only fifteen percent of Turks expressed favorable opinions of the United States, yet Obama has taken Erdogan into his inner-circle of confidents.

As an example, in June 2012, the United States blocked Israel's participation in the Global Counterterrorism Forum's (GCTF) first meeting in Istanbul, even though Israel has one of the most extensive experiences in counterterrorism in the world. A pro-Israeli source in Washington told *Globes* that Israel was excluded from the meeting because of fierce objections by Turkish President Recep Tayyip Erdogan.

Israel tried hard to obtain an invitation to the Global Counterterrorism Forum meeting, and her exclusion greatly disappointed officials in Jerusalem. The diplomatic fallout from the current crisis with Turkey makes Israel even more isolated in an already extremely volatile Middle East.

On all fronts Israel is isolated. On June 28, 2012, well-known Algerian writer Boualem Sansai received a prestigious French literary award; however, he did not get the cash prize of fifteen thousand euros he had been slated to receive. After being named as the winner of the award Sansai was invited to attend the Jerusalem Writers Festival, which he attended as the guest of honor. For the 'crime' of having visited Israel the Arab sponsors of the prize withdrew their support for Sansai.

Commenting on the decision to withdraw the prize money, laureate Sansai said it was "unacceptable," adding that Arab countries – and his home country, Algeria, in particular – had "shut themselves in a prison of intolerance" Sansai also said, according to *France24*: "Yes, there are complicated relations with Israel, but we are not at war with them."

A spokeswoman for the Arab Ambassadors Council claimed:

> the Ambassadors are subject to the official position of **the Arab League which considers itself effectively in a state of war with Israel.**

Another glimpse of how Israel is being isolated can be seen in an offensively biased June 2012 study by the Global Peace Index (GPI) that graded Israel as one of the least peaceful countries in the world. The Index, which has offices in New York, Sydney, and Washington, DC, ranked one hundred and fifty-eight countries in its annual study and listed Israel at number one hundred and fifty – lower than Iran, Egypt, or Syria. Only one other Middle

Eastern country, Iraq – at number one hundred and fifty-five – was ranked lower than Israel.

Israel's ranking placed it behind Iran, where multitudes of pro-democracy protestors have been arrested, hundreds tortured, and many hung for the crime of protesting against the oppressive mullah-controlled regime. And where it was reported by Iranian officials themselves in June 2012, that in 2011 more than six hundred people were executed, including women. Yet Iran was ranked at one hundred and twenty-eight in the Global Peace Index study.

Syria, where almost eighty thousand people have been killed in unrest and massacres in less than twenty-four months, was ranked one hundred and forty-seventh. Egypt, with its sixteen months of turmoil centered around Tahrir Square and more than a thousand dead, was listed at number one hundred and eleven. Even war-torn Ivory Coast outranked Israel at number one hundred and thirty-four.

Israel's Foreign Ministry spokesman Yigal Palmor dismissed the Global Peace Index report and told *The Times of Israel*:

> How is it possible that Israel is a more dangerous place than Syria? Perhaps in some parallel universe, but not in any empirical reality in which real people live.

The Global Peace Index is compiled by the Institute for Economics and Peace, which identifies itself as a nonprofit, nonpartisan research organization dedicated to exploring the relationship between peace and economic stability. Israel's economy, due to her outstanding fiscal skill, weathered the global financial collapse with the minimum of problems and her economy expands at almost twice the rate of nearly all Western countries. The Global Peace Index draws its data from sources that include the various arms of the United Nations, which perhaps answers the fundamental question of why the Index is biased against Israel.

The conclusion of all that has been written above is that while the great majority of countries are intent upon delegitimizing Israel and isolating her from the international community of nations, they are unwittingly fulfilling what the Bible decreed throughout millennia – that Israel shall dwell alone. Everything is under the control of the *"Creator"* and *"Master"* of the universe:

And we know that all things work together for good to those who love God, to those who are the called according to His purpose (Romans 8:28).

We know that Israel is the only nation in the world that has been called according to the LORD's purpose and that today there are tens of thousands of Israeli Jews who love the LORD with a whole heart.

The LORD is taking Israel into the wilderness, a multifaceted wilderness. In this wilderness the LORD will judge Israel severely, but in this wilderness she will not only find salvation, but the LORD will also judge the nations according to how they have blessed, despised, reviled, humiliated, or ridiculed her. The Bible is replete with nations that despised, reviled, humiliated, or ridiculed Israel, and they are no more. Only those with a pure heart toward the LORD and His people Israel will survive what will soon enough befall our sick and dying world.

---

[1] See Chapter 19 of the author's book *When Day And Night Cease: A prophetic study of world events and how prophecy concerning Israel affects the nations, the Church and you* for an in-depth look at the number of armies, troop numbers, tanks, heavy guns, aircraft, *et cetera*, pitted against Israel.

[2] See Chapter 7 of the author's book *SAGA: Israel and the demise of nations* for a full exegesis of this passage.

[3] See Chapter 9 of the author's book *Philistine: The Great Deception* for a fully documented, astonishing exposé of the world's news media.

[4] See Chapter 7 of the author's book *Philistine: The Great Deception* for how the term "Palestinian Arab" came into being.

[5] See Chapter 6 of the author's book *Philistine: The Great Deception* for a complete chapter, fully documented, concerning the United Nations' dealings with the Palestinian Refugees; the United Nation's definition of a "Palestinian Refugee;" and the absurd details of how they are numbered.

[6] See Chapter 7 of the author's book *Philistine: The Great Deception* for the true, heavily documented history of "Palestine."

— *twelve* —

The Wilderness
(Boycott, Divestment, and Sanctions)

In the political climate previously described the campaign to delegitimize Israel is growing – spreading its tentacles throughout the Western world. This delegitimization campaign has given rise to the Boycott, Divestment, and Sanctions movement, which is more widely known by its acronym BDS. It should also be mentioned that there is a corresponding rise in antisemitic sentiment directed against Jewish populations in the Western world.

In addition to the classical forms, antisemitism is now being manifested through boycotts of Israeli goods and academic institutions, and in political faux-legal suits against Israeli leaders and military personnel visiting Europe (more on political faux-legal suits in the next chapter).

There seems to be no end to the creative evil of Israel-hating organizations and no bottom to the depths of the world's inherent antisemitism.

Anti-Israel activity was stepped up in July 2008 on the Google Earth application with the message "Nakba - The Palestinian Catastrophe" appearing when users scroll over orange dots that speckle locations across the entire map of Israel. Google spokesperson, Jessica Powell, said that Google had no plans to restrict the application's content, despite Israel being uniquely and malevolently targeted.

In a poll taken in February 2008, it was found that only fifty-three percent of the Dutch would consider voting for a Jewish prime minister. In the Netherlands rankings, Jews came far behind women who were at ninety-three percent, homosexuals at seventy-eight percent, and blacks at seventy-five percent.

On the eve of Kristallnacht – November 8, 2012, a former Dutch prime minister of the Christian Democratic Appeal, Dries Van Agt, described as "a harsh critic of Israel" and a "pro-Palestinian activist," reportedly said, according to the Dutch daily *Telegraaf*:

> The Jewish state should have been established in Germany because the Middle East had nothing to do with World War II.

Van Agt not only showed cosmic ignorance of history, but the timing of his tasteless remarks on the eve of the anniversary of Kristallnacht rubbed salt into Jewish wounds. Kristallnacht took place on November 9, 1938, and over ninety German Jews lost their lives, hundreds of synagogues were vandalized or looted along with almost eight thousand Jewish businesses in a state sponsored Nazi pogrom. For Van agt to address his remarks to seminar delegates just prior to the remembrance of the "Night of Broken Glass," can only be described as revolting antisemitism.

More revolting European antisemitism took place in Belgium on November 18, 2012, when the Israel Defence Force band arrived for a concert in Antwerp. The band was met at the venue by more than a hundred protestors shouting: "Hamas, Hamas, all the Jews to the gas."

On January 15, 2009, the *Jerusalem Post* reported that Jewish students at York University in Toronto, Canada, were forced to take refuge in an office as anti-Israel protesters banged on the glass doors, chanting, "Die, bitch, go back to Israel," and "Die, Jew, get the hell off campus." In yesteryear the world took aim at Jews as individuals; today, the world takes aim at Jews as a people.

At the other end of the world, in Australia, in 2012, on the Gregorian calendar's celebratory date of Israel's independence – May 15, hundreds of pro-Palestinian demonstrators – including many Muslim immigrants – marched through central Sydney waving placards reading "Break ties with Apartheid Israel."

Similarly, in Melbourne, Australia, on June 5, 2012, a smaller crowd of angry pro-Palestinian demonstrators marred the annual celebration of Israel's Independence day. Again, the crowd was Muslim dominated and had to be held back by police. The Victorian Premier, along with a high-profile gathering of politicians and diplomats, were forced to walk past the unruly, jeering mob that waved signs reading "Israel – an Apartheid state," and "Free Palestine." At one point the demonstrators burnt an effigy of Victorian Premier Ted Baillieu. A newspaper later quoted Baillieu as saying:

> The Boycott, Divestment, and Sanctions campaign, should be re-named "Bigoted, Dangerous and Shameful."

It is interesting to note that all over the world pro-Palestinian activists label Israel an apartheid state. It has already been said, however, that twenty-one percent of Israel's population is Arab. Israel also welcomed and absorbed around a hundred thousand black Ethiopian Jews, and every citizen – including more than a million Israeli Arabs – all receive the same health and welfare benefits, and every citizen is free to rent or purchase property anywhere within the state of Israel.

Conversely, when Israelis by mistake enter Palestinian-controlled areas they are usually greeted with rocks, beaten with iron pipes, and often lynched. Renting properties to Jews is taboo, but selling a property to Jews is a capital offense and offending Palestinians are summarily tried in a kangaroo court and executed soon after.

When Israel handed Yasser Arafat – the godfather of international terrorism – and his cadres in the Palestine Liberation Organization huge swathes of land in May 1994 as her commitment to peace, the first law the Palestinians enacted was for the death penalty to be given to any Palestinian who sold property to a Jew. Since then Palestinian Authority President Mahmoud Abbas and his cohorts have said time and time again – like Arafat did before them – that no Jews will be allowed to reside in a Palestinian state. And it is Israel that the world claims to be an apartheid state? How absurd.

South African Judge, Richard Goldstone, who served for years in South African courts during the days of apartheid, has unequivocally stated that Israel is "not an apartheid state," and that "such a term is both disrespectful and libelous." Apparently, the world has a very large number of pro-Palestinian activists who are themselves ignoramuses and bigots.

For many years Arab suicide bombers and gunmen infiltrated

from Palestinian-heavy areas into Jew-heavy areas, murdering hundreds of innocent Israelis. In June 2002, Israel began building a separation barrier along the boundary of the West Bank in order to distance Israeli civilians from the threat of terrorism. The building of this barrier-fence is ongoing at the time of writing. The mesh fence is three and one half meters (yards) high, topped with razor wire and electrified. Sections of the "barrier" close to Arab villages are constructed with five to eight-meter-high precast-concrete interlocking slabs. The concrete sections – some sections longer than others – are to prevent terrorists from shooting at Israeli vehicles as they pass by the Arab towns and to stop Arab youths from stoning or firebombing Israeli vehicles.

It is the relatively small number of concrete sections that has given rise to what Palestinians and their avid followers call "the apartheid wall." This ridiculous description is propagated by the fantastications of Palestinians and pro-Palestinian activists. The barrier-fence was built to keep Palestinian terrorists and car thieves out of Israel. It has proven to be a most effective tool for reducing terrorism and for slashing the numbers of Israeli cars that were being stolen and driven into Palestinian territory. Car thefts by Palestinians have dropped from several thousand each year to several hundred at the time of writing, and the stolen cars are now being taken to "chop shops" within Israel, primarily operated by Israeli Arabs – Palestinians holding Israeli citizenship.

According to statistics published by the Israeli government, in the thirty months between January 2000 and July 2003, when the first continuous segment of the barrier was built, seventy-three suicide bombings were carried out from the West Bank, killing two hundred and ninety-three Israelis and injuring over nineteen hundred more. However, in the twenty-eight months between August 2003 and the end of 2006, only twelve attacks were carried out, killing sixty-four Israelis and wounding four hundred and forty-five. As work on the separation barrier progresses so the number of attempted attacks continue to drop and are today almost a thing of the past.

Arab terrorists target Israel simply because she exists, and Israel defends herself. The defense is decontextualized and made to seem like arbitrary cruelty. Israeli self-defense becomes an excuse for unending indictments, spurred by antisemites with an avowed agenda of bringing about the destruction of the State of Israel. These indictments criminalize the Jewish state and the Jewish people as presumed supporters of this criminal Jewish state.

Hate-crime statistics in country after country show Jews to be the number one victims by far. Antisemitic hate-fests under the title "Israel Apartheid Week" are springing up on university campuses globally. Graffiti equating the Magen David (Jewish star) with the Nazi swastika are everywhere. Iran at one and the same time threatens Israel with genocide and hastens toward developing a nuclear capacity to realize that threat. In the international arena, resolution after resolution, session after session, conference after conference, focuses on Israel alone.

"Israel Apartheid Week" has grown since it began in Toronto, Canada, in 2005 – the organizers try to prevent media coverage inside the events. In 2009, Golda Shahidi, spokeswoman for Students Against Israel Apartheid, told the *Jerusalem Post* by phone from Toronto that:

> Forty-four international cities held Israel Apartheid Week events, which is twice as much as last year, and in Toronto thousands of people attended events. Almost every building was filled to maximum capacity.

The official website of Israel Apartheid Week said that 2011's Israel Apartheid Week was:

> incredibly successful with ninety-seven cities participating ... we hope you put BDS at the forefront of your campaigns and join together for Israeli Apartheid Week, the pinnacle of action across universities worldwide.

The eighth annual Israel Apartheid Week took place in February and March 2012 with one hundred and sixteen cities participating worldwide:

> It was a more popular, better attended, and with a more aggressive series of anti-Israel rallies and lectures than ever before.

The youth of the world are being indoctrinated in hatred on Western university campuses. What were supposed to be seats of higher learning are now being turned into enclaves of raw antisemitism. Most, but not all, of the organizers of the Israel Apartheid Week are Muslim immigrants foolishly allowed into Western countries. Chancellor Angela Merkel of Germany, Prime Minister David Cameron of Britain, and former President of France, Nicolas Sarkozy, have each said that multi-culturalism has failed in their countries. But it is the Jews who are the big losers in the failure of multi-culturalism. Israel's sports teams have also met hostility and violent protests in Sweden, Spain, Hungary, Romania, and Turkey. Even in her ultimate wilderness, Israel finds no relief, she is constantly subjected to assault.

In a move called "unfortunate and discriminatory," African-American Pulitzer Prize-winning author Alice Walker refused to allow an Israeli publisher to translate her book *The Color Purple* into Hebrew. Walker said she turned down the request because: "Israel is guilty of apartheid and persecution of the Palestinian people."

In a letter to the publisher, which appeared on the website of the Palestinian Campaign for the Academic and Cultural Boycott of Israel, Walker wrote:

> It is my hope that the non-violent BDS (Boycott, Divestment, Sanctions) movement, of which I am part, will have enough of an impact on Israeli civilian society to change the situation.

Abraham H. Foxman, national director of the Anti-Defamation League, said in response:

> It is sad that people who inspire to fight bigotry and prejudice continue to have a biased and bigoted side. For some time Walker has been blinded by her anti-Israel animus.

Walker has apparently been blinded by prejudice since before she wrote her acclaimed 1982 novel based on her childhood growing up in segregated Georgia. Countless tens of thousands have been murdered or mutilated in the Middle East and North Africa by suicide bombers and gunmen in recent years. Yet without a trace of emotion Walker could still say in a 2011 interview: "I think Israel is the greatest terrorist in that part of the world." Prejudice is always stronger that facts, and Walker proves the truth of it. Also, it shows that she is both gullible and naive for having believed Arab and pro-Palestinian propaganda and their rewriting of thousands of years of history.

It was stated in the last Chapter that the European Union's reliance on false information to frame its foreign policy adds to the existing and ever increasing friction between Europe and Israel. The European Union blindly accepts assertions made by not-for-profit non-governmental organizations (NGOs) without verifying them and this, as mentioned before, is a failure to exercise due diligence.

Britain, Finland, the European Union, and Norway, give tens of millions of euros annually to more than a score of anti-Israel non-governmental organizations and hold to the opinion that the organizations' reports are the truth. Due to the anti-Israel bias shown against the Jewish state, Britain, Finland, the European Union, and Norway have been largely shut out from participating in any dialogue concerning anything pertaining to the Israel-Palestinian peace process. To quote Daniel Patrick Moynihan again: "Everyone is entitled to his own opinion, but not to his own facts."

Funding antisemitic, anti-Israel non governmental organizations who can openly operate in Israel and the Palestinian territories, and then acting upon their reports is blatant interference in Israel's politics. It is inconceivable that any European country or Norway would accept a situation where another democratic government provided funds to organizations whose primary aim is to trash that country before hostile audiences.

On August 2, 2012, the Simon Wiesenthal Center expressed its outrage to learn from the *Washington Post* that a 2010 European Union grant for technical assistance to Syria of fourteen million six hundred thousand dollars was in fact used to expand Syria's chemical weapons program. The European Union funds anti-Israel non-government organizational boycotts of Israeli goods while at the same time it funds Syria's chemical weapons program that will ultimately be aimed at Israeli civilian centers.

"Mouthpieces for Europe" was how *YNetNews* headlined an article about anti-Israel non-governmental organizations in November

2011. These non-governmental organizations' submissions are nothing less than propaganda intended to advance a political agenda, and they are causing Israel a great deal of distress.

Non-governmental organizations include numerous Christian groups like Christian Aid and Oxfam. They also include medical non-governmental organizations like Physicians for Human Rights. All show themselves to be biased against Israel – some stridently so.

Between April 2011 and September 2012, Oxfam International and its branches released only three statements condemning the ongoing violence in Syria, in which time some sixty thousand civilians were killed and tens of thousands fled the country as refugees. In comparison, in the same time frame, Oxfam condemned Israel in at least nine statements and, during the three-week 2008-2009 Gaza war in which some three hundred and fifty civilians were killed, Oxfam condemned Israel in ten statements. Heavily biased non-governmental reports and media releases help turn the Western world's masses against Israel.

War on Want, Physicians for Rights-Israel, Keshev, I'lam, and Israel Committee against House Demolitions – whose funders include the European Union, the Finnish and British governments, and the George Soros-funded New Israel Fund – joined a number of extremist non-governmental organizations to promote Israeli Apartheid week.

In 2010, an Israeli non-governmental organization, Breaking the Silence – a group of disgruntled Israeli soldiers – has addressed the Irish Parliament, a crowd in Washington that included the United Arab Emirates Ambassador to the United Nations, the First Secretary of Pakistan to the United Nations, and numerous college campuses in the United States, along with other similar engagements. At one event in Sweden, Breaking the Silence activist Yonatan Shapiro even stated:

> We are the oppressors, we are the ones that are violating human rights on a daily basis. We are creating the terror against us, basically.

On November 20, 2011, Breaking the Silence representative Oded Na'aman spoke at the University of Pennsylvania, at an event sponsored by Penn for Palestine – formerly Students for Justice in Palestine – a pro-boycott, anti-Israel organization. Few seem to question why a group that claims to want to impact Israeli society spends so much time speaking to anti-Israel audiences abroad and reinforcing the image of Israeli soldiers as evil doers and "war criminals"? Breaking the Silence is a patron of several European Governments and more than seventy-five percent of its 2010 budget – the last available public documents – came from funding from European governments, under the pretense of support for human rights and democracy.

In the twelve months from December 2011 to November 2012, Palestinian jihadi groups fired over eight hundred rockets and mortars at civilian populations in Israel. Every rocket and mortar constitutes a war crime. But only after the Israel Defense Force responded to those indiscriminate attacks with an aerial bombardment of Gaza's missile arsenals and launchers did the non-government organizations find their voice. Until then there had been a deafening silence.

On March 22, 2012, the United Nations Human Rights Council adopted a resolution calling for:

> an independent international fact-finding mission, appointed by the President of the Council, to investigate the implications of the Israeli settlements on the civil, political, economic, social and cultural rights of the Palestinian people throughout the Occupied Palestinian Territory, including East Jerusalem.

As with the 2009 United Nations Fact-Finding Mission on the Gaza Conflict – Operation Cast Lead – (led by Judge Richard Goldstone), the 2002 pseudo-investigation on the basis of the "Jenin massacre" myth, and many other examples, this new resolution reflects the role of non-governmental organizations working with the powerful Organization of Islamic Cooperation (OIC).

That alliance was also responsible for the infamous United Nations Durban Conference, dealt with in the previous chapter, in which the Non-Governmental Organization Forum adopted a strategy for the "complete isolation of Israel" using totally false allegations of "war crimes" and pseudo-investigations, and the one-sided 2004 International Court of Justice advisory opinion on Israel's security barrier.

Before the latest United Nations Human Rights Council session, the Ram'allah-based Al Haq funded by Norway, Ireland, and the Non-Governmental Development Center (NDC) – a Palestinian mechanism for providing support to the non-governmental organizations sector and jointly funded by Sweden, Denmark, Switzerland, and the Netherlands – submitted a written statement on behalf of eleven Palestinian non-governmental organizations, lobbying for:

> a United Nations Fact-Finding Mission to investigate the widespread and systematic nature of Israel's policies and practices that lead to the forcible transfer of the protected Palestinian population.

These non-governmental organizations include European-funded Palestinian activist groups, Al-Dameer, Al-Mezan, BADIL, and Defense for Children International-Palestine Section.

Additionally, during the session, non-governmental organizations – Al-Haq, BADIL, Commission of the Churches on International Affairs of the World Council of Churches, International Federation for Human Rights Leagues (also on behalf of Palestinian Center for Human Rights), and North-South XXI – made oral statements in support of the anti-Israel resolutions, using demonizing rhetoric and advancing their one-sided, biased agendas.

As a result of this and similar campaigns, these non-governmental organizations and their European government sponsors share in the responsibility for the exploitation of the United Nations Human Rights Council as a framework for political warfare and discrimination against Israel.

Israel has made many overtures to the Palestinians in her attempts to revitalize Israeli-Palestinian dialogue, and the establishment of further United Nations Human Rights Council probes harms these efforts and pushes the sides further apart.

In March 2012, when the probe into Israeli settlements was announced, Israel cut her ties with both the United Nations

Human Rights Council and the Office of United Nations Human Rights chief Navi Pillay. *The Times of Israel* reports that a senior Israeli Foreign Ministry official said:

> From now on, we will no longer work together in any way, shape or form with any officials from the council, including the High Commissioner. If anyone from the council calls us, we just won't answer the phone.

Israel felt it was important to remind the international community that she is not going to cooperate with a biased fact-finding mission, the outcome of which is decided in advance. The investigators would not be allowed to enter the country or go to the West Bank.

It should be noted that this investigation would constitute the third probe by the United Nations Human Rights Council into Israeli activities in the past four years. These investigations into Israeli actions are not about the subjects under investigation – they are political tools used to attack and delegitimize Israel.

With all the demonizing of Israel over settlements, which only exist due to the Arab's 1967 Khartoum rejection of any negotiations with Israel, a surprising turn of events came to light in July 2012.

In January 2012, Prime Minister Binyamin Netanyahu called for a legal commission – made up of former Supreme Court justice Edmund Levy, former Foreign Ministry legal adviser Alan Baker and former deputy president of the Tel Aviv District Court Tchia Shapira – to rule on the legality of unauthorized Israeli outposts and settlements. In July the three legal experts submitted their report to the government. The report contains an in-depth analysis of the entire settlement issue, not just that of the illegal outposts.

The report criticized the actions of past governments that led to the creation of illegal West Bank (biblical Judea and Samaria) Jewish communities, while recommending transforming them into new settlements where possible. The report noted that some one hundred outposts, built from 1991 to 2005, had occurred with the help of government offices and ministries and that Jewish building was:

carried out with the knowledge, encouragement, and tacit
agreement of the most senior political level – government
ministers and the prime minister.

The three legal experts found that such activity is to be seen
as "implied agreement" and concluded that this "implied agreement"
opened the door for Netanyahu's government to legalize this
construction if it chose to do so.

The report did not overly focus on Israel's diplomatic con-
siderations with respect to the peace process, instead it looked at
Israel's obligation under international and domestic law.

The prospect that a legal opinion opened the way for outposts
to be made into permanent settlements was a surprising turn of
events for Israel, but the outpost report also concluded that the
classical laws of occupation:

as set out in the relevant international conventions cannot be
considered applicable to the unique and *sui generis* historic and
legal circumstances of Israel's presence in Judea and Samaria
spanning over decades.

Similarly, the report said the 1949 Fourth Geneva Convention
against the transfer of populations is not applicable to the Israeli
settlement activity in Judea and Samaria:

Israelis have the legal right to settle in Judea and Samaria and
the establishments of settlements cannot, in and of itself, be
considered illegal.

In a nutshell, the report concludes that the establishment of
settlements in the West Bank does not breach international law,
and that Jews can legally make their homes there. It also states
that Israel does not meet the criteria of "military occupation" as
defined under international law in the West Bank, and therefore
the settlements and outposts are legal, since there is no provision
in international law prohibiting Jewish settlement in the area.

The findings in the commission's report have to be approved
by the Ministerial Committee on Settlements or the government.
Its findings, at this stage, are only recommendations, but the
report immediately led to a resurgence of calls to annex the West
Bank and give the approximately two million Palestinian Arabs

Israeli citizenship. However, such a move would certainly set the Israeli cat among the nations' pigeons. It remains to be seen if Netanyahu has the cojones to run the United Nations' gauntlet.

Non-Governmental Organizations (NGOs) have become a substantial headache and also a big heartache for Israel. The damage executed against Israel and the injustices suffered by Israel due to the abundance of lies and misinformation spread widely by non-governmental organizations is incalculable.

As befitting the prevailing circus atmosphere in Durban (dealt with in the previous Chapter), and the ambiance of lynch and Israel-baiting within and around the Durban conference (including violent anti-Israel demonstrations in the streets of Durban), the parallel conference, a scandalous event, adopted in its own declaration such formulations on Israel as:

> "a colonial military occupant," "a racist, apartheid state in which Israel's brand of apartheid is a crime against humanity."

It declared Israel guilty of:

> racist crimes including war crimes, acts of genocide and ethnic cleansing.

The conference's Program of Action called for implementation of measures against Israel as employed previously against the South African apartheid regime: deployment of an independent international protection force; reinstatement of the United Nations' Zionism Equals Racism Resolution 3379; the repeal by Israel of its Law of Return by which all Jews have right of aliyah to the Jewish homeland; the establishment of a special United Nations committee to deal with Israeli apartheid and other racist crimes; the launch of an international anti-Israel apartheid movement; and a call to the international community to totally isolate Israel.

The content of the appalling conference remains in the records of the United Nations, and as such has entered into history. It was but a taste of the mounting hatred of Israel by non-governmental organizations in Europe, Scandinavia, and the Islamic world.

One non-governmental organization that garners a great deal of media attention is the London-based Amnesty International. Amnesty seems to have a scheduled order of protests against Israel, which it trundles out with monotonous regularity. On the surface Amnesty appears to be an active, impartial, and independent charitable group that does a great deal of good in third-world countries, and the media and diplomats consider the non-governmental organization to be upholding the universal principles of human rights.

But when it comes to Israel, Amnesty throws ethics, impartiality, and fairness out of the window by only listening to those who hold anti-Israel views. Israel's documented coverage of events are ignored completely. One does not have to dig down very far in order to find the reason for this.

Amnesty's public image is misleading. Contrary to what the Amnesty implies on its website and in other public relations materials, Amnesty is not an independent charity. Amnesty International and its local branches accept government funding and is therefore not neutral, but influenced by donors. Amnesty International has received many millions of GB Pounds and Euros from Europe, with Britain being the biggest donor.

Amnesty Israel claims on its website:

> We are independent of all governments, political persuasions and religious creeds. We are funded by our members and donors, and no funds are sought or accepted from governments.

This is patently untrue. Between 2008 and 2010, Amnesty Israel received four hundred and twenty nine thousand seven hundred and ten Israeli sheqels (one hundred and ten thousand dollars) from the Netherlands and the United States. It is not the amount of funds, it is the deceit of denying receiving it.

Amnesty claims that it maintains a policy of "impartiality" and is unbiased in its research of allegations of human rights violations. Despite making this claim, Amnesty employs an anti-Israel activist as a researcher in its "Israel, Occupied Palestinian Territories and Palestinian Authority" section. This individual, Deborah Hyams, has a well-documented history of radical activism in the context of the Arab-Israeli conflict and, correspondingly, weakens Amnesty's credibility and claims of neutrality.

Deborah Hyams volunteered as a "human shield" in Beit Jala (near Bethlehem) to deter Israeli military responses to gunfire and mortars. In 2008 she signed a letter claiming Israel is:

> a state founded on terrorism, massacres and the dispossession of another people from their land.

Another Amnesty Israel activist, Saleh Hijazi, a Palestinian born in Jerusalem and raised in Ramallah, and also working as a Public Relations official for the Office of the Ministry of Planning in Ram'allah, and who, in 2007, was listed as the contact for the non-governmental organization Another Voice – under the group's signature "Resist! Boycott! We Are Intifada!"

In November 2012, a tweet with Amnesty International's logo, posted by Kristyan Benedict, Amnesty-UK's, Middle East campaign manager, targeting three Jewish members of the British parliament, overtly suggesting that the Jewish parliamentarians (Louise Ellman, Robert Halfon, and Luciana Berger) supported bombing Gaza and the killing of its civilians. The "offensive" tweet raised the ire of the British Jewish community which demanded a "proper apology" from Benedict and "disciplinary action" from Amnesty.

Benedict's activities have been the source of controversy in the past and the Jewish community has raised concerns previously with Amnesty. For instance, in July 2012, Benedict stated that Israel:

> was now included in the list of stupid dictatorial regimes who abuse peoples' basic universal rights, along with Burma, North Korea, Iran, and Sudan, its government has the same wanton attitude to human beings.

The façade of Amnesty's impartiality is as hideous as it is extensive.

Another large non-governmental organization that has shown itself to be anti-Israel is the George Soros-funded Human Rights Watch (HRW), which has a powerful influence on governments, newsrooms, and classrooms worldwide. Human Rights Watch, like Amnesty International, is portrayed as a human rights protector, but, like Amnesty, it bares its teeth at Israel. The world is unaware of how it is duped by myriads of assorted organizations, of which all have their agendas to pedal, but who need public and taxpayer money to remain operative.

Human Rights Watch promotes the strategy of the 2001 Durban Non-Governmental Organization Forum (discussed in the previous chapter), whose goal is that of isolating Israel through the language of human rights. Detailed research shows that Human Rights Watch alone has issued at least **sixty-eight** calls for "independent investigations" of Israel.

Marc Garlasco was Human Rights Watch's "senior military expert" and coauthor of numerous reports condemning Israel. Following a research report by NGO Monitor,[1] Garlasco was shown to be an avid collector of Nazi memorabilia. This revelation provided the rational for Human Rights Watch's pattern of false and unsupported claims used to condemn Israel, and a history of anti-Israel ideology among Human Rights Watch officials.

Garlasco was suspended by Human Rights Watch in September 2009 following NGO Monitor's embarrassing allegations that he collected Nazi memorabilia. Garlasco resigned from Human Rights Watch in February 2010. Human Rights Watch also removed Richard Falk, the United Nations special rapporteur for human rights in the Palestinian territories (mentioned in the previous chapter), from one of Human Rights Watch's committees and updated its website to reflect Falk's expulsion from the committee. Falk's ousting followed a number of complaints from several countries and an open letter from UN Watch calling for Falk's removal due to his overt animus toward Israel.

In May 2009, while Marc Garlasco was still Human Rights Watch's "senior military expert," leaders of Human Rights Watch visited Saudi Arabia to raise funds for the organization. Saudi Arabia is one of the major violators of the norms that Human Rights Watch claims to promote. Arab news reported that "senior members" of Human Rights Watch – including Middle East Division director Sarah Leah Whitson, and Hassan Elmasry, a member of the International Board of Directors and the Middle East Division's Advisory Committee – attended a "welcoming dinner" and encouraged "prominent members of Saudi society" to finance their work. Human Rights Watch's anti-Israel activities were given as the major reason for holding the Saudi fundraiser:

> The group is facing a shortage of funds because of the global financial crisis and the work on Israel and Gaza, which depleted Human Rights Watch's budget for the region.

Sarah Whitson's appeal for Saudi support and money acknowledged and cited Human Rights Watch's extensive anti-Israel focus.

Similarly, Whitson told the Saudi leaders about Human Rights Watch's role in anti-Israel activities in the United States Congress and the United Nations, boasting that this propaganda campaign was instrumental in the United Nations "fact-finding mission to investigate the allegations of serious Israeli violations during the war on Gaza," to be headed by Justice Richard Goldstone, who was also a member of Human Rights Watch's board at the time. (He resigned after the investigation began; as NGO Monitor had noted, Goldstone's membership on Human Rights Watch's board was a conflict of interest.)

Judge Goldstone gathered his 'facts' about the Gaza war from a number of non-governmental organizations, including Amnesty International and Human Rights Watch. Goldstone swallowed everything hook, line, and sinker. Goldstone's findings were delivered at the United Nations and the media carried them around the world: Israel was guilty of "war crimes" and "crimes against humanity."

After some months, Goldstone began to recant his findings that were based upon briefs by non-governmental organizations. In an April 2, 2011, *Washington Post* opinion piece Goldstone wrote:

> We know a lot more today about what happened in the Gaza war of 2008-09 than we did when I chaired the fact-finding mission appointed by the U.N. Human Rights Council that produced what has come to be known as the Goldstone Report. If I had known then what I know now, the Goldstone Report would have been a different document.

Goldstone went on to say:

> I regret that our fact-finding mission did not have such evidence explaining the circumstances in which we said civilians in Gaza were targeted, because it probably would have influenced our findings about intentionality and war crimes.

That Goldstone, as a judge, could bring such a report, one that blackened the name of Israel around the world without all the facts is mind boggling. In the absence of facts he should have refrained from bandying about such loaded terms as "war crimes" and "crimes against humanity." Goldstone's feelings of remorse for having found out the facts post report is a travesty of justice and brings little comfort to Israel. Ultimately, it was the non-governmental organizations' falsified reports that are to blame for the Goldstone Report, but Goldstone should hang his head in shame for being so credulous. As a Jew, Richard Goldstone is another example of embedding Jews into organizations and groups hostile to Israel. As mentioned in the previous chapter, this exercise has been coined "Jew Washing" and provides "believability" to biased reports concerning Israel.

Blame for the Human Rights Watch bias against Israel lies squarely with its Jewish executive director Kenneth Roth, yet another example of "Jew Washing" that the author introduced in the previous chapter. David Feith, assistant editorial features editor of the *Wall Street Journal*, wrote an opinion piece for December 4, 2012, entitled "Dancing Around Genocide." In his article Feith portrayed a divide within Human Rights Watch on the subject of the incitement to genocide against the Jewish state. Quoting from emails obtained from Human Rights Watch, Feith shows the organization's vice chairman writing to his collegues:

> Sitting still while Iran claims a 'justification to kill all Jews and annihilate Israel' . . . is a position unworthy of our great organization.

Roth, who runs the organization, strenuously disagrees: On the subject of Iranian President Mahmoud Ahmadinejad's statement that Israel "must be wiped off the map," Roth claims that this and other Iranian rhetoric does not qualify as "incitement" – which is illegal under the United Nations Genocide Convention of 1948 – but rather that it amounts only to "advocacy," which is legal. Roth defends his position by saying that Iran is merely advocating the destruction of Israel, but since no one has actually acted on that advocacy, Iran has nothing to answer for!

In an October 20, 2009, *New York Times* opinion piece, under the heading, "Rights Watchdog, Lost in the Mideast," Robert L. Bernstein, the founder of Human Rights Watch and its active chairman for twenty years and today the founding chairman emeritus, pointed out to the English-speaking world his grave disappointment in the organization he had founded:

> I must do something that I never anticipated: I must publicly join the group's critics. Human Rights Watch had as its original mission to pry open closed societies, advocate basic freedoms and support dissenters. But recently it has been issuing reports on the Israeli-Arab conflict that are helping those who wish to turn Israel into a pariah state. . . .
>
> When I stepped aside in 1998, Human Rights Watch was active in seventy countries, most of them closed societies. Now the organization, with increasing frequency, casts aside its important distinction between open and closed societies.
>
> Nowhere is this more evident than in its work in the Middle East. The region is populated by authoritarian regimes with appalling human rights records. Yet in recent years Human Rights Watch has written far more condemnations of Israel for violations of international law than of any other country in the region.
>
> Israel, with a population of 7.4 million, is home to at least eighty human rights organizations, a vibrant free press, a democratically elected government, a judiciary that frequently rules against the government, a politically active academia, multiple political parties and, judging by the amount of news coverage, probably more journalists per capita than any other country in the world – many of whom are there expressly to cover the Israeli-Palestinian conflict.
>
> Meanwhile, the Arab and Iranian regimes rule over some three hundred and fifty million people, and most remain brutal, closed and autocratic, permitting little or no internal dissent.

The plight of their citizens who would most benefit from the kind of attention a large and well-financed international human rights organization can provide is being ignored as Human Rights Watch's Middle East division prepares report after report on Israel.

Human Rights Watch has lost critical perspective on a conflict in which Israel has been repeatedly attacked by Hamas and Hizb'allah, organizations that go after Israeli citizens and use their own people as human shields. These groups are supported by the government of Iran, which has openly declared its intention not just to destroy Israel but to murder Jews everywhere. This incitement to genocide is a violation of the Convention on the Prevention and Punishment of the Crime of Genocide.

Leaders of Human Rights Watch know that Hamas and Hizb'allah chose to wage war from densely populated areas, deliberately transforming neighborhoods into battlefields. They know that more and better arms are flowing into both Gaza and Lebanon and are poised to strike again. And they know that this militancy continues to deprive Palestinians of any chance for the peaceful and productive life they deserve. Yet   Israel, the repeated victim of aggression, faces the brunt of Human Rights Watch's criticism.

The organization is expressly concerned mainly with how wars are fought, not with motivations. To be sure, even victims of aggression are bound by the laws of war and must do their utmost to minimize civilian casualties. Nevertheless, there is a difference between wrongs committed in self-defense and those perpetrated intentionally.

But how does Human Rights Watch know that these laws have been violated? In Gaza and elsewhere where there is no access to the battlefield or to the military and political leaders who make strategic decisions, it is extremely difficult to make definitive judgments about war crimes. Reporting often relies on witnesses whose stories cannot be verified and who may testify for political advantage or because they fear retaliation from their own rulers. Significantly, Col. Richard Kemp, the former commander of British forces in Afghanistan and an expert on warfare, has said that the Israel Defense Forces in Gaza "did more to safeguard the rights of civilians in a combat zone than any other army in the history of warfare."

Only by returning to its founding mission and the spirit of humility that animated it can Human Rights Watch resurrect itself as a moral force in the Middle East and throughout the world. If it fails to do that, its credibility will be seriously undermined and its important role in the world significantly diminished.

Only a person from another planet would not think it odd to see someone take to task the human rights group he founded, and that for being biased against Israel. Bernstein could obviously see through the façade of impartiality by the Middle East division of Human Rights Watch. However, there is little difference between the way the Organization's Executive Director and the entire Middle East division of Human Rights Watch treats Israel and the way the United Nations and the herd of anti-Israel non-governmental organizations treat Israel. It is a disgrace. Unfortunately, millions believe these groups to be beyond reproach and swallow the lies and disinformation they propagate.

In mid-June 2012, some fifty non-governmental organizations and United Nations bodies issued a joint appeal, calling on Israel to end to her blockade of the Gaza Strip that is ruled by the Hamas terror group. The petition claimed:

For over five years in Gaza, more than 1.6 million people have been under blockade in violation of international law. More than half of these people are children. We the undersigned say with one voice: "end the blockade now."

Amongst the signatories were Amnesty International, Save the Children, the World Health Organization, Oxfam, the Office of the High Commissioner for Human Rights and five other United Nations agencies.

Israel's blockade of Gaza has been declared legal by international law experts and even by her most bitter critic – the United Nations. Therefore, the charge of the blockade being in violation of international law is a fabrication of a multifarious group of anti-Israel know-nothings.

Israel imposed restrictions on trade to Gaza in 2001 following the outbreak of the second *intifada* and tightened them further in 2007 after Hamas seized power in the coastal enclave adjacent to Egypt, which also enforced a blockade until shortly after Hosni Mubarak's overthrow in 2011.

Israel has relaxed her stringent rules over the past two years in the face of heavy international pressure, but insists on checking all goods entering the territory to prevent arms or weapons-making equipment from reaching Hamas.

Hamas's charter calls for the destruction of Israel. It has launched thousands of rockets and mortars at Israeli cities and towns, therefore all cargo going into Gaza must be checked. Without question it is unfair to expect Israel to remove the restriction on military use items while the terror groups in Gaza are as hostile and aggressive as they are.

In June 2012, two Christian groups were calling on the British government to boycott produce that stems from Israeli settlements, claiming it would promote peace between Israelis and Palestinians. Christian Aid and the Quakers told the Foreign Affairs Committee in the House of Commons that the government should implement a total ban of settlement produce by introducing legislation.

It has been alluded to previously, that Britain is a fertile ground for the Boycott, Divestment, and Sanctions (BDS) movement. There appears to be a goodly amount of animus toward Israel residing in the British psyche. The author, who was born and raised in England, believes this deep-seated ill will toward Israel stems from small groups of militant Jews having been instrumental in driving the British to relinquish to the United Nations the Mandate of Palestine. A serious wound had been inflicted on British military and political pride and, as the British lion licked its wound, the *New Statesman* reflected the mood of the nation by publishing a full front page editorial on June 23, 1946, entitled, "**War for the White Paper**?" which stated *inter alia*:

> in fighting the Jews, the Government had the help of the B.B.C. and probably most of the widely-read papers, and there would

be a flood of anti-Jewish "atrocity" stories and editorials on the righteousness of liquidating the obstinate survivors of Hitler's gas chambers.

Nothing much has changed over the last sixty plus years. Many of the "widely-read" British newspapers, along with the *BBC* (British Broadcasting Corporation), still print or broadcast a "flood of anti-Jewish atrocity stories." The *BBC* was obviously broadcasting "anti-Jewish atrocity stories" long before the State of Israel was declared, and it remains today one of the most unreliable sources of news concerning the Middle East. The *BBC* has tried numbers of times to explain away its shoddy journalism when it comes to reporting on Israel and was denied broadcasting rights in Israel for a time due to its overt bias.

An organization named BBC Watch was established in 2012 in order to monitor the *BBC*'s news output and examine the broadcaster's adherence to its legal obligation to produce accurate and impartial reports. Following two successive scandals in November 2012 – over which the *BBC*'s director-general was forced to resign – *BBC* chairman Chris Patten said the scandals were marked by "unacceptably shoddy journalism," that the organization was in a "ghastly mess" and that it was in need of a "fundamental shake-up." Patten also said:

> The BBC is one of the things that has come to define and reflect Britishness, and we shouldn't lose that.

If there is one thing "that has come to define and reflect Britishness" it is anti-Israelism. Many millions of Israelis and supporters of Israel around the globe would very much like to immediately see the *BBC*'s particular reflection of Britishness lost.

In something less than coincidental, the *BBC*'s former director-general, Mark Thompson, who served in that capacity until September 2012, reported for work as the chief executive of the *New York Times* on November 12, 2012. The *New York Times* is America's premier Israel-bashing daily in addition to being the Bible of the liberal left.

According to BBC Watch ninety-seven percent of the population of the United Kingdom and approximately two hundred and twenty-five million more people worldwide watch and listen to *BBC* broadcasts every week. Its pronounced anti-Israel bias can have serious injurious impact on its listeners and it has to stop.

To make matters worse in the Israel-United Kingdom diplomacy stakes, in Israel's 1948-49 War of Independence, Israel's largely untrained farmer-soldiers defeated the seven British-trained and equipped Arab armies that took part in the multi-nation attack against the nascent state – three of the seven British-trained and equipped armies were led by British officers. It must have been extremely humiliating for Britain, which was once the world's preeminent military and maritime power, to be humbled by less than twenty thousand Jewish farmer-soldiers using, for the main part, homemade weapons.[4] (Ian V. Hogg, a war historian and one of the leading British authorities on military activities, claims that Israel could only muster "around eighteen thousand troops, ten thousand rifles and three thousand six hundred machine guns" against the combined force of seven armies).

In Britain today, hating Israel has apparently become a valid criminal defense. In July 2010, five people charged with destroying property valued at more than one hundred and forty-three thousand pounds (two hundred and twenty-five thousand dollars) at an arms factory in Brighton during a January 2009 break-in were found not guilty of all charges. They were found innocent although all five admitted to having committed the crime.

As the *Guardian* reported, the defendants boasted in on-line forums at the time of the incident, their crime was premeditated. It took place during Israel's twenty-two-day Operation Cast Lead against Hamas in Gaza. The jury found the five innocent because it accepted as a valid defense their claim that they vandalized the plant because they wanted to stop Israel from carrying out war crimes in Gaza. The arms factory did some business with the Israel Defense Force, therefore, the defendants claimed and the jury agreed, it deserved to be attacked.

In August 2012, four hundred and fifty London buses were being shamefully driven around the city displaying large anti-Israel posters advertising the *"Al Quds Day"* annual march –

the brainchild of Ayatollah Ruhollah Khomeini who led Iran's Islamic revolution. The posters declare: "Our Freedom is incomplete without the Freedom of the Palestinians." The Transport for London said on August 10 that it would not remove the posters until after the march had taken place on August 17.

It was announced on August 17, 2012, that an Israeli professor, Motti Crystal, was suing the British National Health Service for discrimination. Professor Crystal was to have led a May 8, 2012, National Health Service seminar in Manchester, but the invitation was withdrawn at the last minute due to complaints "about his nationality."

In mid-November 2012, a performance by Israel's Batsheva Dance Company in Britain's city of Birmingham was completely disrupted by anti-Israel protestors. Birmingham was the fourth stop in England for the troupe, which had been picketed and disrupted at every venue. The next stop on the tour was cancelled due to the high security costs.

In December 2011, while visiting friends in Yorkshire, England, the author suffered a heart attack following an address to an assembly in Sheffield. While the author was undergoing heart surgery, his wife completed all the necessary paperwork, which included all our Israel details.

Three days later, still in the cardiac ward, the author had a visit from the ward's cardiac rehabilitation specialist. In her possession were a sheaf of papers containing the author's records. The author's Israel address had been altered and was shown as being in Jerusalem, "Palestine." It seems to be a knee-jerk reaction with the British to replace the name Israel with a non-existent country of "Palestine" at every opportunity. When the author pointed out that he lived in Israel and that there was no such country as "Palestine," the cardiac specialist stared at the author with the most vacant expression on her face – she did not know what to say.

Similarly, the official *BBC* website for London's July 2012 Olympic Games had no capital city listed for Israel in its profile of countries, the space was blank. Of the two hundred nations profiled on its website, only Israel did not have a capital city. But the profile for "Palestine" listed East Jerusalem as its capital, and United States dollars as its accepted currency.

Israel, with more than three thousand years of history in Jerusalem, was left without a capital city, while her holy city – *the city of the great King* (Psalms 48:2) – was given as the capital of a county that does not exist at the time of writing. Also, the Israeli sheqel is the accepted currency in the Palestinian Authority-controlled territories, not the United States dollar.

Following strong protests from the Israeli government, the organizers of the *BBC*'s Olympic Games website changed Israel's country profile to say that "the seat of government is Jerusalem," but refused to own to the fact that Jerusalem is the capital of Israel.

The Mayor Jerusalem, Nir Barkat, attacked the *BBC* directly:

> We will not accept those who deny our history, our sovereignty, and our right to determine our own capital. Irrespective of the BBC's political agenda, Jerusalem was, is, and will always be the capital of Israel and the spiritual, political, and physical center of the Jewish people.

Mark Regev, spokesman for the Prime Ministers Office, wrote a second time to the *BBC*'s Bureau Chief. In his letter Regev said:

> I am afraid that despite your efforts, Israel is still discriminated against on the BBC's London 2012 Olympics website. I kindly request that Israel's capital be identified accurately on your website.

In similar fashion neither the *BBC* nor *SkyNews* ever show the temperatures for Jerusalem in their televised weather forecasts, they show the temperatures for Tel Aviv instead. (*Kol Hakavod* to *France24*, which bucks the European trend and shows Jerusalem temperatures in its forecasts). It is unsurprising that Britain has fallen from its perch today as the preeminent world power to merely being a European nation-state playing second-fiddle to Germany. Britain's downward spiral began when Britain, under Neville Chamberlin, turned against the Jews by issuing the White Paper in 1939, abandoning the recommended partitioning of Palestine and limiting the number of Jews allowed into the country.

In July 1922, Britain was tasked by the Council of the League of Nations (forerunner of the United Nations) with the Mandate to establish the Jewish National Home in all of Palestine, which had formerly been part of the then defunct Ottoman Empire. However, Britain went on to deal treacherously with the Jews due to the amount of oil that was beginning to flow in the Middle East.

Britain cut off some seventy-seven percent of the land intended for the Jewish National Home and created an Arab country that is today known as Jordan, from which Jews were banned. Britain went on to severely limit the number of Jews it allowed to enter the Mandate area, and even went so far as to prevent ships carrying thousands of desperate Jews fleeing Nazi Germany's death camps from reaching the shores of their ancient land. The gates of the ancient Jewish homeland, which were to have been opened to them again through the Mandate Britain had been given by the League of Nations, had in fact been slammed shut by Britain.

Some of the boatloads of Jews escaping the Nazi Germany's hell were escorted to Cyprus by the British navy, where the Jews were offloaded and locked in huge steel cages until after the end of the war. Some Jewish refugee ships were simply turned away by British warships – those ships with their pitiful human cargoes wallowed in inhospitable seas and a number sank with few or no survivors. In what must be one of the cruelest, most inhuman acts of all time, Britain sent one ship's desperate Jewish human cargo – more than four thousand five hundred Holocaust survivors, including almost one thousand seven hundred children – back to Germany.

Winston Churchill, the inspiring leader who took Britain through the dark days of the war and who was probably the greatest British statesman ever, was repaid for his noble efforts by being thrown out of office in 1946 before he was able to establish the Jewish National Home in Palestine. The Labour Party came to power with Clement Attlee as prime minister and Ernest Bevin as foreign secretary. Neither man supported their party's commitment to establish the Jewish National Home and worked against it, which ultimately led to a great deal of blood shedding in Palestine.

On May 16, 1948, Christopher Mayhew, a faithful supporter of Ernest Bevin, wrote into his diary *inter alia*:

> I must make a note about Ernest's anti-Semitism. There is no doubt to my mind that Ernest detests Jews. He makes the odd wise-crack about the "chosen people" and declares that the Old Testament is the most immoral book ever written and makes a snide reference to Jews having been elected to Parliament, but no Arabs. He says the Jews taught Hitler the technic of terror and even now were paralleling the Nazis in Palestine. ... I allow him only one point, that in giving voice to his irrational and indefensible prejudices, he is speaking for millions of British people.

Apparently, little has changed in the majority of British hearts – as shown previously, a *BBC* poll reported that sixty-eight percent of Britons held negative views of Israel. With its tragic history vis-à-vis the Jews it is indeed regrettable that a full sixty-four years after the founding of the modern state of Israel Britain continues with a low-grade political war against the Jewish state. It remains anti-Jew and staunchly pro-Arab. It is an even sadder fact that numerous Christian denominations and groups in Britain have gotten involved in the BDS – Boycott, Divestment, and Sanctions – movement against Israel. Without Israel's highly technological advances Britain's entire financial, business, and telecommunications worlds would collapse.

Britain's Christian Aid's advocacy officer for Israel and the Palestinian territories, William Bell, has said that:

> the settlements are illegal under international law, a major cause of poverty among Palestinians and an obstacle to peace.

The author has shown[2] that the settlement movement was caused by the Arab refusal to negotiate a peace with Israel in return for the land she captured in a war of self-defense. On September 2, 1964, the Soviet daily *Pravda* published what the Supreme Soviet had formulated, which specifically referred to the Soviet Union's occupation of Eastern Europe during and after World War II when it defeated invading Nazi forces:

A people which has been attacked, has defended itself and wins wars, is bound by sacred duty to establish for itself in perpetuity a political situation which will ensure the liquidation of the sources of aggression. It is entitled to maintain this state of affairs as long as the danger of aggression does not cease.

A nation which has attained security at the cost of numerous victims, will never agree to the restoration of the previous borders. No territories are to be returned as long as the danger of aggression still prevails.

The Soviet formula was fully acceptable to the international community. However, what was good for the Soviet Union apparently does not hold good for Israel. Apparently, the so-called international community is nothing less than an international community of hypocrites.

In the face of Arab rejectionism; and after pouring billions of dollars into building prosperous cities and towns where some three hundred thousand Israelis live today, the Palestinians are now pleading with the international community to force Israel to cede all the land, cities, and towns back to them. Back to those who wish only to destroy the Jewish state.

In August 2005, Israel ceded the Gaza Strip to the Palestinians. Israel razed the homes of nine thousand four hundred and eighty Israelis, but left all the green houses and synagogues intact. The logic behind leaving the green houses was in order for the Palestinians to inherit an agricultural system worth millions of dollars, which would be a major boost to their economy. It was also felt the that Palestinians would show the synagogues reverence and not destroy them, perhaps even turning them into mosques with the blessing of Israel. But once the Palestinians had access to the vacated land they looted the greenhouses of all the irrigation and other equipment, and afterward destroyed the structures, looting anything of value. The synagogues suffered the same fate and were all totally destroyed.

And from the vacated land Palestinian terrorists have launched thousands of rockets and mortars into Israeli cities and towns. And the Palestinians, along with the international community, think Israel is foolish enough to try the experiment again, but on a far more massive scale. It will not happen, period.

The boycotts of Israeli goods manufactured in the industrial areas beyond the Green Line[3] affects the livelihood of over fifteen thousand Palestinians in the West Bank's Area C where all Israeli companies are situated. Area C is the area where Israel is, by recognizable international treaties, responsible for civilian law and security and where most Israeli settlers live. However, Palestinian President Mahmoud Abbas is encouraging Palestinians in an illegal "building intifada," slowly impinging on Israel's legal right to Area C.

Much space is given by the world's media about how difficult it is for Palestinians to obtain building permits from Israeli authorities. If the truth be known, the great majority of Palestinians are only applying for permits in areas where they know Israel does not allow Palestinian building, and the denial of permits in those areas provide headline-making fodder for the anti-Israel media. Under the Oslo Accords Israel was given full administrative and security control over Area C. Allocation of final sovereignty over the area was to be determined by negotiations between Israel and the Palestinian Authority. But the Palestinians have illegally built more than fifty thousand homes in Area C and on Israel's state lands – creating what is known as "facts on the ground."

The boycotts certainly affect Israeli manufacturers in Area C, and also the small Israeli farmers that produce flowers, fruit, and vegetables in other small settlement towns. However, the greatest loss will be to the Palestinians who will lose their jobs and struggle to put something to eat on the family table.

The Quakers said that they see boycotts "as a non-violent action to support efforts to build peace in the region." When will folk begin to learn from history? History shows us again and again that the most peaceful times were when the nations' leaders least pursued peace. If the nations attempt to impose their will upon Israel it will come back to haunt them, possibly by way of the battlefield. The LORD is the only one who can settle the Israeli-Palestinian question, and He is already working this out by bringing Israel into the wilderness and allowing the nations to exercise their free wills against her.

Numbers of Christian denominational Churches and organizations in the Western world are heavily involved in the BDS movement. In the last decade, BDS aimed at Israel developed as a key issue in mainline Christian denominations in the United States, Europe, Canada, and elsewhere.

A number of European governments, together with the United States and Canada, provide funds for these church-based efforts that delegitimize Israel. The taxpayer funds are disbursed as grants to church-based humanitarian non-governmental organizations, which then transfer the funds to highly politicized pro-Palestinian non-governmental organizations, including Christian groups that promote BDS, the one-state solution and, in many cases, antisemitic replacement theologies within mainline churches.

On July 9, 2012, the Church of England's General Synod, which is the church's highest legislative body, voted to support "the vital work" of the Ecumenical Accompaniment Program in Palestine and Israel (EAPPI). The project brings church members to the West Bank to "experience life under occupation" for three to four month periods and expects the members to campaign on their return for:

> a just and peaceful resolution to the Israeli-Palestinian conflict through an end to the occupation, respect for international law and implementation of United Nations resolutions.

The church members only spend a few days, up to a week in Israel, inside the Green Line – the rest of the groups' time is spent with the Palestinians. Israel says the Church of England's support of this anti-Israel project is heavily biased in favor of the Palestinians.

Perhaps these churches, groups, and individuals need to learn what the LORD has to say about His people Israel, and activities that delegitimize His *"special treasure:"*

> *For thus says the LORD of hosts: "He sent Me after glory, to the nations which plunder you; for **he who touches you touches the apple of His eye"***
> (Zechariah 2:8).

Those who touch Israel in a harmful way, whether they be secular or "Christian," jab their fingers into the LORD's eye – Israel's *"Maker,"* and the consequences of such actions are too dreadful to dwell on. It is impossible to love Jesus, *"born King of the Jews"* (Matthew 2:2), while despising His brethren. Thought should be given to what was explained in the fifth footnote at the conclusion of Chapter two.

Marisa Johnson, of the Ecumenical Accompaniment Program in Palestine and Israel (EAPPI) that is managed by the Quakers says: "The problem goes beyond the obvious effects on Palestinian livelihoods and damages prospects for peace."

Jerusalem-based research organization NGO Monitor says the Ecumenical Accompaniment Program in Palestine and Israel harbors an anti- Israel stance, in that it supports the BDS (Boycott, Divestment and Sanctions) campaign against Israel as well as the right of return for all the estimated seven million Palestinian refugees into Israel, inside the Green Line.

Quaker meeting houses in the United Kingdom are regularly used by groups who question Israel's right to exist and support boycott action against Israel. In 2007, the Quakers joined a coalition of anti-Israel groups to mark the "40th anniversary of Israel's military occupation of Gaza and the West Bank, including east Jerusalem."

The boycott war against Israel is rapidly gaining ground. After South Africa instructed commercial importers not to use the label "Product of Israel" (see below) for goods manufactured in Judea and Samaria's Jewish communities, the Danish government also announced the adoption of this policy. Then Irish Foreign Minister Eamon Gilmore proposed that the European Union consider banning products from the settlements. The move follows a British decision to allow retailers to distinguish whether goods are "Israeli settlement produce" or "Palestinian produce."

If Europe labels goods as "Israeli settlements produce," it will become impossible for the Israeli companies to reach sales points abroad. Other European countries will adopt this racist policy. According to a decision taken in 2010 by the European Union high court: the "disputed areas" are not part of Israel, so

Israeli goods made there are subject to European Union import duties. The historic ruling stemmed from a German case filed by Brita GmbH, a German company that imports drink-makers for sparkling water from Soda Club, an Israeli company based in Mishor Adumim, one of Israel's industrial areas in the West Bank.

During the first *intifada*, then-industry, trade and labor minister Ariel Sharon said there had been a "drastic reduction" in the consumption of Israeli-made goods from Judea and Samaria during the violent uprising after Western activists stepped up their campaign for a boycott.

Sales of Israeli agricultural products dropped by some sixty percent between 1987 and 1988. Production of other goods has also declined, including textiles, rubber and plastic, non-metallic minerals, clothing, and quarry-stone.

Since then the boycott campaign has flourished in the West. If yesterday the orders came from Damascus, where the Arab League headquartered the Arab boycott operations, today the boycott virus is spreading through Europe's pension funds, supermarkets, commercial companies, labor unions, food co-ops and industrial firms.

European governments, including Britain's, have received legal opinion from an international counsel who argues that they would be fully within their rights to ban trade with Israeli settlements in the West Bank. The opinion was to be published in July 2012 by the Trades Union Congress, which has mounted a sustained campaign for a ban on goods from Israeli settlements. Brendan Barber, general secretary of the Trades Union Congress, said that the United Kingdom had made a "real difference" by ensuring supermarket goods from settlements were properly labelled.

Agrexco, Israel's leading flower exporter, declared bankruptcy, partially due to the boycott of its produce. More than twenty organizations in Europe, in thirteen countries, endorsed a boycott of the company, partially owned by the Israeli government and which had farms in the Jordan Valley and in Tekoa, a settlement at the entrance of the Judean desert.

Norway's oil fund withdrew its investment from Africa-Israel and Danya Cebus citing involvement in "settlement construction." A Swedish co-op terminated all purchases of Soda carbonation devices.

Major Dutch pension fund Pensioenfonds Zorg en Welzijn, which has investments totaling ninety-seven billion euros, has divested from almost all the Israeli companies in its portfolio (banks, telecommunication companies, construction companies and Elbit Systems). The British supermarket chain Co-Operative Group approved a boycott of goods from Judea and Samaria. A large Swedish pension fund also divested from Elbit over the latter's role in building Israel's West Bank security barrier. A New Zealand government fund has divested from Israeli companies that have involvement in construction on Israel's Security Barrier or with settlements in Judea and Samaria.

The Ethical Council of four Swedish buffer pension funds urged Motorola "to pull out of the Israeli-occupied territories in the West Bank" or face divestment. Norway's governmental pension and Germany's Deutsch Bank divested from Elbit. The flagship London outlet of Israeli company Ahava, which produces cosmetics and creams has been closed after years of protest.

The food manufacturing giant, British and Dutch-owned multinational Unilever, withdraw from Ariel, Israel's largest settlement. Unilever, which makes household staples such as Sunsilk shampoo and Vaseline, sold its fifty-one percent stake in the Beigel Bakery's factories in Judea and Samaria.

The settlements' products are targeted not just because these are political symbols, but also because Yesha and Golan businesses are an important part of the Israeli economy with firms such as Oppenheimer, Super Class and Shamir Salads, Golan Heights Dairies, Ahava and Hlavin, Beitili, and Barkan Brackets.

Most settlers' businesses are centered in Barkan (Ariel), Mishor Adumim (east of Jerusalem), Atarot (northern Jerusalem) and Ma'aleh Efraim (Jordan Valley). Despite Barkan being an industrial zone fully integrated with the Gush Dan economy, several companies, such as the Swedish firm Assa Abloy and the partly Dutch owned Barkan Wine Cellars, already pulled out of Ariel.

But targeting the settlements is just an excuse to destroy Israel's economic life as such. The boycott campaign is not about Israel's size, it is about her very existence. The list of Israeli products targeted worldwide for the boycott reveals the hatred for the existence of the Jewish state in any borders. The boycott movement also targets Teva, a company established in Jerusalem forty-seven years before the re-establishment of Israel, only because it is today one of the world's largest pharmaceutical companies.

The BDS movement targets Delta Galil Industries, located in pre-1967 Israel, only because Delta Galil is Israel's largest textile manufacturer. They target Sabra, only because Israel's second largest food company supplies food for the Israel Defense Force. They target Intel, because its first development center outside the United States was in Israel and employs thousands of Israelis.

The economic boycott of the German Jews in business and employment was the first step toward bringing in the Holocaust. The same *"Raus mit Uns"* (Out with us) boycott is now bleeding the State of Israel. The Nazi appeal *"Kauft nicht bei Juden"* (Don't buy from Jews) is back – and it is coming predominantly from Europe and Scandinavia. That it also comes from the Arab and Muslim worlds is a given.

Union boycotts of Israeli academia, boycotts of Israeli manufactured items, fruit, produce, and flowers have today become the norm in the United Kingdom. Pro-Palestinian activists have picketed large supermarket chains, accosting customers with requests that they not buy Israeli products. Anti-Israel fervor has reached boiling point and is spilling over into other countries .

In May 2012, a deepening crisis in Israel's relationship with South Africa saw the Foreign Ministry's spokesman in Jerusalem accuse Pretoria's trade minister of "unbelievable ignorance" in pushing to ban the use of "Made in Israel" labels on settlement goods, while a South African university cancelled a lecture by Israel's deputy ambassador because it could create "negative publicity" and damage the institution's reputation.

The deputy ambassador, Yaakov Finkelstein, was scheduled to speak at the University of KwaZulu-Natal (UKZN), but the university's deputy vice chancellor, Joseph Ayee, announced the preceding afternoon that the lecture was canceled. Ayee said, according to a press release issued by a South African group advocating a boycott of Israel:

> I have re-considered the sensitivities that the visit of the Israeli
> deputy ambassador have generated.

Ayee scrapped the event in light of the "negative publicity" and "likely reputational damage" it would bring the university.

The press release went on to cite politics professor Lubna Nadvi, who specializes in political Islam, who said the university's decision represents the general sentiment among students and staff. Nadvi was quoted as saying:

> Israel is fast becoming a pariah state, like Apartheid South
> Africa did, that no one really wants to be associated with —
> including academics and students..

A spokeswoman at the Israeli Embassy in Pretoria, Hila Stern, said the event – a regular lecture appearance – was canceled in coordination with the university. A pro-Palestinian campaign of "intimidation and threats" reached a level where "there was a genuine threat to the diplomat's well-being," she said. Stern added:

> Anti-Israeli elements have embarked on a campaign of
> intellectual terror which rejects everything that academia
> believes in, meaningful dialogue, discussions, research,
> understanding and freedom of speech. The use of bullying to
> silence freedom of expression in an academic setting is a very
> sad development.

Last year, the University of Johannesburg withdrew from a joint research project with Ben-Gurion University of the Negev, becoming the first academic institution to formally cut ties with an Israeli university.

At the bidding of a pro-Palestinian organization called Open Shuhada Street, South African Trade and Industry Minister Rob Davies said he intended to issue an official notice:

to require traders in South Africa not to incorrectly label products that originate from the Occupied Palestinian Territory (OPT) as products of Israel.

Davies said that Pretoria recognized the State of Israel "only within the borders demarcated by the United Nations in 1948."

As a matter of interest and a point of clarification: no "borders" were ever demarcated by the United Nations in 1948. As mentioned before, the so-called Green Line[3] is a ceasefire line – an armistice line, but not a border. When the Palestinians and the international community refer to Israel's "1967 borders," they are, by default, referring to the Green Line which was drawn in 1949, not 1948, and which is not a legal "border," only the line that was held by Israeli forces when hostilities ended when the Arab nations called for a truce.

There is concern among some in South Africa and many in Israel that, on the basis of representations made by one pro-Palestinian lobby group – a non-governmental organization – the South African minister had already pre-judged the issue and was in favor of adopting a labeling policy that specifically refers to "Occupied Palestinian Territories" and which would accordingly be extremely partisan.

The South African Zionist Federation, for its part, said it deeply regretted that Davies was singling out Israel for censure –

a country that has become a leading example in the fields of agricultural, water, technological and entrepreneurial innovation and a country that has remained committed to partnering and sharing with South Africa that expertise in which it excels.

The Federation charged that the minister had:

relied on the narrow views of lobby groups whose stated aims are to enforce a regime of boycotts and sanctions against Israel and had refused to meet and consult with interest groups opposed to his position.

If the proposal takes effect, South Africa would become the first country to legally prohibit businesses from labeling products from beyond the Green Line as made in Israel.

The Foreign Ministry in Jerusalem said Davies's plan unfairly singled out Israel and "smacked of racism." The ministry added that it would express its indignation to the South African ambassador, Ismail Coovadia.

According to Israeli law, the West Bank is not legally part of the State of Israel, as it was never officially annexed. However, in light of the aforementioned findings of the legal commission on settlements, annexation of the West Bank – biblical Judea and Samaria – might yet take place.

A Foreign Ministry spokesman, Paul Hirschson, noted that there are more than two hundred territorial conflicts in the world. He said the fact that South Africa has chosen to focus:

> on one side of one of these many conflicts raises very harsh questions about South Africa's policies. There are forty-seven territorial disputes in Africa alone.

Hirschson also told *The Times of Israel*:

> South Africa itself is in a territorial dispute with Swaziland, with that country claiming that Pretoria is occupying Swazi territory. We understand that there is a territorial dispute in the West Bank. But to pick one party in one dispute raises uncomfortable questions about your motivation.

Another Foreign Ministry spokesman, Yigal Palmor, told *The Times of Israel* that the very wording of Davies's notice displays "unbelievable ignorance" about Israel's history and has the potential to confuse South African customers to the extent that they will boycott all Israeli products. As the author pointed out earlier, Davies had mentioned Israel's borders as having been demarcated by the United Nations in 1948, but Palmor confirms what the author said earlier when he said the United Nations never demarcated any borders that year. Palmor said it appears that Davies was referring to the 1947 partition plan, which the Arabs rejected. "This ignorant statement adds insult to injury," Palmor said.

Relations between Jerusalem and Pretoria have been strained for the last few years, but the tone is becoming increasingly rough. Israel's foreign ministry chose harsh words to respond to the labeling issue because it is merely the latest in a long line of insults and undiplomatic behavior toward Israel.

On December 21, 2012, South Africa's ruling party, the African National Congress (ANC), voted to make boycotts, divestment, and sanctions of Israel part of its official government policy, handing a decisive victory to the anti-Israel BDS campaign.

Following hard on South Africa's decision to label Israeli products produced in Area C of the West Bank as coming from "Occupied Palestinian Territories" was Palestinian Authority Prime Minister Salam Fayyad's June 3 call for Palestinians to boycott West Bank products made by Israeli companies. Fayyad's call sealed the initiative by South African Trade and Industry Minister Rob Davies to label these products as such. Fayyad thanked the South African official for his support.

Iraqi-born Middle East columnist Linda Menuhin Abdul Aziz believes the boycott will fail as it did in 2010, because Palestinians will not buy into it. "Palestinians are caught in a vicious cycle," she said:

> On the one hand they cannot afford to lose their jobs and benefits, neither now nor in the future. On the other, they cannot stand up against the boycott lest they be labelled as traitors. The Arab world applies double standards and behaves in a two-faced manner. In public they say exactly the opposite of what they say in private.

In 2011, it was reported that seventy-six thousand seven hundred and twenty-three Palestinians work in Israel and the settlements. Compared to Israel's unemployment rate of just over five percent, unemployment in the West Bank in 2011 was twenty-two and a half percent. According to the CIA World Factbook this amount is out of a total labor force of seven hundred and forty-five thousand six hundred.

Unemployment in the Gaza Strip is estimated at forty-five percent. Israel has had no presence in Gaza since 2005, other than facilitating the freight forwarding of produce out of and into the enclave.

Back in Europe, Swissinfo reported that Switzerland's largest supermarket chain, Migros, has announced that it will label products originating in West Bank settlements and east

Jerusalem. Migros stated that it wanted to offer customers greater transparency, adding that the Swiss government and the United Nations consider Israel's settlements illegal. Company spokeswoman, Monika Weibel, stated on May 29, 2012 that Migros does not support boycotts, but rather wants to let customers make informed decisions.

In 2009, the British government issued an official, but non-binding recommendation, urging retailers to place labels on products produced in the West Bank telling whether they were made by Palestinians or in Israeli settlements.

On the weekend of April 28-29, 2012, Britain's fifth-largest retailer, the Co-operative Group, announced that it would stop doing business with four Israeli companies due to their ties to and operations in the West Bank. The Group's business with the four Israeli companies amounted to some three hundred and fifty thousand GB pounds (five hundred and fifty thousand dollars) annually. In its statement the Group said that it will "continue to actively work to increase trade links with Palestinian businesses."

Denmark appears to be following Britain's lead, with the Foreign Ministry spokesman telling the *Associated French Press* (AFP) that the government was:

> preparing a system of information based on retailers' voluntary participation, identifying food products coming from Israeli settlements.

Sweden is also considering following Britain's lead on labeling.

The Irish government has suggested that the European Union should consider an all-out ban on settlement goods while Trócaire, an Irish church-based non-governmental organization that received eighteen million euros just from the Irish government alone in 2012, has launched a campaign to lobby the European Union to end trade with Israeli settlements.

And on October 22, 2012, popular Irish broadcaster, Vincent Browne, said, during a broadcast: "Israel is the cancer in foreign affairs." No complaints were lodged against the broadcast and Browne said that he would not apologize. Israel's deputy ambassador to Ireland, Nurit Tinari-Modai, told the *Chronicle*:

I would have never believed that the day would come when a presenter on Irish TV would make racist, antisemitic remarks.

Ireland rode high financially while it regarded Israel as a friend, but since Ireland began to lash out at Israel its economy has tanked and the country is bankrupt at the time of writing.

In June 2012, Germany's Social Democratic, Left Party, and Christian Democratic politicians, rejected Jena Mayor Albrecht Schröter's campaign for a wide-ranging boycott of Israeli products. Critics accused Schröter, the Social Democratic mayor of Jena in Thuringia state, of fostering modern antisemitism with his support for a call by the German branch of Pax Christi, an international Catholic "peace movement," to not buy Israeli goods.

On June 6, according to the *Jerusalem Post*, the local branch of the neo-Nazi party NPD expressed solidarity for Schröter's and the non-governmental organization Pax Christi campaign calling for a boycott of Israeli products.

The neo-Nazis wrote that Schröter is "courageous" for his anti-Israel conduct and noted:

as nationalists who have to deal every day with these Jewish/ left-liberal defamation tactics, we think of Goethe's sorcerer's apprentice, who couldn't get rid of the spirits he called.

But is this not merely symptomatic of Germany almost as a whole? At the 1972 Munich Olympics eleven members of the Israeli Olympic team were murdered by the Black September faction of the Palestine Liberation Organization (PLO). On August 26, 2012, the German magazine *Der Spiegel* reported that following the massacre at the Olympic village German government officials had gotten in contact with the terror group and had remained in contact with it for years. *Der Spiegel* reported that the German government had cut a deal with the Palestine Liberation Organization in which it would be diplomatically upgraded on condition it did not carry out further terrorist attacks on German soil. Later, Paul Frank, the state secretary in the German Foreign Ministry, sent a message to the Palestine Liberation Organization informing that the "Munich chapter" is now "closed."

At the time, the author was a little astonished at the German government's refusal to act on irrefutable evidence presented to it showing Yasser Arafat's involvement in the Munich massacre. The German government dismissed the evidence by saying that taking action again Yasser Arafat "was not in Germany's best interest."

Rather than catch and punish the Palestinian murderers of the greater part of Israel's Olympic team at the world's premier sporting event, the German government forged a deal with the murderers and for all intents and purposes exonerated them. The author and the rest of the world can now understand the German government's actions in 1972.

According to German journalists and intelligence officers, and made public in the *Jerusalem Post* on August 26, 2012, Germany today maintains a *quid pro quo* policy toward the Lebanese terrorist group Hizb'allah that is similar to its posture toward Black September. The Federal Republic allows Hizb'allah's nine hundred and fifty active members to work legally in Germany in exchange for not engaging in terrorism on German soil. With friends like Germany, who needs enemies?

In light of governments, companies, supermarket chains and the like boycotting and promoting boycotts of Israel and Israeli goods, the author asks sympathetic readers to themselves boycott all countries boycotting and promoting boycotts of Israel and Israeli goods by denying those nations lucrative tourist dollars. Companies, supermarket chains and goods from countries enforcing boycotts against Israel should be boycotted in return. It would be a gift of kindness toward Israel if concerned readers were to stand alongside her as a friend.

With the influx of millions of Arabs and other Muslims into the Western world so the anti-Israel demonstrations and clamor increases in direct correlation to the influx. Governments, pro-Palestinian advocacy groups, and scores of non-governmental organizations have taken the Palestinian side and are beating on Israel. With rare exceptions, these governmental groups and non-government organizations are grossly ignorant of the true facts and show no interest in obtaining them. Apparently, their sole aim is to bring as much harm to Israel and the Israelis as possible

– to bring the Jewish nation to her knees. But they do not factor into the equation the God of Israel – Israel is, and will always be, *"the apple of His eye"* (Deuteronomy 32:10), and whoever touches Israel *"touches the apple of His eye"* (Zechariah 2:8).

Israel is as eternal as day and night; however, the nations are not. They are playing right into the hands of the most powerful and the most destructive force in the universe. The nations are heading for a confrontation with *the Holy One of Israel*, and He never loses in any confrontation.

---

[1] Much of the information on Non-Governmental Organizations (NGOs) in this and the following chapter was provided by NGO Monitor, a Jerusalem-based organization that acts as Israel's watchdog of human rights bodies. NGO Monitor's web address is: http://www.ngo-monitor.org.

[2] See Chapter eleven, page 147

[3] The Green Line refers to the demarcation lines set out in the 1949 Armistice Agreements between Israel and her neighbors. The name derives from the green ink used to draw the line on the map while the talks were in progress.

[4] See Chapter 19 of the author's book *When Day And Night Cease: A prophetic study of world events and how prophecy concerning Israel affects the nations, the Church and you* for documentation of armies, troop numbers, tanks, heavy guns, aircraft, *et cetera*, pitted against Israel.

— *thirteen* —

The Wilderness
(Lawfare)

It was stated in Chapter three that in the waning days of December 2008, following eight years of missiles and mortars raining down upon Israel's southern cities and towns, Israel launched the twenty-two-day Gaza War entitled Operation Cast Lead.

As part of the political war against Israel during the Israel Defense Force's operation in Gaza, some fifty non-governmental organizations issued more than five hundred statements accusing Israel of "wanton killing," "deliberately targeting civilians," and "war crimes."[1] Many of the statements called for boycotts and international sanctions against Israel and suspension of European Union-Israel upgrade talks. Another aspect included demands for international investigations and "lawfare." Despite the vast majority of previous lawfare cases having been dismissed, the damage – including the public perception of Israel, the interference with Israel's diplomatic relations, and the restrictions placed on the movement of Israelis singled out for this harassment – is considerable.

Before proceeding further, the author would like to repeat here what Robert L. Bernstein, the founder of Human Rights Watch, wrote in his *New York Times* opinion piece[2] concerning Colonel Richard Kemp, the former commander of British forces in Afghanistan and an expert on warfare. Bernstein quoted what Colonel Kemp said publicly on air with the *BBC* (British Broadcasting Corporation) that the Israel Defense Force in Gaza:

> did more to safeguard the rights of civilians in a combat zone than any other army in the history of warfare.

Non-governmental organization researchers are not trained professionals in evidence or forensic collection. Non-governmental organizations rarely name their researchers, specify the collection methodology, or identify witnesses. It is, therefore, simply mind-boggling that non-governmental organizations, which have no military experience and have had little or no access to the actual fighting between Palestinian terror organizations and the Israel Defense Force, claim to know better than real military experts. The only possible reason for this can be a smoldering hatred of Israel.

The author should explain at this point what "lawfare" is. Lawfare is the exploitation of courts in democratic countries in order to harass Israeli officials with civil lawsuits and criminal investigations using allegations of "war crimes," "crimes against humanity," and other alleged violations of international law. These cases claim to be about obtaining "justice" for Palestinian victims, but they are actually part of the larger political war.

The tactic of lawfare against Israel was adopted at the Non-Governmental Organization Forum of the 2001 Durban Conference[3] and is an integral part of the Durban Strategy that seeks to demonize and delegitimize Israel. Although Israel is not the only country that has been subject to lawfare (the United States and Britain have also been subject to suits arising out of the Iraq war), Israel is a primary target.

Non-governmental organizations exploit universal jurisdiction statutes in Europe and North America to bring these cases. These statutes allow courts to preside even though the parties and events at issue are entirely foreign. In some countries, such as Spain, a non-governmental organization can apply to a court directly for an arrest warrant or to launch a criminal investigation without the knowledge or approval of the government. Since the adoption of the lawfare strategy at least ten cases have been filed against Israelis in England, New Zealand, Spain, Belgium, Switzerland, and other countries.

Non-governmental organization superpowers such as Amnesty International and Human Rights Watch support lawfare against Israel by providing publicity, organizing demonstrations, and issuing reports crafted as legal briefs to coincide with court hearings.

Israel is not a party to the International Criminal Court or the International Court of Justice due to the overtly political nature of these bodies, mainly due to them being part of the United Nations network of anti-Israel organizations. Consequently, non-governmental organizations do not petition those courts. However, the United Nations Security Council can refer a case to the International Criminal Court and the United Nations General Assembly can refer cases for advisory opinions to the International Court of Justice.

In 2004, working on a Palestinian-initiated United Nations resolution, the General Assembly referred a case to the International Court of Justice for an advisory opinion regarding the "legality" of Israel's separation barrier. Apart from some pro-Palestinian Israelis, no one in Israel had any illusions how the biased United Nations agency would rule. The international Court of Justice's absurd consideration was that:

> Israel cannot rely on a right of self-defense or on a state of necessity in order to preclude the wrongfulness of the construction of the wall.

The Court asserted that "the construction of the wall, and its associated régime, are contrary to international law." However, Israel is not party to the International Court of Justice, and advisory opinions issued by the Court are not legally binding.

An Indian newspaper reported on January 25, 2009, that the Palestinian Center for Human Rights was preparing cases in six countries at that time, targeting eighty-seven Israelis for harassment. In the article, Palestinian Center for Human Rights's Director claimed that "dozens of arrest warrants have already been issued." Numerous other non-governmental organizations are calling for lawfare in the wake of Israeli responses to Palestinian rocket fire from the Gaza Strip.

One anonymous group has established a website, entitled "Wanted," with pictures of Israeli government and military officials. The website asks those with "information about the suspect[s] when [they] are outside of the Israeli borders" to contact the Prosecutor of the International Criminal Court.

Non-governmental organizations also distort international law by claiming Israel committed "war crimes" by attacking military targets located within civilian infrastructure such as homes, schools, mosques, hospitals, and United Nations facilities. Under the Geneva Conventions, the presence of civilians does not render military targets immune, and any civilian deaths resulting from terrorist groups' use of human shields in these areas are the responsibility of the terror organizations and not Israel.

It may surprise some to know that Israel has approximately twenty international lawyers, plus a number of reserve lawyers incorporated into the Israel Defense Force. These lawyers are held in high regard by the top brass of the Israel Defense Force and the lawyers' opinions are valued and taken into account before the execution of any Israel Defense Force operation.

Modern warfare has become a legal minefield. Israel Defense Force lawyers are employed specifically to keep the Israel Defense Force out of that minefield. It was very likely that in the eight-day Pillar of Defense war with Hamas in November 2012, the fifteen hundred targets struck by the Israel Defense Force would have been studied and approved by the international law department as valid targets prior to the operation.

In contrast to the many appeals for lawfare against Israel, very few, if any, of these non-governmental organizations call for the filing of cases against Hamas, Islamic Jihad, or Hizb'allah. Hamas's, Islamic Jihad's, and Hizb'allah's war crimes, such as deliberately attacking Israeli civilians with thousands of rockets and mortars; the widespread use of human shields within Gaza and Lebanon; and the killing and maiming of Gazan and Lebanese civilians from premature detonation of Hamas and Hizb'allah weaponry and "work accidents" are completely ignored.

Israel has been subject to a systematic assault on the very legitimacy of its existence. The continuing assaults on the state's legitimacy threaten to push Israel towards the status of a pariah state and therefore pose a real threat. These assaults are being promoted by a coalition of pro-Palestinian, anti-Zionist and antisemitic groups.

The issue of the Jewish State's political legitimacy was considered to be permanently off the table following the League of Nations General Assembly Resolution one-eight-one (The Partition Plan) in November 1947. However, Israel's legitimacy is under assault from every quarter.

Israel's defense establishment is concerned at the intensifying legal campaigns in foreign courts that aim to deter Israel from using force against Hamas and Hizb'allah. Still reeling from four damning reports in one week from human rights organizations about the Israel Defense Force's conduct in Operation Cast Lead in December 2008 to January 2009, the sense among Israel's senior defense officials is that the "legal front" against Israel is growing at an alarming rate.

There are hundreds of petitions, cases, legal opinions and actions cropping up across the world. The phenomenon is very wide and growing. A slew of lawsuits against Israeli officials in European courts and the singling out of Israel for condemnation in the United Nations are but two examples of the campaign to quietly destroy the Jewish State. The other side has a lot of money that comes from countries and people not friendly to Israel. This is another front in the war against Israel.

It was said in Chapter eleven that the Palestinian leadership only wants a state in order to gain access to the International Criminal Court and the International Court of Justice. With United Nations recognition the Palestinians will be able to file a plethora of faux-legal actions against Israel – for alleged war crimes, crimes against humanity, state terrorism, occupation of a neighboring state, *et cetera* – actions that will require an army of Israeli lawyers to defend against.

The Palestinians are not shy about what they intend to do following an upgrade of their status to Non-Member State at the United Nations. Nabil Sha'ath, a senior Palestinian official, said on November 3, 2012, in a *Times of Israel* interview, that the Palestinians have political goals behind the decision to lobby for being a non-member state at the United Nations. There are political advantages:

> including that we will become full members of international organizations, mainly the International Criminal Court.

Sha'ath said that upgraded status at the United Nations "would allow for suing Israel for 'its crimes.'" The interview with Sha'ath makes Palestinian intentions crystal clear.

With the United Nations already working towards recognizing

"Palestine" in its General Assembly – which will give Palestinians access to the World Courts that are affiliated with the United Nations – the war against Israel will quickly escalate.

The European Union's non-governmental organization alliance destabilizes not only Jerusalem, but the entire region. Jerusalem is the most complex and sensitive issue in the Arab-Israeli conflict. For over three thousand years *the city of God* (Psalms 46:4) has been the focus of intense religious and national importance..

Tragically, the diplomats and officials of the European Union, and some of its member states, appear to have failed to learn any of the true facts regarding Jerusalem. These officials, based primarily in Arab east Jerusalem and Ram'allah, have prepared two "policy documents" that present ill-considered analyses and dangerous recommendations for the division and future of the city.

The European Union's draft documents, written between 2009 and 2011, were never presented for public debate, thus failing to follow democratic procedures that Europe preaches to others. Instead, they were strategically leaked in *Ha'aretz*, the *Guardian*, and the *European Observer* newspapers.

Worse, the claims that served as the foundation for the European Union documents on Jerusalem were provided by a small number of political advocacy groups, or non-governmental organizations, which, despite their self-identification as "non-governmental," are funded by the governments of Europe. In the European Union, budgets for political non-governmental organizations, amounting to tens of millions of euros annually, are provided through entirely secretive processes, with no information on who makes these choices or the basis for their decisions.

The European Union copied much of the text and recommendations in its "policy documents" from European-funded anti-Israel groups. Repeating the ideological objectives of these fringe non-governmental organizations, the 2011 report presents a simplistic picture: Palestinians are victims and Israel is the aggressor.

The battle for Jerusalem is no longer being fought in the trenches, but in the European Union's capital of Brussels; in courtrooms, in places like the International Court of Justice in the Hague, and in the conference halls of the United Nations in New York and Geneva. Avigdor Lieberman, the then Israeli foreign minister, called it "diplomatic terrorism." The anti-Israel brigades call it "international lawfare" and, as in any war, the first casualty has been and will continue to be – truth.

If it were not bad enough that the European Union funds groups whose leaders promote "one-state" polices and use demonizing rhetoric that incites hatred, the fact that this becomes the basis for European policy is even worse yet. Anti-Israel sentiment serves as a thin guise for Jew-hatred.

Ten years ago, false allegations of a "massacre" and "war crimes" against Palestinian civilians in Jenin provided the first example of a new type of warfare that exploited the principles of human rights. This was the first application of the strategy developed earlier at the Non-Governmental Organization Forum of the 2001 United Nations World Conference Against Racism – the infamous Durban Conference.[3]

On April 3, 2002, following a spate of Palestinian suicide bombings, including an horrendous Palestinian attack in Netanya at a Passover seder, in which thirty civilians were killed and over one hundred and forty injured, the Israel Defense Force launched Operation Defensive Shield – the first major counter-terrorist operation. Palestinian officials immediately accused the Israel Defense Force of committing a "massacre" in the Jenin refugee camp – the epicenter of the terror operations. In parallel, a number of officials from "human rights" non-governmental organizations echoed the allegations, while being devoid of any credible independent investigation.

Amnesty International and Human Rights Watch, both deeply involved in the United Nations Durban fiasco, leapt in and immediately repeated the "war crimes" accusations and demanded the appointment of an "independent investigative committee."

On April 16, *Le Monde* cited Human Rights Watch, and on April 18, the *BBC* (British Broadcasting Corporation) quoted Amnesty International official Derrick Pounder, who repeated the "massacre" allegations. Although Amnesty had no information, it issued a statement that declared:

> The evidence compiled indicates that serious breaches of international human rights and humanitarian law were committed, including war crimes.

Like Human Rights Watch and Palestinian officials, Amnesty International also called for an "independent inquiry." Other influential non-governmental organizations published similar condemnations.

On May 3, one month after the operation began, Human Rights Watch launched a fifty-page "investigative report" – "Jenin: IDF Military Operations," based for the most part on unverifiable "eyewitness testimony" from Palestinians. No credible analysis could have been produced in such a short time, but the goal was purely political. Only one sentence mentioned the context of mass terror, while the rest consisted of overtly false allegations that "IDF military attacks were indiscriminate . . . failing to make a distinction between combatants and civilians . . . and vastly disproportionate . . . ." Human Rights Watch's acknowledgment that no massacre occurred was thereby nullified by the use of language that portrayed the Israel Defense Force as cruel and wicked. The fact that Palestinians had located this terror center in the middle of a densely populated neighborhood – a clear violation of moral and legal standards, was not mentioned.

Human Rights Watch and the other political non-governmental organizations totally ignored the Israel Defense Force decision to use ground forces in the operation, rather than air attacks, which they did in order to minimize civilian casualties among the Palestinians. As a result, twenty-three Israeli soldiers were killed in booby-trapped buildings. However, in accordance with their ideological agenda, Human Rights Watch's leaders such as Kenneth Roth repeated the spurious allegations that the Israel Defense Force had killed civilians indiscriminately. Wikipedia notes that:

> Jenin remained sealed throughout the invasion and claims of a "massacre" were circulated in the mass media by Palestinian officials. Stories of hundreds or thousands of civilians being killed in their homes as they were demolished spread throughout international media. Subsequent investigations

found no evidence to substantiate claims of a massacre, and
official totals from Palestinian and Israeli sources confirmed
between fifty-two and fifty-four Palestinians, mostly gunmen, as
having been killed in the fighting.

For the international media, as well as foreign diplomats,
political leaders, academics and others, the allegations and faux-
research reports of non-governmental organizations such as
Human Rights Watch and Amnesty International were repeated
without question. And each time the allegations were repeated,
as occurred in many of Human Rights Watch's fifteen press
releases and reports condemning Israel in 2002, this triggered
further rounds of anti-Israel headlines.

Human Rights Watch only undertook to publish a single report
– at the end of October 2002 – criticizing the Palestinian terror
campaign that took hundreds of Israeli lives. Even this report
ignored most of the evidence in order to absolve Yasser Arafat of
responsibility for his direct involvement in mass murder.

The non-governmental organizations' campaign accompanied
the Islamic bloc's initiative, which resulted in the appointment of
a distinctly biased United Nations "fact-finding team" to "investigate"
the allegations of Israeli war crimes. As a consequence, the
Israeli government refused to cooperate. The United Nations
report followed the lead of Human Rights Watch and other non-
governmental organizations and, as Israel had anticipated, the
report was equally as one-sided.

The "Jenin Massacre" report proved that the Durban Strategy
could be used successfully to wage political warfare. The Israeli
government and military were unprepared for this political
assault and could not defeat the attack. Eventually, the facts began
to replace the myths, but by then the demonization campaign
had already achieved its goals. On the foundation of the Jenin
fabrications, the first round of BDS (Boycotts, Divestment, and
Sanctions) efforts began.

The Jenin template was later repeated time and again, and
was perfected in the selection of Judge Richard Goldstone
– a confidant of Human Rights Watch's Kenneth Roth – to
head another pseudo-investigation based yet again on non-

governmental organizations' allegations and inventions. The Israeli government also refused to work with Judge Goldstone. The 2009 "Goldstone Report" on the twenty-two-day Gaza War was based on the strategy used in Jenin. Once again, the "Jenin Massacre" fabrication had proved that the Durban Strategy could be successfully used to wage political warfare against Israel.

The United Nations-sponsored Goldstone Report accused Israel of war crimes during operation Cast Lead in the Gaza Strip. However, the report's main author, Judge Richard Goldstone, belatedly retracted the accusations of "war crimes" against Israel and shifted the blame to Hamas, the terror organism that controls Gaza, as being the responsible party for transgressions of human rights and international law.

In May 2011, NGO Monitor released a report detailing the activities of several non-governmental organizations such as Al Haq, Palestinian Center for Human Rights, FIDH (France), Badil, and Defense for Children International-Palestine Section. All of these non-governmental organizations receive funding from European governments and are actively involved in pursuing a strategy of targeting the Israeli Supreme Court by "flooding the Court with petitions in the hope of obstructing its functioning and resources." In their efforts to overwhelm the Court with faux-legal actions against Israelis they hope to discredit the Israeli judicial system and further isolate Israel internationally.

The report says these anti-Israel organizations have also been pursuing a strategy at the United Nations and the International Criminal Court in hopes of charging Israeli officials of war crimes.

On September 15, 2005, Doron Almog, an Israel Defense Force general with an illustrious military career, landed in London on an El Al flight. He was traveling to London to fundraise for a charity that provides residential facilities for disabled children. General Almog did not expect to have any difficulties passing through airport control in London. But in fact the British police were waiting for him with an arrest warrant. A lawyer in London had asked a local court to issue an arrest warrant for General Almog and the police were waiting at passport control to take him into custody.

General Almog had a narrow escape. He was warned before the plane landed that the police were waiting for him and he stayed on the plane. El Al did not permit the British policemen to board the plane, and General Almog flew back to Israel without stepping on British soil.

Under international law, some crimes are considered so serious that a person who has committed them may be arrested and tried in any country, not just the place where the crime was committed or where the person lives, which is normally the rule. Such crimes include piracy, torture, and war crimes. The legal principle is called "universal jurisdiction" because a court in any country will consider itself to have jurisdiction over the whole world when it comes to these crimes.

In conformity to that universal jurisdiction, General Augusto Pinochet, the eighty-two-year-old former president of Chile, was accused of torturing people in a seventeen-year reign of terror in his own country and was arrested in London in October 1998 on a warrant issued by a Spanish judge.

Until 2011, England and Wales had permissive rules about who could ask the courts for an arrest warrant in relation to a crime subject to universal jurisdiction. Any person could put information before a magistrate that a crime had been committed, even one committed outside the court's jurisdiction, and the magistrate could issue an arrest warrant. In the case of Israel's General Almog a pro-Palestinian group was responsible for obtaining the warrant.

There were exceptions for foreign politicians in the country on a "special mission," but not for ordinary soldiers. This situation resulted in Israeli politicians, including Foreign Minister Tzipi Livni, canceling planned trips to the United Kingdom for fear of being arrested.

In September 2011, following pressure by the Israeli government and pro-Israel groups in the United Kingdom, the law was amended so that "the consent of the Director of Public Prosecutions will be required before an arrest warrant can be issued." The Israeli government was demanding the change, but Amnesty International opposed the amendment tooth and nail, stressing before and after that such a change would:

hamper victims' attempts to bring private prosecutions through the British courts against perpetrators of torture and war crimes.

In September 2011, the British Parliament finally passed the "Police Reform and Social Responsibility Act" to deal with the problem of universal jurisdiction. According to an *Ha'aretz* June 1, 2012, article and reprinted in Britain's *Independent*, a "senior Israeli official" speaking to the paper anonymously, claimed that the British government promised the law would be changed so that only the Attorney General, who is a trusted political figure, would authorize universal jurisdiction arrests. However, the government assigned this responsibility to the Director of Public Prosecutions (DPP).

Under the new law the prior permission of the Director of Public Prosecutions is required before a warrant can be issued against foreigners suspected of war crimes committed outside of the United Kingdom. The Director of Public Prosecutions is a lawyer employed by the government to decide, according to strict criteria, which suspected criminals should be prosecuted. In particular, only cases which have a realistic prospect of conviction and where prosecution is in the public interest should be pursued.

In October 2011, Tzipi Livni, by now the former foreign minister, visited the United Kingdom at the invitation of the United Kingdom's Foreign Secretary, William Hague. An arrest warrant was applied for under the new law, and the Director of Public Prosecutions stated that "it had not concluded whether to prosecute her or not," because she was in England on a "special mission" with diplomatic immunity from prosecution.

Apparently, Livni only avoided an arrest warrant due to a legal assessment by the Foreign and Commonwealth Office (FCO) that she was on a "Special Mission." In other words, the new law had not actually been tested and Livni's visit was defined "as official, in order to guarantee her protection under diplomatic immunity." *Ha'aretz* reported that in an interview in London, Livni worried that the changes to the law could not entirely protect an individual with a case to answer. Apparently, that is the case, and

General Almog and other top-tiered Israelis are being wise in not throwing caution to the winds and visiting the United Kingdom anytime soon.

With this new law in operation, General Almog cancelled a planned trip to England in June 2012 because he was advised by Israeli government lawyers that the British Director of Public Prosecutions might decide that the he should be arrested. Obviously, for General Almog and others, the new law offers little assurance that British policemen will not be waiting at passport control.

In January 2011, before the universal jurisdiction law was amended in the United Kingdom, Tzipi Livni, in her capacity as Israel's leader of the government opposition and head of Israel's largest political party – Kadima, cancelled a scheduled visit to South Africa. The official reason for the cancellation was given as being due to a strike by workers at the foreign ministry; however, the unofficial reason was said to be Livni's fear of arrest in Johannesburg under South Africa's version of universal jurisdiction law.

Some credence must be given to the unofficial version. The Palestine Solidarity Alliance welcomed the news of the cancellation and thanked all those who provided the "groundswell" of support against the visit, specifically expressing gratitude to Amnesty International, Congress of South African Trade Unions, the Muslim Judicial Council, and Coalition for a Free Palestine.

An August 10, 2012 article in *The Times of Israel* reported that a pro-Palestinian California-based organization, describing itself as a non-government organization "accredited" to the United Nations, published a list of about one hundred Israel Air Force pilots, their names, birth dates, ranks, and Identification Numbers. The website says:

> it may be possible to use the data to bring the pilots to justice for alleged war crimes.

The site recommended that its readers use the data to:

> gather more information, possibly including questioning and potential prosecution of the named individuals when they travel abroad.

The Israel Defense Force did not comment as to whether it intended to take legal or any other kind of action against the site.

---

[1] Much of the information on Non Governmental Organizations (NGOs) in this and the previous chapter was provided by NGO Monitor, a Jerusalem-based organization that acts as Israel's watchdog of human rights bodies. NGO Monitor's web address is: http://www.ngo-monitor.org.

[2] See Chapter twelve, pages 189-191 for Bernstein's complete *New York Times* Opinion Piece.

[3] See Chapter eleven, pages 131-134 for details concerning the United Nations' Durban I, II, and III Conferences.

— *fourteen* —

The Wilderness
(Warfare)

It is not a comforting thought, but the worst wars prophesied and depicted in the Bible are yet to come. We only get a glimpse of the catastrophic nature of these horrific wars, but apparently weapons of mass destruction (WMD) are used in at least two of them. And, of course, these wars all involve and revolve around Israel. Only the atomic bombs dropped on Nagasaki and Hiroshima in 1945 come anywhere close to the description of the human devastation that will take place:

> *And this shall be the plague with which the LORD will strike all the people who fought against Jerusalem: their flesh shall dissolve while they stand on their feet, their eyes shall dissolve in their sockets, and their tongues shall dissolve in their mouths*
>
> (Zechariah 14:12).

> *It will come to pass in that day that I will give Gog a burial place there in Israel, the valley of those who pass by east of the sea; and it will obstruct travelers, because there they will bury Gog and all his multitude. Therefore they will call it the Valley of Hamon Gog.* **For seven months the house of Israel will be burying them,** *in order to cleanse the land. Indeed* **all the people of the land will be burying,** *and they will gain renown for it on the day that I am glorified, says the Lord GOD.*
>
> *They will set apart men regularly employed, with the help of a search party, to pass through the land and bury those bodies remaining on the ground, in order to cleanse it. At the end of seven months they will make a search. The search party will pass*

> *through the land; and when anyone sees a man's bone, he* **shall set up a marker by it, till the buriers have buried it** *in the Valley of Hamon Gog*
>
> (Ezekiel 39:11-15).

The Bible does not indicate to us how many of the people of Israel are killed in these future wars, but it is obvious that Israel, with the help of her *"Maker,"* prevails throughout. The Bible tells us that the LORD will bring all nations against Jerusalem, to *"the Valley of Jehoshaphat,"* which begins on the outskirts of the city and runs all the way to the Dead Sea, and that He will judge them there:

> *I will gather all nations, and bring them down to the Valley of Jehoshaphat; and I will enter into judgment with them there on account of My people, My heritage Israel* (Joel 3:2).

At the close of Chapter twelve it was said that the nations are heading for a confrontation with *"the Holy One of Israel,"* and that He never loses in any confrontation. Apparently, the nations' impression of Israel's God seems to be that He either does not exist or is some sort of a wimp with no more power than a morning mist. However, Israel's God is *"clothed with power"* (Psalm 65:6; *"He rules by His power"* (Psalm 66:7); true *"power belongs to God"* (Psalm 62:11) and, more definitively, He is *"the Power"* (Matthew 26:64; Mark 14:62), which means to say that He is the power that created the universe and the power that holds it together. If the nations underestimate the power of the One who introduced Himself as *"God Almighty"* (Genesis 35:11), they do so at their own peril.

The preceding five chapters of this book have shown that Israel has many enemies – in the Middle East, North Africa, Europe, and even within states that are outwardly friendly toward the Jewish state. At some point in time – squarely in the domain of *"God Almighty,"* Israel's *"Maker"* – Israel must face-off against many of these enemies. Israel can only do what is humanly possible; her *"King"* will do the impossible. Israel is a small country, but is militarily powerful. She will not be alone on any battlefield, her *"Creator"* long ago decreed that Israel will be inordinately strong militarily:

Arise and thresh, O daughter of Zion; for I will make
your horns iron, and I will make your hooves bronze;
you shall beat in pieces many peoples (Micah 4:13).

The Israeli government, strategists, and the Israel Defense Force plan and prepare for war – they have no option. Israel exists in vast sea of hostility – many Arab nations remain in a state of war with her, and others declare their cherished goal and reason for existing to be that of "wiping Israel from the map."

Following Israel's conquest of the Promised Land under Joshua we find that sizable numbers of fighting men from eight nations still remained in the land:

Now these are the nations which the LORD left, that
He might test Israel by them, that is, all who had not
*known any of the wars in Canaan (**this was only so***
that the generations of the children of Israel might
***be taught to know war,** at least those who had not*
formerly known it) (Judges 3:1-2).

The LORD's strategy at that time was to leave some of the nations of Canaan in the land so that there would be continual wars between them and Israel in order for subsequent generations of Israelis to learn the art of waging war. Little has changed since the days of yore.

Israel's *"Maker"* could just as easily given all of the Promised Land to the Jews in 1947, but He chose to give them half of what Britain, and its ally France had left to be divided by the League of Nations. Of the total area of Palestine, Britain gave over seventy-seven percent to the Hashemites who established the Kingdom of Trans-Jordan (now called Jordan) and the French took all of the Golan (biblical *Bashan*) and gave it to Syria, leaving only a small part of Palestine to be divided into two states – one Jewish, one Arab. The Partition Plan resolution was passed in the General Assembly of the League of Nations by a majority of thirty-three to twelve on November 29, 1947.

The Jews accepted the Partition Plan, even though it meant they would only receive eleven percent of the Promised Land. The Jews felt that a small piece was better than no piece, but the Arabs refused to accept it.

The Jews declared statehood on May 14, 1948, and seven armies invaded the embryonic State of Israel the following day. Thus Israelis began to learn the art of war.

Having been forced to wage six defensive wars, four against overwhelming odds, the Israel Defense Force is today recognized as one of the most powerful militaries in the world.

Jane's Defense Weekly, arguably the world's most highly respected military journal, ranked Israel as the world's third most powerful military force. And later, in 2010, Jane's ranked Israel as the world's sixth nuclear power, alongside Britain, with up to three hundred nuclear warheads.

Israel has not signed onto the Nuclear Non-Proliferation Treaty (NPT), and the holds to a deliberate policy of nuclear ambiguity insofar as her nuclear capabilities are concerned. Israel also has five Dolphin class submarines fitted with missiles capable of carrying nuclear warheads. In April 2012, Israel's defense minister signed an agreement to procure a sixth submarine.

And as far back as 1987, according to Leonard Spector, then of the Carnegie Endowment, Israel had sufficient nuclear weaponry to destroy every urban center in the Middle East with a population of one hundred thousand. Spector also said that Israel had a large chemical weapons stockpile and an efficient means of delivery. That was in 1987. A further twenty-five years of progress with her weapons proficiency must be left to the imagination.

Very few Israelis have any illusions about what lies ahead for their country. Many believe there is an almost certain probability of abnormally large numbers of dead among families and friends and widespread destruction throughout the land. It is a cost Israel is prepared to pay for survival. Israel can read the writing on the wall yet fails to understand it was her *"Maker"* that wrote it.

We have seen in past chapters that Israel appears to be bewildered by the many assaults against her. Israel has no answer for what is happening against her. For Israel, it is like being in a box whose walls and ceiling are slowly moving inwards, ever trying to crush the life out of her. But it is God's hand that is working the mechanism of the box. In Hosea 2:14, the Lord said He would bring Israel into the wilderness because she had forgotten Him. After all her *"Creator"* has done for her, Israel has turned her back on Him, again. But *"God requires an account of what is past"* (Ecclesiastes 3:15).

In contravention of the word of the LORD, Israel has ceded huge areas of her divine inheritance to those who hate her and work toward her extinction. The LORD specifically commanded Israel:

> *The land shall not be sold* **permanently,** *for* **the land is Mine;** *for you are strangers and sojourners with Me* (Leviticus 25:23).

But in order to cut a peace agreement with her enemies, Israel's leaders collaborated to give away the LORD's land, to those with whom it was forbidden to make treaties with:

> *And you shall make no covenant with the inhabitants of this land; you shall tear down their altars*
> (Judges 2:2).

Israel has made covenants (treaties) with the inhabitants of the land in violation of what God commanded, neither did Israel tear down the altars. However, the Arabs have torn down scores of Israeli synagogues and used ancient Jewish gravestones for building military latrines.

As it was in Bible times, so today has the LORD cut off parts of Israel and given it into the hands of her enemies – because Israel has forgotten her *"Maker."*

In Joshua's day the 'leaders' – ten of the twelve spies – brought back a faithless report and were the cause of Israel's forty years of wandering in the wildernesses of Sin and Sinai, and the death of an entire generation in the desert. Modern Israeli leaders, in their misguided pursuit of peace with Israel's warring neighbors, and the overt willingness to cede the LORD's land to the enemies of Israel, have played a large part in causing Israel to wander in an ultimate wilderness where more than one generation may perish. Because *"God requires an account of what is past"* (Ecclesiastes 3:15).

Israel desires peace, but her many adversaries compel her to plan and prepare for war, which she does continuously. In an address at the Institute for Contemporary Affairs of the Jerusalem Center for Public Affairs[1] in January 2012, Major-General Amir Eshel, Commander of the Israel Air Force and former Head of the Israel Defense Force Planning Directorate said:

> From an Israel Defense Force planner's perspective, it is a nightmare to prepare for the unknown. The Planning Directorate of the Israel Defense Force has three major tasks: the first is strategic planning. We have a lot of interaction with the government related to national security, policy, and strategy. The second task is to provide yearly and multi-year plans for the force structure of the Israel Defense Force in terms of procurement, organization, and resource allocation. There is a clear relationship between strategy and force structure. The strategy should direct the force structure, but the force structure has an influence on strategy as well because not everything can be implemented, so they go together.
>
> The Middle East is going through a time of dramatic change, a process that has not been experienced in centuries. Looking through the lens of national security, this creates many new challenges and unknowns that we have to take into consideration. We have two options: one is to sit on the fence and see what will happen and try to prepare ourselves in order to address these new challenges. On the other hand, we would like to be proactive in order to have some kind of influence, even though Israel's ability to address these changes in the Middle East is limited. Even superpowers have only limited ability to influence this arena. The toolbox is not empty, but the tools needed to address the emerging currents are limited.

From Israel's perspective, the Arab Spring has turned into an Islamic winter. In June 2011, Israel's assessment of the regional turmoil was that the revolutions in the Arab states would be hijacked by others. This has proven correct and for the most part radical Islamists are now in control of most Arab states involved in the Spring, the revolutions were hijacked by well-organized Islamic groups with a solid agenda and an anti-Israel ideology.

On the military level, every component of Israel's national security strategy faces challenges. There is the need for deterrence

– a number of countries in the Middle East are working to acquire weapons of mass destruction.

Syria is known to have chemical and biological weapons and its pursuit of nuclear weapons is ongoing; however, Israel set back Syria's nuclear program when the Israel Defense Force destroyed a secretly constructed complex containing a joint Syrian-North Korean nuclear reactor near al-Kibar. Israeli commandos first gathered evidence of nuclear activity from the site and then seven Israeli air force fighter-jets carried out a bombing raid on September 6, 2007.

A lesson some mid-eastern leaders learned from the Arab Spring was to get nuclear capability. This they believe will make them practically immune to outside pressure. They consider Libya's Colonel Mu'ammar al-Qaddafi to have made a very big mistake when he gave up his nuclear program. They believe no one would have dared to use force in dealing with him if he had nuclear capability. Similarly, they believe no one would have dared to use force against Saddam Hussein in 1991 or 2003 if he would have had a nuclear capability.

The growing numbers of surface-to-surface missiles and rockets are another major challenge to Israel's deterrence. In the past, Israel's early-warning capability was for large-scale wars. Today, Israel needs a warning for a single terrorist and, because of this, Israel built the separation barrier between Israel and the Palestinians with watch-towers each two hundred meters (yards) on the concrete sections.

With the rise in attacks against Israelis from the Sinai Peninsular across Israel's border with Egypt, Israel is building a two hundred and sixty-six kilometer (one hundred and sixty-five miles)-long fence along the border. Originally built to stop illegal African economic migrants entering from Egypt, the fence was later adapted to halt both terrorist and economic infiltrators. The fence is three-meters (yards)-high, built of concrete and wire mesh, bolstered from top to bottom on the Egyptian side with razor wire. The fence stands several meters (yards) into Israeli territory and includes the installation of advanced surveillance and motion-detector equipment.

Delegations of security officials from a number of countries, including India, which wishes to seal its border with Pakistan, and the United States, which wants to seal its border with Mexico, have come to Israel to closely study the fence in order to adapt Israeli technology for their own border fences.

Israel is a small country and the national security strategy of David Ben-Gurion, Israel's first prime minister, was to strive to achieve a decisive outcome in a very short time and to take the war to the other side of the border. However, Israel has seen enormous efforts by her enemies to arm themselves with surface-to-surface missiles and rockets. Therefore today, Israel faces more than one hundred thousand missiles and rockets, which of late have longer-ranges, are more lethal and more accurate. The second Lebanon War, Israel's longest war, began in July 2006 and ran for thirty-four days. During that time Hizb'allah showered Israeli cities and towns with almost five thousand rockets and, despite the damage the Israel Air Force inflicted upon Hizb'allah's infrastructure from the air, it could not prevent it from launching rockets at Israel's civilian centers.

There was no decisive outcome to that conflict and it showed that future wars will be waged against Israeli civilians and the enemy could well be the one to fire the last shot. This scenario also played out in November 2012 against Hamas and Islamic Jihad in the Gaza Strip. In response to almost two hundred rockets fired into Israel within less than a week, the Israel Defense Force pummeled the missile arsenals and underground launchers in Gaza for eight days, but was unable to prevent missiles being fired from Gaza into Israel, and in this skirmish missiles reached the outskirts of both Tel Aviv and Jerusalem. A ceasefire was negotiated by Egypt, but Hamas was a clear winner in the negotiations, having most of its demands met. Two rockets were fired into Israel hours after the ceasefire went into effect and this showed Hamas was not in the least cowed by Israel's destructive onslaught.

It is for situations like the two instances immediately above that the Israel Defense Force hierarchy have said the destruction wrought in Gaza during Operation Cast Lead would pale in comparison to the destruction that will overtake Lebanon if

Hizb'allah starts another war. There will be a decisive outcome and it will take Lebanon a decade to recover – if it does. A senior Israel Defense Force officer says destruction in Lebanon will be extensive due to Hizb'allah establishing command posts and bases within civilian villages.

On August 14, 2012, it was announced that Avi Dichter had been appointed to the post of Home Defense Minister, a position in which he is eminently qualified to serve. Dichter, a former Director of Israel's General Security Service (Shin Bet) also served in the Israel Defense Force élite *Sayeret Matkal* unit along with Prime Minister Binyamin Netanyahu. With Israel's home front being the expected target in future wars the government has sought to place the best of the best at the head of its defense arena.

We have seen in previous chapters that there are many fronts in the war against Israel. It is not just a military war, but also a political, legal, and economic war incorporating diplomatic isolation, BDS, and Lawfare.

Israel is preparing for the unknown. And in order to prepare for the unknown Israel must enhance her core robust, versatile, and flexible capabilities in order to address challenges that she does not even know about today. Further, it is crucial for Israel to have people who can adjust themselves to new situations. Israel needs to be flexible in order to change things as she sees them emerging.

Wide media coverage was given to the Stuxnet virus, a computer malware program created in tandem by the United States and Israel and which became the bane of the Iranian nuclear program. Undetected until June 2010, it sabotaged over a thousand Iranian uranium-enrichment centrifuges and beamed back to its operators Iranian nuclear scientists' conversations, photographs, and data on Iran's nuclear program. Some one hundred and thirty computers were infected, almost all of them were part of Iran's nuclear program.

Some weeks after its detection Stuxnet was found to have an encoded, predetermined shutdown date and it duly shut itself down at one second past midnight on June 25, 2012. The age of powerful, sophisticated computer superbugs has arrived.

In May 2012, another cyber superbug was found in Iranian computers. This malware virus, called Flame, was twenty times more powerful than Stuxnet and had been running undetected for several years before Stuxnet was born and is the most sophisticated cyber-spying program ever discovered. Some small sections of Flame's code is identical to that of Stuxnet, giving rise to speculations that the two superbugs may be related.

The Obama administration gave Israel a drubbing for "unilaterally" launching Flame against Iran's oil industry, which clearly suggests Israel used Flame against Iran's oil industry without consultation with the United States.

Flame wiped numbers of Iranian computers clean and shutdown much of Iran's oil industry by erasing its computer software. Iran lodged a complaint with the United Nations due to the very malicious nature of the cyberweapon. The Moscow-based Kaspersky Lab uncovered Flame after the security firm was asked by a United Nations agency to look for a virus that Iran said had sabotaged its computers, deleting valuable data. Apparently, it was the damage done to Iran's oil industry that ultimately uncovered Flame and brought the slap upon Israel's wrist by the United States.

The Flame virus was designed to do all its malice while masquerading as a routine Microsoft software update. It evaded detection for years by using a sophisticated program to crack an encryption algorithm. Flame not only conducted espionage, but also completely sabotaged computer systems. It has the ability to turn computer microphones and cameras on and off, record key strokes, and take screen shots.

While the huge majority of Flame's infections happened in Iran, infections also happened throughout the Middle East, North Africa, and parts of Europe. Flame supports a 'kill' command that wipes all traces of the malware from the computer. The initial infections of Flame stopped operating after its public exposure, and the 'kill' command was sent, effectually bringing the virus 'home.' No one knows, apart from the controllers, whether other computers in other countries remain infected.

In some recent email exchanges published by Wikileaks were claims that Israeli commandos had sabotaged and significantly damaged Iranian nuclear facilities. Also, in a recently published book, *Spies Against Armageddon: Inside Israel's Secret Wars*, co-authors Dan Raviv and Yossi Melman tell how Israeli commandos from the "super-secret" élite unit *Kidon* (Spear) clandestinely entered Iran and were responsible for the assassination of at least four of Iran's nuclear scientists.

Obviously, both the Stuxnet and Flame viruses were aimed at delaying Iran's ability to develop a nuclear weapon and were part of a covert war against Iran's nuclear program. Intelligence estimates assessed Iran as being able to produce a nuclear bomb by 2011; however, these assessments have been extended to 2013-2014, which means the cyberweapons, assassinations of nuclear scientists, and sabotaging of facilities effectively slowed Iran's pace by up to three years.

Without question the creators of Stuxnet and Flame are already working on creating other malware. Only agencies like America's National Security Agency (NSA) and Israel's Mossad would have the capabilities to produce such sophisticated viruses. New malware is likely to be even more destructive than anything known thus far and could cause malfunctions in military operations, air-traffic control, cellular phone grids, electricity grids, waterworks and dams, sewerage pumping stations, chemical plants, *et cetera*. Warfare has now entered the world of science fiction.

State of the art weapons continue to flow unabated to Hizb'allah in Lebanon and to Hamas and Islamic Jihad in Gaza. Israel has learned lessons from past wars and skirmishes with these terror organizations and is responding accordingly.

Following the 2006 Second Lebanon War, in which Israeli tanks came under heavy advanced anti-tank missile fire from Hizb'allah, the Israel Defense Force sped up development of the Trophy anti-missile defense system designed for battle tanks. The Trophy, developed by Rafael Advanced Defense Systems, is an active protection system that creates an hemispheric protected zone around armored vehicles such as Israel's Merkava tanks. The system employs sensors and radar to identify and track incoming missiles and dispatches interceptor missiles that neutralize the hostile weapons before they can hit the tank.

The Israel Defense Force has completed the installation of the Trophy system on the 401st Brigade whose Merkava MK 4 main battle tanks served prominently in Gaza during Operation Cast Lead and in Lebanon during the Second Lebanon War. The Trophy's first actual battlefield test came in February 2011, when Hamas targeted a Merkava MK 4 tank with a wire-guided anti-tank missile along the Israeli-Gaza border – the activated system successfully intercepted and destroyed the missile. A second battlefield success was notched up in August 2012 when an activated Trophy system intercepted and destroyed an advanced Russian-made anti-tank missile fired from Gaza, near the Israel-Egyptian border.

In 2010 the Defense Ministry decided to combine the Trophy system with a similar system called the Iron Fist, developed by Israel Military Industries. The Iron Fist launches a projectile that is effective in intercepting tank shells, thus the combined systems affords a tank protection against both tank shells and anti-tank missiles.

It was stated above that Israel faces some one hundred thousand missiles and rockets. The majority of these missiles will emanate from Gaza and Lebanon, but Israel's archenemy, Syria, is known to have medium range ballistic missiles capable of carrying chemical and biological warheads that can hit every part of Israel. Iran also has a vast array of ballistic missiles that can strike anywhere in Israel. Iran is also working to develop intercontinental ballistic missiles that can carry nuclear, chemical, or biological warheads and has stated that Israel "must be wiped off the page of time" – a Persian phrase often translated as "wiped off the map."

Facing such an array of missiles in the hands of hostile nations and entities, Israel has spent a great deal of money and time in developing anti-missile systems. At the time of writing Israel has three levels of missile defense: the Iron Dome, David's Sling, and the Arrow. These systems form part of the multilayered missile defense system Israel is putting in place to meet the growing threat of a sustained bombardment, possibly lasting several weeks, by missiles and rockets of all calibers and ranges.

Iron Dome: five batteries are in operation at the time of writing. The Iron Dome constitutes the bottom tier of the multilayered missile defense system. Designed to intercept short-range missiles, rockets, mortar shells, and one hundred and fifty-five millimeter (six inch) shells fired by the Iranian-armed Hizb'allah into northern Israel and by the Palestinians into the south.

The Iron Dome was developed by Rafael Advanced Defense Systems and uses two radar units to calculate the trajectories of incoming missiles within moments of launch. The system's computer decides whether the incoming missiles will hit an inhabited area or not. If they do not, the system ignores them and pursues missiles that could cause casualties. Each Iron Dome battery has 20 Tamir interceptors and can cover an area of up to one hundred and fifty-five square kilometers (sixty square miles). Israel's military acknowledges that it could take fifteen to twenty Iron Dome batteries to effectively cover the northern and southern border areas.

The Israel Air Force will take delivery of two Iron Dome batteries with extended ranges by the beginning of 2013. The Israel Air Force would not reveal the new range of the upgraded system, but officers said that it would lead to a reduction in the number of batteries Israel will ultimately require to protect against short-range rockets fired from Lebanon and the Gaza Strip. The Iron Dome was originally designed to defend against rockets at ranges from four to seventy kilometers (two and a half to forty-four miles).

The new batteries will come equipped with new software and a new radar system that will enable each battery to protect a larger area. In addition, the Israel Air Force plans to soon take delivery of an upgraded and improved interceptor that will also contribute to the extension of the Iron Dome's range.

Iron Dome scored its first kills in April 2011, when it made its combat debut in southern Israel. The mobile system downed at least nine one hundred and twenty-two millimeter (four point eight inches) Grad rockets aimed at the Negev Desert city of Beersheba and the port of Ashkelon, the first ever destroyed in mid-flight by counter-missile fire anywhere in the world.

In November 2012, during the eight-day Pillar of Defense operation against missiles being fired from Gaza by Hamas and Islamic Jihad, Israel's Iron Dome was a game changer and awed many in the Western world. Iron Dome proved to be as good as its name by destroying four hundred and twenty-one rockets in mid-air – an eighty four percent success rate. According to the Israel Defence Force information, eight hundred and seventy-five rockets from Gaza landed in open areas – only fifty-eight landed in Israel's urban areas, killing five Israelis and injuring two hundred and forty.

Patriot missiles built by Raytheon Corporation attempted to shoot down Scud-type ballistic missiles during the 1990-91 Gulf war, but had no success at all. Until Iron Dome came along there was no way of intercepting short-range missiles like the Qassam and Grad rockets and the mortar shells that Hamas and Islamic Jihad use.

David's Sling, sometimes referred to as the Magic Wand, the middle tier of Israel's missile defense system will be based in central Israel sometime in 2013. David's Sling is designed to intercept medium-range missiles with ranges of forty to three hundred kilometers (twenty-five to one hundred and eighty-five miles). David's Sling has been jointly developed by Rafael Advanced Defense Systems and United States defense contractor Raytheon. The interceptor, known as Stunner, is a two-stage missile that can change course in mid-flight and can operate in all weather conditions.

According to Israeli media reports, David's Sling would also be capable of intercepting long-range missiles like the Shahab at lower altitudes if they evaded the Arrow batteries.

Hizb'allah and the Palestinians in Gaza are acquiring longer range weapons that can reach Israel's narrow central region. This makes Tel Aviv, Israel's main urban conurbation containing two-thirds of Israel's population, its industrial heartland and many strategic installations, increasingly vulnerable.

Thus, David's Sling is needed to provide some defense in that region, but when the shooting starts multiple batteries could be needed.

The Arrow system, developed by state owned Israel Aerospace Industries, forms the top layer of the defense shield. The Arrow system consists of the joint production hypersonic Arrow anti-missile interceptor, an early-warning Active Electronically Scanned Array (AESA) radar and the Israel Aerospace launch control center. The system is transportable and can be moved to other prepared sites.

The Arrow is considered one of the most advanced missile defense programs currently in existence. It is the first operational missile defense system specifically designed and built to intercept and destroy ballistic missiles. The first Arrow battery was declared fully operational in October 2000. Arrow-2, the variant currently deployed, is primarily designed to knock out Shahab-3b ballistic missiles currently deployed by Iran, and the more advanced solid-fuel Sejjil-2 that Tehran is now developing.

On August 5, 2012, the *Jerusalem Post* reported that the Israel Air Force will take delivery in the coming weeks of a new and improved Arrow-2 interceptor. The report said the upgraded missile contains new software aimed at improving the systems ability to defend against long-range missiles such as Iran's Shahab and Sejjil and Syria's Scud-D missiles.

Arrow-3, which would be able to intercept ballistic missiles in space earlier in their trajectory, is currently under development and is expected to be operational in 2014.

Israel's Space Agency keeps track of the movements of the nation's enemies via its many eyes in the sky. The Israel Space Agency is a governmental body that coordinates all Israeli space research programs with scientific, military, and commercial goals. Outside of Israel little attention is given either to Israel's active space program or its prolific satellite production and launch capabilities. Israel is the smallest country in the world with indigenous launch capabilities for satellites, and only the eighth nation to gain an indigenous launch capability.

The Israel Space Agency has put a number of satellite series into orbit atop its Shavit rockets and thirteen satellites have collectively accumulated sixty-six orbiting years. Israel's satellites are for research, communications, reconnaissance, and observation – the latter two series being more generally referred to as spy satellites. One series of reconnaissance satellites, the Ofeq, has several satellites orbiting the earth every ninety minutes, which means there is constant surveillance of nations posing a threat to the Jewish state. The cameras on the reconnaissance and observation satellites are capable of reading vehicle licensing plates on the ground. Currently, there are six satellite series in orbit and four additional series are under development. The Israel Space Agency also produces custom-made satellites for other nations, and the Agency is also advancing the 'SPACEIL' program, whose mission is to deliver the first Israeli spaceship to the moon by 2014.

Nuclear Weapons – it was mentioned above that Israel holds to a deliberate policy of nuclear ambiguity insofar as her nuclear capabilities are concerned. However, almost all bona fide Western intelligence agencies and *Jane's Defense Weekly* are convinced that Israel has a substantial arsenal of nuclear warheads and the means to deliver them. In 1986, Mordechai Vanunu, a former Israeli nuclear technician was paid a "gratuity" of sixty thousand British pounds (one hundred and twenty-five thousand five hundred dollars allowing for inflation at the time of writing) to reveal information concerning Israel's nuclear arsenal to the *London Sunday Times*. Vanunu told the *Sunday Times* that Israel had around two hundred warheads at that time.

Electromagnetic Pulse Weapons. The region is unstable and Israel has many enemies. When Israel looks to the future the first factor she must consider strategically is Iran. A nuclear Iran will create a dramatic change in the region – first, by having such a capability, and the outcome of having that capability. New intelligence information obtained in early August 2012 by Israel, the United States, Britain, France, and Germany shows that Iran has made greater progress on developing its nuclear weapons program than the West had previously realized.

Israel has to imagine the behavior of radical non-state actors under an Iranian nuclear umbrella. They will be more aggressive and will dare to do things that perhaps they are not willing to do at the time of writing.

The Iranian threat against the Jewish state is echoed in the words of Iranian President Mahmoud Ahmadinejad – the words he spoke on October 26, 2005, saying Israel "must be wiped off the map." These words have been cited by Israel to show the international community how allowing Iran to get nuclear arms would be a threat to the existence of the Jewish state.

Ahmadinejad has made many other threats against Israel since 2005, the latest (at the time of writing) being published on his website on August 2, 2012. He said: "the ultimate goal of world forces must be the annihilation of Israel." It is therefore understandable why Israel has long been planning an attack upon the Iranian nuclear program if diplomatic negotiations fail to halt Iran's nuclear drive.

If Israel appears to be obsessed with Iran it is because Iran is a very real existential threat to the Jewish state. Some readers may tend to dismiss statements from Iran threatening to wipe Israel from off the face of the earth as mere bellicose rantings from radical Muslim leaders of a fanatical Islamic regime. If that were really the case Israel would not care two hoots about Iran, but the fact of the matter is that Iran's leadership truly believe it is Iran's destiny to annihilate Israel.

It was noted in Chapter ten that in the Qur'an Mohammed calls for the destruction of all Jews. It was further noted that the *Hadith*, the sayings attributed to Mohammed and handed down through the centuries, also calls for the death of all Jews. That the *Hadith* goes as far as saying that it is a Muslim obligation to liquidate the Jews; that the Muslim messiah cannot come "unless there is first a great slaughter of the Jews."

The Muslim messiah is known by three terms: the Mahdi; the twelfth Imam; and the hidden Imam. Iranian President Mahmoud Ahmadinejad frequently mentions the Mahdi in the various terms and believes the Islamic world is now in the era of "The Coming," which explains Iran's total preoccupation with developing atomic weapons with which to annihilate Israel. Simply put: Iran needs nuclear weapons to ensure Israel's demise otherwise the Mahdi, the Muslim messiah cannot come. Israel has good reason to consider an attack against Iran's nuclear facilities.

A *New York Times* report on August 1, 2012 said there was "feverish speculation" in Israel that Prime Minister Benjamin Netanyahu "will act in September or early October." And former Mossad chief and national security advisor, Efraim Halevy, said, in an *Israel Radio* interview the following day, that Israel's threats of military action had a certain "credibility" and "seriousness." He added, "If I were an Iranian, I would be very fearful of the next twelve weeks."

It is a well-worn saying among high-level Israeli officials that: "Those who talk, don't know. Those who do know, don't talk." As this book nears completion in January 2013, we now know the pundits that forecasted an imminent strike by Israel were not prophets at all, merely talking heads who "don't know."

Amongst the substantial volume of media hype concerning a possible Israeli strike at Iran's nuclear program have been several "leaks" from high-ranking Israeli military officials. These leaks began to surface in August and September 2012. One "leak" concerned a "secret weapon" that Israel supposedly began developing in the 1990s, and which Israel could well use in a planned strike against Iran.

Israel is thousands of kilometers (miles) from Iran and the Israel Air Force would need to fly through hostile airspace and refuel the fighter-jets in the air. So many "leaks" have been made public about Israel's plans for a strike, both by the Obama administration and also Israeli officials opposed to such a strike, that Iran has had plenty of time to secure its nuclear program and reinforce its air defenses.

The latest information from Israel's security establishment at the time of writing is that Iran has completed its fortification of its nuclear facilities, putting them beyond conventional air attacks, even with the biggest of "bunker-buster" bombs. According to Israel's security establishment only tactical nuclear weapons or ground forces can now stop Iran.

Apparently, because of these advance warnings to Iran, Israel has, according to one "leak," considered using a "secret weapon," an electromagnetic pulse (EMP) bomb that would effectively cripple Iran's air defenses and all electronics within a radius of tens of kilometers (miles). The effect from an electromagnetic pulse weapon would be on a lesser scale than a pulse from a high-altitude nuclear explosion.

On September 9, 2012, the *London Sunday Times* claimed that:

> the use of the new technology by Israel was brought up in discussions regarding an attack on Teheran's nuclear facilities.

An American expert told the *Sunday Times* that this type of electromagnetic bomb operated on the "non-lethal technology of gamma rays" and that the outburst of energy would "fry" Iran's electric network and "disrupt all the technological devices on the ground." *The Times of Israel*, which carried the *London Sunday Times* report, headlined its own report **"Israel could send Iran 'back to the stone age' with electromagnetic bomb."**

Prime Minister Binyamin Netanyahu pledged on November 5, 2012, that Iran will not develop nuclear weapons on his watch. Netanyahu said:

> As long as I am prime minister Iran will not have nuclear weapons ... if there is no other choice and our back is to the wall, we will do what we need to do to defend ourselves. If there is no other way to stop Iran, Israel is prepared to act.

Netanyahu continued and said:

> When the Jews were being murdered by the Nazis, they were unable to save themselves, but I, as Israel's prime minister, do have the capacity to protect the Jewish nation. When we didn't have a state, we begged others to defend the Jews. Today, we're not begging, we are preparing.

Iran is the world's biggest exporter of terror and its terror has no boundaries. On September 17, 1992, three Iranian-Kurdish insurgent leaders and their translator were assassinated at a Greek restaurant in Berlin, Germany. In July 1994, in perhaps the worst of Iran's terror atrocities, was its bombing of Argentina's Jewish Community Center in Buenos Aires – eighty-seven people died and hundreds were injured. It was Argentina's deadliest bombing and followed an earlier bombing by Iran of the Jewish Community Center in March 1992, when twenty-nine people died and two hundred and fifty were injured.

In October 2011, Iran sent its men to assassinate the Saudi ambassador with a bomb on American soil, at a restaurant. Fortunately, the plan went awry and the leader was arrested. During interrogation he confessed that the would-be assassins planned to bomb the Saudi Embassy and Israeli Embassy in Washington, D.C.

In 2012, Iranian agents carried out terror attacks in Azerbaijan, Thailand, Georgia, India, Kenya, and Bulgaria. The bombings and plots all fitted the pattern of previous attacks by Iranian agents, mostly against Israeli interests. Officials in Kenya say that two Iranian agents arrested with explosives planned to attack Israeli, American, British, and Saudi Arabian targets inside Kenya. The two agents arrested in Kenya were members of Iran's Islamic Revolutionary Guards Corps Quds Force, an elite and secretive unit.

In June 2012, Daniel Benjamin, the United States State Department's coordinator for counterterrorism said Iran's support for terrorism and the activities of its proxy Hizb'allah are at their highest levels in more than a decade. He said:

> We are increasingly concerned about Iran's support for terrorism and Hizb'allah's activities as they've both stepped up their level of terrorist plotting over the past year.

Benjamin characterized Iran as "the preeminent state sponsor of terrorism in the world," and said the United States was "deeply concerned" about Iran undertaking violent activities directly through its Iranian Revolutionary Guards Corps Quds Force.

Iran is behaving like a great power. On July 2-4, 2012, the Aerospace Force of the Iranian Revolutionary Guard Corps (IRGC) conducted its annual missile exercise, dubbed Great Prophet 7. It involved the firing of dozens of missiles and rockets of different kinds and ranges at a target on Iranian soil that resembled a foreign – i.e. United States – airbase situated in one of Iran's neighbors (such as Afghanistan, Bahrain, Kuwait, or Saudi Arabia).

Iran is signaling, and not for the first time, that it is prepared and deployed for a military clash with the West and Israel, and possesses a fitting, rapid, and devastating "second-strike" response capability against any attack on its nuclear sites. Iranian spokesmen also warned during the exercise that if Israel attacked Iran it would be "destroyed."

With the missile exercise and the terminology used by its various spokesmen, Iran wants to present the profile of a great power – one capable of a rapid, symmetrical missile response to threats against it, and of projecting power toward the neighboring states. Add to this the ongoing emphasis on the naval components of the asymmetrical response Iran would mount in case of a naval clash with the United States – swarms of rocket-equipped speedboats, suicide speedboats, and naval mines – and on preparing terror cells for the "day of reckoning" at various spots on the globe. The recent exposure of Iran's terror infrastructure in Kenya, as well as in India, Georgia, Thailand, Azerbaijan, and Bulgaria, should be seen in this light.

Iran claims to have already amassed information on thirty-five United States bases in the region and have deployed missiles to destroy them within minutes of an attack. "All of these bases are within the range of our missiles."

Iran continues to develop ballistic missiles that can reach regional adversaries, Israel, and Eastern Europe, including an extended-range variant of the Shahab-3 and a two thousand kilometer (twelve hundred and fifty mile) medium-range ballistic missile, the Ashura. Beyond steady growth in its missile and rocket inventories, Iran has boosted the lethality and effectiveness of existing systems with accuracy improvements and new submunition payloads. And Iran may be technically capable of flight testing an intercontinental ballistic missile by 2015.

During the last twenty years Iran has placed significant emphasis on developing and fielding ballistic missiles to counter perceived threats from Israel and Coalition forces in the Middle East and to project power in the region. Iran also has developed medium-range ballistic missiles to target Israel and continues to increase the range, lethality, and accuracy of these systems.

At the same time, Iran is dispersing these missiles throughout the country – deep in the interior, along the coast, at sea, and even beyond Iran's borders. Iran has a broad concept of the use of force that also encompasses missiles located in Syria, Lebanon, and the Gaza Strip. Iran's missile exercises also make clear (as does the rain of missile fire from Gaza, Sinai, and Lebanon) Iran's reliance on missiles as one of the main components of its national-security strategy and the answer to the threats it faces.

Iran is working to complete Israel's encirclement with missiles of different ranges; some of those fired during the recent exercise are also possessed by Hizb'allah. Iran made no reference during the exercise to the broader context of the missiles and rockets held by Hizb'allah, Hamas, Islamic Jihad, Syria, and, latterly, Sudan that originate in Tehran. However, Iran sees these as part of its response in case it is attacked. It also continues to regard Hizb'allah in Lebanon as its "first line of defense" in its national-security doctrine, both as a deterrent and a response factor, and views such missile fire as an asymmetrical answer to Israel's superior technological capability – particularly her air force.

Iranian officials adamantly assert that their controversial nuclear program is meant solely for peaceful purposes. Israel, the United States, and much of the Western world's nations claim the opposite is true, especially in light of Iran's many threats to annihilate Israel. Iran is without doubt bearing down on its goal of developing nuclear weapons.

In the first week of August 2012, Hizb'allah Member of Parliament Walid Sakariya told Lebanese television that the nuclear weapon Iran is developing is "intended to annihilate Israel." In one segment recorded and translated by the Middle East Media Research Institute (MEMRI), Sakariya, also a retired general, told his interviewer on Hizb'allah's *al-Manar* network that:

> should Iran acquire a nuclear weapon it would serve Syrian as well as Iranian interests, namely the eradication of the Jewish state. This nuclear weapon is intended to create a balance of terror with Israel, to finish off the Zionist enterprise, and to end all Israeli aggression against the Arab nation.

By "Arab nation" Sakariya is meaning the whole Arab world. Iran is today challenging the United States, intensifying its threats against Israel, and is trying to behave like a superpower. Given the rapid changes in the Middle East, any concession by Iran, particularly on the nuclear issue, is no longer seen as an option.

The format of the latest Iranian missile exercise sent a clear message both to the United States and the regional states that Iran is prepared for any scenario and does not fear a confrontation.

Some Western political pundits dismiss Iran's professed military capabilities with a *bon mot*, but that is worse than foolish. Iran must be treated with respect – its Supreme leader Ali Khamenei is not a clone of Saddam Hussein.

Egypt, Israel's immediate neighbor to the south west, has undergone an unprecedented political upheaval. Hosni Mubarak, the Egyptian president who autocratically ruled the Arab world's largest state for thirty years, was toppled by the Arab Spring in January 2011. To his credit, Mubarak steadfastly kept the peace with Israel, albeit it was a cold peace. Mubarak once said that "the Egyptian government made peace with Israel, the people did not." Mubarak kept a stable situation in Egypt by suppressing the Islamists and controlling the Sinai, which in turn allowed Israel to reduce its defense spending and also its troop numbers.

Mubarak was staunchly pro-American and the United States considers Egypt a key ally in the Middle East. The United States has rewarded Egypt with billions of dollars in military aid and sells it state-of-the-art weaponry, military equipment and fighter jets. The Egyptian media is government controlled and numerous times Israel has been depicted as Egypt's "only enemy." Thus the advanced American weapons will likely be turned against Israel.

Following Mubarak's overthrow the Sinai became a hotbed for terrorism and brazen attacks on Egyptian border-guard soldiers and policemen. And, as previously mentioned in Chapter eleven, the gas pipeline that carried Egyptian natural gas to Israel through the Sinai was blown up fourteen times in fifteen months after the fall of Hosni Mubarak – prior to the interim Islamist government illegally canceling the gas contract with Israel in its entirety.

On August 5, 2012, some thirty-five Islamists dressed in bedouin clothing attacked an Egyptian checkpoint near Israel's border, killing sixteen Egyptian border policemen and soldiers and wounded seven others as they sat down to eat the traditional meal at the end of the Ramadan fast day.

Israel had warned Egyptian security officials that a major terror attack was in the planning and had also warned Israelis vacationing in Sinai to return home immediately, and advised those planning a trip to the Sinai to cancel their plans. The Egyptians pooh-poohed Israel's warnings and accused Israel of seeking to harm Egypt's tourism industry.

After killing the border-guards at the checkpoint the jihadists commandeered two armored Egyptian military vehicles and stormed the Kerem Shalom border crossing into Israel. The Israel Defense Force was prepared and had closed a watch tower three hours prior to the attack. Israel Defense Force opened fire on the vehicles as they raced toward the crossing causing one vehicle, an armored jeep, to crash into the vacated guard tower, detonating half a ton of explosives.

The second vehicle, an armored personnel carrier, burst through the crossing, evaded Israeli tanks, and raced down Israel's border road at seventy kilometers (forty-four miles) an hour toward an Israeli kibbutz. An Israeli commander called for air support, deciding to bomb the armored vehicle from the air – marking the first time that an Israel Air Force aircraft has fired on a target inside Israel. The vehicle managed to drive some two kilometers (less than one and a half miles) into Israel before the Israeli Air Force was able to get a clear shot and blow up their armored vehicle without risk to civilian traffic on the road. An Israeli tank fired two additional shells into the burning wreckage.

Israeli forces killed five jihadist gunmen on the Egyptian side of the border and three bodies were found amidst the wreckage of the vehicle bombed from the air – all eight gunmen were wearing explosive vests. Obviously, a major saving of Israeli life was effected by the alertness of Israeli intelligence and defense forces.

News of the attack brought knee-jerk reactions from the terrorist world. From the Gaza Strip, Ismail Haniya, the Hamas terror-group leader could find nothing to say apart from: "Israel is somehow behind yesterday's attack on Egyptian guards in Sinai." In Egypt itself, the reactions to the attack were mixed. Predictably, the Egyptian Muslim Brotherhood said on its website the following day:

This crime can be attributed to the Mossad, which has been seeking to abort the revolution since its inception and the proof of this is that it gave instructions to its zionist citizens in Sinai to depart immediately a few days ago.

While acknowledging that jihadists carried out the attack, former Egyptian Islamist Member of Parliament Mustafa Bakri told the Egyptian daily *Al-Youm A-Sabi'* that it was:

a Zionist plot to bring Israel back to Sinai and expel Palestinians to Egyptian lands in Sinai.

On his Twitter account, Bakri speculated that Israel would seize the opportunity and reoccupy Sinai. He cited Israel's warning to her citizens to leave the Sinai Peninsula as proof that Israel was aware of the terrorists' plan.

The main Egyptian *Al-Ahram* newspaper reported that some Egyptian social media commentators were furious that Egypt's security chiefs dismissed Israel's terror warning, issued three days earlier, as unfounded and as an attempt to sabotage tourism to the area.

On August 7, Egypt's intelligence head Murad Muwafi admitted that he received prior warnings of the deadly attack on the border police station in Sinai. Muwafi said:

Yes, we had detailed information about the attack, but we never imagined that a Muslim would kill a Muslim on the hour of breaking the fast in Ramadan.

The following day (August 8) Egyptian officials called for changes to be made in several clauses of the peace treaty with Israel. Officials in Cairo said that the 1978 Camp David Accords, under which Israel withdrew from the Sinai Peninsula and which set limitations on the Egyptian army's rights to deploy forces and operate there, prevent Egypt from effectively exerting control in the Peninsula.

The terms of the treaty prevents the Egyptian army from operating more effectively in the areas where it is currently confronting Islamic terrorists. Amr Moussa, the Secretary of the Arab League and a vehement critic of Israel, said:

Changes are required in order to allow Egypt to control the
Sinai border areas.

One day earlier, Dan Meridor, Israel's Deputy Prime
Minister and Minister of Intelligence and Atomic Energy, said
Jerusalem would not object to Egypt moving heavier forces
into the peninsula to carry out anti-terror operations. The same
day, and following a terrorist attack against Egypt's Al-Risa
checkpoint near Rafah – already attacked twenty-eight times
since the fall of Hosni Mubarak in January 2011 – Egyptian
forces mobilized tanks, attack helicopters, and fighter jets and
struck at terrorist bases and cars in Sinai killing twenty suspected
terrorists. By August 9, the terrorist kill count had risen to sixty.

By August 9, Egypt had positively identified the body of one
of the attackers as a member of the Gazan-based Army of Islam.
Egypt called upon Hamas to hand over three more gunmen
who were connected to the attack. Despite vehement denials by
Hamas (an offshoot of the Egyptian Muslim Brotherhood) of any
involvement in the deadly attack upon the Egyptian checkpoint,
Egyptian troops began sealing the Gaza border with Egypt. The
Rafah crossing, which had remained closed under Mubarak but
opened again by Egypt's Islamist government, was closed once
more – "indefinitely." Egyptian heavy earth-moving equipment
began destroying the hundreds of smuggling tunnels under the
Gaza-Egypt border, from which Hamas receives its weapons
from Iran and levies heavy taxes on all other smuggled goods.
The brief honeymoon between Hamas and Egypt seemed to be
over, but Hamas soon sweet-talked the Muslim Brotherhood into
opening the Rafah crossing and has been arresting terrorists from
rival Gaza factions as a peace offering to Egypt.

In the latest skirmish between Israel and Hamas and Islamic
Jihad in November 2012, called Pillar of Defense by Israel,
Hamas and its jihadi cadres fired fifteen hundred and six missiles
at Israeli cities, including Tel Aviv and Jerusalem. In return
Israel pounded the terror groups' missile arsenals, underground
launchers, and Hamas's infrastructure.

Egyptian President Mohammed Morsi's immediate reaction
was to recall Egypt's ambassador and demand meetings of the

United Nations Security Council and the Arab League. Morsi aligned himself with Hamas and sent Egyptian Prime Minister Hisham Kandil to Gaza to boost Hamas's moral and denounce Israel's "unprovoked aggression." The Israel Defense Force said it would hold its fire during Kandil's visit providing Hamas held back the missiles, but the Kandil had to cut short his visit due to several missiles being fired into Israel and Israel responded with heavy air attacks. During his visit to Gaza Kandil pledged Egypt's support for the Palestinians and urged all the jihadi factions to unite. Kandil said:

> The strength of the Palestinian people lies in its unity. That is the way to achieve victory."

Morsi, a former head of the Muslim Brotherhood, said Egypt and Hamas – an offshoot of the Egyptian Muslim Brotherhood – said:

> We are one people. Our blood is Palestinian blood and Palestinian blood is Egyptian blood.

This adds yet another new twist to the ongoing Israeli-Arab conflict.

The Egyptian offensive against the terrorists in the Sinai Peninsular was the first time since the 1973 Yom Kippur War that Egyptian forces used air power and missiles in the Sinai. Apparently, for Egypt, the killing of so many fellow Egyptian Muslims by Muslim terrorists was the proverbial straw that broke the camel's back. Israel is concerned the Egyptians, especially in light of Morsi's recent ouster of the military's top brass, may exploit the attack on their border checkpoint to remilitarize the Sinai Peninsular. Israel allowed Egypt to bring troops, tanks, armored vehicles, attack helicopters, and fighter-jets into the Sinai Peninsular on a temporary basis in order for Egypt to deal with the ballooning terrorist situation. Israel must now wait to see whether President Mohammed Morsi will withdraw everything back to the mainland in accordance with Egypt's treaty with Israel, or whether Morsi will take control of the Sinai Peninsular as was the situation prior to the Yom Kippur War. A demilitarized Sinai was an essential buffer against another surprise attack against the Jewish state.

The election of the Muslim Brotherhood candidate Mohammed Morsi as Egypt's president on June 24, 2012, caused Israel to enter a deeply problematic period in ties with her powerful neighbor. Zvi Mazel, Israel's ambassador to Cairo in the late 1990s, says Egypt's new president, Mohammed Morsi seeks the destruction of Israel. Mazel says: "He has said he wants to conquer Jerusalem."

"During the presidential election campaign," said Mazel in an *Israel Radio* interview, Morsi was deliberately vague on the issue of ongoing relations between Egypt and Israel, which signed a peace treaty in 1979. Mazel predicted that Morsi and the Brotherhood would swiftly widen and tighten their grip on Egypt.

On August 12, 2012, Morsi consolidated the Muslim Brotherhood's hold on Egypt when he sacked the entire leadership of the country's defense establishment. Morsi forced Egypt's top brass, its military élite, to retire and issued a decree consolidating his presidential authority. The military had been the force that had curtailed Morsi's authority, but he has turned the tables and ousted Egypt's military strongman Mohammed Hussein Tantawi, Chief of Staff Sami Anan and other security chiefs. Morsi also ordered the retirement of the commanders of the navy, air defense, and air force. The move has cemented Morsi's authority over the armed forces, a move similar to Turkish Prime Minister Recep Tayyip Erdogan's expulsion of dozens of his generals. However, while Erdogan achieved his control of the Turkish military in a gradual process, Morsi did so in a matter of days. With the Muslim Brotherhood exercising total control over the Egyptian armed forces, Israel has reason to be troubled.

Mohammed Morsi's recent election as president of Egypt is indeed proving to be a matter of concern for Israel. A candidate from the radical Islamist Muslim Brotherhood – a former leader until being required to step down in order to be eligible for election – many fear that Morsi's victory, along with the Brotherhood's many parliamentary successes, will threaten the Egyptian-Israeli peace. Part of the Muslim Brotherhood's statement of belief is:

> Allah is our objective; the Qu'ran is our law, the Prophet is our leader; jihad is our way; and death for the sake of Allah is the highest of our aspirations.

The question that is being asked in Israel at the time of writing is how can Morsi commit to keeping his country's treaty with Israel when his religious beliefs preclude it? Part of Morsi's acceptance speech, widely interpreted as a reference to future relations with Israel, emphasized "the state of Egypt's commitment to international treaties and agreements." More broadly, he declared that "we carry a message of peace to the world."

Encouraging as these statements may be, they do in fact fit neatly with the Brotherhood's sophisticated strategy for dealing with outsiders. That strategy is laid out comprehensively in Mustafa Mashhur's *Jihad is the Way*. Mashhur, leader of the Brotherhood in Egypt from 1996 to 2002, explains the movement's religious beliefs and aspirations in detail – especially the role of violent jihad in bringing about a world under a unified Islamic Caliphate. It gives reason to doubt Morsi's reassurances. Mashhur explains:

> Jihad and preparation for jihad are not only for the purpose of fending-off assaults and attacks against Muslims by Allah's enemies, but are also for the purpose of realizing the great task of establishing an Islamic state, strengthening the religion, and spreading it around the world.

"Martyrdom for Allah," Mashhur writes, "is our most exalted wish." Jihad is indeed the way, and not only has Morsi never rejected this Muslim Brotherhood ideology – he is now its most senior political representative in Egypt and is also standing with Hamas against Israel in the Gaza Strip.

So how are these contradictions to be understood? Why does Morsi talk peace when he explicitly adheres to an ideology of war? Because Morsi's statements are really stratagems. Nullifying Egypt's treaty with Israel might isolate Egypt politically and bring it economic ruin. Instead, Morsi can apply the Brotherhood's principle, as learned from Muhammad: *"Sabr"* – patience and resolve. Standing by Egypt's international commitments now does not preclude war later; and assurances of peaceful intent do not jettison jihad from the agenda – in fact, as far as the Brotherhood is concerned, they advance it. Morsi does not have to change his opinions, nor does he have to reject the

Brotherhood's fundamental beliefs when he speaks of peace.

The necessity to strengthen and stabilize Egyptian society is a priority now – it is, moreover, the very means by which to prepare Egypt to lead the Islamic world and to fulfill Islam's perceived global destiny. Peaceful statements released from Egypt over the next few years should not deceive observers into believing that the Brotherhood has abandoned its religious ideology and its comprehensive Islamic vision. Talking peace, while preparing for jihad, is an integral part of jihad.

On October 19, 2012, Mohammed Morsi participated in prayers at the el-Tanaim Mosque in the coastal area of Matrouh, the footage of which was shown on Egyptian state television. Morsi was shown in fervent prayer as Islamist cleric Futouh Abd al-Nabi Mansour declared:

> Oh Allah, absolve us of our sins, strengthen us and grant us victory over the infidels. Oh Allah, destroy the Jews and their supporters. Oh Allah, disperse them, rend them asunder. Oh Allah, demonstrate your might and greatness upon them.

Morsi could be clearly seen mouthing "Amen" (Arabic – "Amin") to the cleric's sentiments – an obvious window into Morsi's soul.

In August 2012, a senior member of Egypt's Muslim Brotherhood refused to participate in a panel with Israeli participants at an international Security and Peace conference. Amr Darrag, head of foreign relations at President Morsi's Freedom and Justice Party, told the Egyptian media that a delegation from his party participated in the international Security and Peace conference in Prague and that a number of Israelis attending the conference tried to approach the Egyptians, but the Egyptians refused to speak to them.

"We at the Freedom and Justice party reject normalization" with Israel, Darrag said, adding that he notified the conference organizers that his delegation would not share the stage with any Israelis or speak on a panel with them. Egypt rejects Israel completely. Darrag said:

> Egypt must abide by its international agreements, but we as a faction of the people refuse any normalization or dialogue with Israel.

Morsi will follow Mohammed's calculation: Egypt will break its treaty with Israel – "when conditions are right."

Disturbing for Israel are the media reports that Morsi said in his acceptance speech that he would make a warming of ties with Iran a priority of his presidency (Iran severed diplomatic relations following Egypt's signing of its peace treaty with Israel). Iran, for its part, invited Morsi to visit Teheran for talks on closer ties, and this took place in August 2012. An Egyptian Islamist government, with a former head of the Muslim Brotherhood as its president underpinning Hamas, is bad enough, but link that with warm ties with the world's foremost exporter of terror is almost too much to contemplate. A September 2012 poll conducted by *Foreign Policy Magazine* found that sixty-two percent of Egyptians interviewed agreed that Iran and its president Mahmoud Ahmadinejad were friends of Egypt and that eighty-seven percent want Egypt to have its own nuclear bomb.

On October 11, 2012, Sheikh Mohammed Badie, Egypt's most influential Muslim Brotherhood official (the Brotherhood's Supreme Guide), in a speech published by the Egyptian daily *Al-Ahram*, called on the Arab world to liberate Jerusalem from Israeli rule by jihad – holy war. Badie said *inter alia*:

> The jihad for the recovery of Jerusalem is a duty for all Muslims – the liberation of the Holy City will not be done through negotiations. Jerusalem is Islamic. The Zionists only understand force and the Arabs cannot hope to achieve justice from the Jews through the corridors of the United Nations.

Israel's backyard is already surrounded by fanatical Islamists working to eradicate the Jewish state, now everything points to Egypt complicating things even further. Israel lives in an extremely rough neighborhood.

Syria After Bashir Assad is also an unknown. Israel does not know what will happen in Syria the day after Assad's regime comes to an end. Syria is not coherent like other countries – the Sunnis in Damascus and the Sunnis in Aleppo are different, and then there are the Druze, the Kurds, and the Alawis.

One immediate cause for concern is the huge stockpile of strategic chemical and biological weapons capabilities inside

Syria. As aforementioned, Israel does not know who will be in control the day after. What weapons have been and will be transferred to Hizb'allah, what will be divided among the factions inside Syria, and what this is going to mean are all major concerns.

Syria has invested more than two billion dollars in air defenses over the last few years because it understands it has a problem with the Israel Air Force. The most destructive missiles that were falling on Haifa and central Israel in 2006 were Syrian missiles, supplied by Syria to Hizb'allah. Syria has been an implacable enemy of Israel and fights a proxy war through Hizb'allah.

In a September 2006 speech, Hassan Nasr'allah, the fanatical Islamic leader of Hizb'allah, said Syria had similarly supplied rockets smuggled into the Gaza Strip to be used by the Palestinian terrorist group Hamas against targets in southern Israel. Nasr'allah boasted:

> The missiles delivered to Gaza managed to force more than a million settlers to stay in bunkers and frightened Tel Aviv.

The British *Times* newspaper reported on August 21, 2012, that Syria has also given Hizb'allah several Ss-1 Scud missiles and allowed them to be based in Lebanon. The Ss-1 Scud missile is a large and powerful missile – eleven meters thirty-five centimeters (thirty-seven plus feet) – long and can inflict serious damage. In the 1991 Gulf War Saddam Hussein hit Israel with thirty-one Ss-1 Scud missiles and destroyed or damaged some five thousand Israeli homes. Weapons like this in the hands of Hizb'allah is a serious addition to Hizb'allah's death-dealing arsenals. And for this Israel must thank Syria.

When the Arab regimes were barring bread and money from entering the Gaza Strip, Syria was sending in weapons and food.

Arab armies have a propensity for being savage toward their prisoners, but Syrian soldiers excel in their butchery – Israeli captives in the 1967 war were found on the Golan Heights with their genitals cut off and stuffed in their mouths. Who will be in control after Assad is a cause for concern in Israel.

Lebanon: Brigadier-General Herzi Halevy, commander of Israel Defense Force Division 91, said on July 5, 2012, that Israel's 2009 offensive against Hamas in the Gaza Strip will pale in comparison to what will happen to Lebanon in a future war with Hizb'allah. What the Israel Defense Force will do in that nation will take Lebanon a decade to recover from – if it does recover. Halevy also said:

> The destruction will be greater in Lebanon than in Israel and the amount of explosives which will fall there will be far more than what will fall here. We will need to be strong and aggressive.

Halevy clarified the remark and told reporters that the destruction will be widespread due to Hizb'allah's decision to establish its command posts and bases inside villages and towns throughout Lebanon. Hizb'allah is Iran's self-declared "first line of defense" against Israel.

Halevy, who headed the Paratroop Brigade during Operation Cast Lead in 2009, said Israel would take immediate action – from the air and on the ground – in a future war that would cause "extensive damage, not as a punishment but rather to hit the enemy where it is." He said that the damage in Lebanon will be far greater than the 2006 Second Lebanon War.

An attack on Iran's nuclear facilities – no matter by whom – or the ongoing civil war in Syria could spark a conflict between Israel and Hizb'allah. Increased tension between the Israel Defense Force and the Lebanese Armed Forces could also spark a conflict.

According to the Beirut newspaper *Al Joumhouria*, the secretary of Iran's Supreme National Security Council, Saeed Jalali, visited Lebanon in August 2012 and gave a green light for the immediate use of Hizb'allah's military force against Israel in the event of an Israeli attack on Iran's nuclear program.

The Israel Defense Force has spent the past twelve months (at the time of writing) upgrading its defenses along the Israeli-Lebanese border. A short while ago it completed the construction of a concrete wall between the Israeli border town of Metulla and the Lebanese town of Kafr Kila. The army decided to build a wall along that section of the frontier to minimize friction between the sides.

Since the war in 2006, in addition to Hizb'allah's extensive rearmament and procurement of tens of thousands of rockets and missiles, the Israel Defense Force has noticed a concerted effort by the terror group to gather intelligence on Israeli military positions along the border. The army released photos on July 5, 2012, showing Hizb'allah operatives with surveillance gear along the border filming Israel Defense Force movements and deployments.

During the war in the summer of 2006 (referenced by Brigadier-General Herzi Halevy above) – triggered by a cross-border raid by Hizb'allah fighters who killed eight Israeli soldiers and kidnapped two others – Hizb'allah fired some five thousand rockets into Israel, reaching as far south as Hadera, around fifty miles (eighty kilometers) south of the border. The war killed twelve hundred Lebanese, according to the Lebanese government, and one hundred and fifty-nine Israelis, according to the Israeli government.

Within three years of the end of hostilities – and despite United Nations Security Council resolutions calling for Hizb'allah to be disarmed – Hizb'allah has rearmed under the nose of the United Nations twelve-thousand-man Peacekeeping Force. Hizb'allah is preparing for a future conflict with Israel and has a stockpile of tens of thousands of missiles and rockets. Blind eyes have to be purposely turned in order for thousands of ten-meter-long (thirty-three foot) missiles weighing more than three tonnes (tons) to be transported throughout Lebanon. The importing and transportation of these missiles was carried out in the presence of those of the United Nations Peacekeeping Force that was specifically assigned to Lebanon in order to prevent Hizb'allah from rearming.

Set up with Iran's assistance in the early 1980s and sponsored both by Tehran and Damascus, Hizb'allah has been listed by the United States as a "foreign terrorist organization" ever since Foreign Terrorist Organization designation was first established under 1996 legislation.

Hizb'allah's deadliest attacks included suicide bombings in Beirut in 1983 that killed more than three hundred people, including two hundred and forty-one United States servicemen and fifty-eight French troops. And at the time of writing the European Union still persists in its refusal to classify Hizb'allah as a terrorist organization. Despite its history of violence, Hizb'allah and its allies control sixteen of the thirty seats in Lebanese Prime Minister Najib Mikati's cabinet, giving it virtual veto power over the government.

Hizb'allah's existence as an armed militia violates two Security Council resolutions – resolution 1559 of 2004, which calls for "the disbanding and disarmament of all Lebanese and non-Lebanese militias," and resolution 1701 of 2006, which requires:

> the disarmament of all armed groups in Lebanon, so that ...
> there will be no weapons or authority in Lebanon other than
> that of the Lebanese state.

On July 2, 2012, the Beirut newspaper *Al-Joumhouria* cited a 'security study' saying the terror group has upgraded underground structures. *Al-Joumhouria* said its source was a diplomatic report issued by an unspecified European embassy, which it said contained information from "a number of Western security agencies."

Claimed in the *Al-Joumhouria* report was that "Iranian experts" had supervised the digging of a new tunnel network in Lebanon's Beqa'a Valley region, which borders with Syria, following the 2006 Second Lebanon War.

The *Al-Joumhouria* report also said Hizb'allah had dug a new network of tunnels in an area south of the Litani River. The tunnels, according to the report, are equipped with state-of-the-art ventilation, lighting and communication networks and are built to resist land and air operations. The report also claimed that the tunnels contain underground stores of weapons and ammunitions, which have been stashed at various locations. And, according to *Al-Joumhouria*, the tunnels are also equipped with dormitories, medical facilities, kitchens, toilets, water, and heating systems that allow dozens of terrorists to live underground for weeks at a time.

The report added that years ago Hizb'allah had purchased large tracts of land in the Hermel region near the Syrian border and had drilled tunnels though the mountains of the Beqa'a area, reaching deep into Syrian territory. The report also claimed Israel had conducted maneuvers in tunnels similar to Hizb'allah's, which could help the Israel Defense Force excel in a future conflict. However, the report said, it is "no longer an issue of tunnels, but of missiles," which are hidden all over the country.

Next to Iran, its proxy, Hizb'allah, has the greatest potential for creating havoc against innocent Israeli civilians. The Israel Defense Force will be compelled to deal assertively with Lebanon's terrorist masters.

On December 17, 2012, a large explosion hit southern Lebanon near the border town of Tair Harfa, adjacent to the border with Israel. Lebanese authorities and the United Nations peacekeepers are at a loss as to what caused the explosion. Three days following the explosion a Kuwaiti newspaper claimed it was the result of a planned attack and that the Hizb'allah facility housed Syrian-made missiles with biological and chemical warheads. The Kuwaiti report did not directly finger Israel for carrying out a strike against the weapons cache, but said the Israel Air Force had carried out such attacks in the past. Referring to the explosion in Lebanon, Israel's air force commander Major General Amir Eshel told *The Times of Israel*:

> Someone who goes to bed with rockets should realize that is a very unsafe place to be in.

The Government of Jordan committed itself to implementing a Treaty of Peace between the State of Israel and the Hashemite Kingdom of Jordan on October 26, 1994. And indeed, the Israeli-Jordanian border has itself been the quietest of all Israel's borders. However, there has been a number of large Muslim Brotherhood-instigated protests against the ruling Jordanian monarchy similar to the protests in other Arab nations during the Arab Spring (Teheran better describes the "Arab Spring" as the "Islamic Awakening").

Many Jordanians would like to see an end to the Hashemite monarchy and Jordan's King Abdullah is pragmatically instituting a number of reforms in an effort to appease those who call for his overthrow. Annulling the practice of citizenship revocation of Palestinians (mentioned at length in Chapter two) is undoubtedly a major reform – if the seventy to eighty percent of Jordanians of Palestinian origin rose up against him, King Abdullah and other Hashemites could be removed almost overnight.

While relations are cordial between King Abdullah and Israel, the Jordanian Embassy in Tel Aviv was without an ambassador for over two years, since King Abdullah appointed Ali al-Ayed, the former envoy, as Jordan's minister of media affairs and communications in July 2010.

Amman did name a replacement, Walid Obeidat, on October 1, 2012, and he presented his credentials to Israel's President Shimon Peres on October 17. However, Obeidat is a member of one of Jordan's largest tribes that rejects normalization with Israel and the tribe denounced and condemned the appointment. The tribe announced that it was cutting all ties to the new ambassador and marked October 17 as an annual day of mourning.

On September 13, 2012, *Agence France-Press* reported that King Abdullah was exasperated with Israel for blocking Jordan's plans to develop a nuclear energy program. Abdullah charged that Israel was trying to thwart the development of a Jordanian nuclear program, a charge Israel diplomatically denied.

Although Abdullah is steadfast in his adherence to the treaty with Israel, he does not shy away from criticizing Israeli policies, especially concerning the Palestinians. And Jordan's peace treaty with Israel should be placed in the same category as Mubarak's description of Egypt's treaty with Israel that was quoted before: "Israel had made peace with the Egyptian government, not with the people of Egypt." Similarly, Israel has made peace with the Hashemite monarchy, not with the people of Jordan.

Following the sacking of the Israeli embassy in Cairo, Egypt, in September 2011, Jordanians massed in protest outside the Israeli embassy in Amman, burning Israeli flags and calling for the cancellation of the treaty with Israel.

Israeli tourists to Jordan have also been assaulted for the crime of being Israelis. For example, in June 2012, six Israeli tourists were assaulted in a market in southern Jordan. The six men and women arrived at a market in the town of Rabba, a hundred kilometers (sixty-two miles) south of the capital Amman. One of the vendors identified the tourists as Israelis and proceeded to assault the men with shoes, a symbol of disdain in Arab culture. The Israeli tourists fled the area in their cars as buyers joined the attack, the local media reported. "Israelis are not wanted in the market," a shopper told *Al-Arab Al-Yawm*, then added:

> Those who talk about peace between Israelis and Jordanians are delusional. The signed agreements are nothing but ink on paper. They are meaningless.

Article 11 of the 1994 Israel-Jordan peace treaty calls on both countries:

> to abstain from hostile or discriminatory propaganda against each other, and to take all possible legal and administrative measures to prevent the dissemination of such propaganda by any organization or individual present in the territory of either party.

On December 12, 2012, the Jordanian Tourism Ministry warned Israeli tourists to the Hashemite Kingdom not to provoke the "sensibilities" of the Jordanians by "outwardly wearing Jewish garb" such as skull caps or *tzitzit*.

But on March 23, 2012, the Jordanian imam Ghaleb Rabab'a delivered a Friday sermon to worshippers that was carried live on state television, according to recently released video footage translated and released by the Middle East Media Research Institute (MEMRI). The Imam's message to his flock in his sermon was that Jordan's army will destroy Israel and regain Jerusalem from the "killers of prophets. The arrogance of the Jews will be defeated, Allah willing." Rabab'a went on to say:

> The [Jordanian] army is invincible. Its units are filled with people who pray, with imams, and with people who memorized the Qu'ran. This army will never be defeated, Allah willing. Jerusalem will be regained, Allah willing, by these modest and pure hands, which hold the Qu'ran high and recite it day and night. This is an army that bows before none but Allah. Today, we must take pride in our country and its army, which descends from the Prophet Muhammed."

It remained unclear whether the sermon was delivered from a state-run or private mosque and requests to the Jordanian

Embassy in Israel for comment went unanswered at the time of writing.

The border with Jordan is quiet and Jordanian soldiers are vigilant in their keeping of the status quo. Albeit, some members of the Jordanian parliament have from time to time expressed opposition to the peace treaty with Israel. If the Hashemite Kingdom is overthrown, the peaceful border situation would soon come to an end.

The Palestinian issue is ongoing and has been so for decades. At the time of writing it appears to be heading for a showdown in the very near future.

Unless an agreement with the Palestinians is based on solid security arrangements, it will not last. People are inclined to think that peace provides security, but in the Middle East security provides peace. Any Israeli-Palestinian peace treaty must be protected by a solid security arrangement due to the proximity of the West Bank and the Gaza Strip to Israel's heartland, and the exposure of her population to potential threats.

However, Palestinian Authority President Mahmoud Abbas is using everything in his box of tricks to stave off all pretense at negotiating a peace treaty with Israel. He is convinced that, given the climate of antisemitism and overt anti-Israel sentiment in the United Nations, he will be able to get the United Nations to impose a sovereign State of Palestine upon Israel, a state that would force Israel to withdraw to the 1949 Armistice Lines. For this we can thank the incompetent United States President Barack Hussein Obama. During his 2008 election campaign Obama repeatedly said that he would make the Middle East peace initiative a priority of his administration. Instead of moving peace negotiations between Israel and the Palestinians forward, Obama brought them to an abrupt halt and there has been no movement since.

Obama came into office intent on creating "daylight" between himself and Israel, believing that by tilting toward the Palestinians, they would be more accommodating. The opposite happened. When Obama insisted on a building freeze in Jerusalem (that no United States government had ever demanded and no Israeli government would ever accept), the Palestinian Authority (PA) saw its way clear to become altogether recalcitrant.

In June 2009, Obama said that the United States "does not accept the legitimacy of continued Israeli settlements." Abu Mazen made that his mantra and refused to hold talks with Israel until it froze all settlement construction in the West Bank (biblical Judea and Samaria) and east Jerusalem. Never, in all the years the talks had been in progress, had settlement construction been an issue – everything had been on the table and up for negotiation.

As a concession to both Obama and the Palestinians, Israel relented and froze all construction in the West Bank for ten months, not even allowing an additional bathroom to be built for expanding Jewish families, but Abbas found excuse after excuse for not meeting with Prime Minister Binyamin Netanyahu and never once met with him during that time.

Syndicated columnist Charles Krauthammer wrote on July 28, 2012, that Palestinian Authority President Mahmoud Abbas openly told the *Washington Post* that he "would just sit on his hands and wait for America to deliver Israel." As a result of Obama's political blunders Abbas has refused to negotiate with Israel. And in September 2011, Abbas tried to undermine the fundamental principle of United States Middle East diplomacy – a negotiated two-state solution – by seeking unilateral United Nations Security Council recognition of Palestinian statehood, without talks or bilateral agreements.

Having already wrecked the Israel-Palestinian talks, Obama did what the author observed elsewhere: he removed one foot from his mouth and replaced it with the other, when, in May 2011, he said that as a concession for peace with the Palestinians the the basis of a deal between Israel and the Palestinians should be the lines Israel held before the 1967 war.

Netanyahu met with Obama in the White House the following day, right on the heels of the president's public call to return Israel to the 1967 lines. Netanyahu told Obama, amid no small amount of tension, that he was willing to make some compromises to achieve peace, but that returning to Israel's 1967 lines was not an option.

But Abbas seized on Obama's public call to return Israel to the 1949 Armistice Lines (which are the 1967 lines) and made that his second demand. He vowed never to return to talks with Netanyahu unless Israel commits to a complete settlement building freeze and accept the Armistice lines as the borders for a Palestinian state. Needless to say, Israel refused Abbas's terms.

In April 2011, even Mahmoud Abbas was showing frustration with President Obama. In an April 24 interview with the *Daily BEAST*, Abbas said:

> It was Obama who suggested a full settlement freeze, I said okay, I accept. We both went up the tree. After that, he came down with a ladder and he removed the ladder and said to me, jump. Three times he did it."

Thirteen months later, on May 14, 2012, Abbas said that he himself "cannot be less Palestinian than Obama." He was in a predicament. Obama had indeed left him up the tree with no way down out of it. Obama could have said that he had been wrong in making the statements that had derailed the talks and that would have gotten Abbas out of the tree, but apologizing is not something Obama does – he is too much in love with his image reflecting in a pool.

Peace talks between Israel and the Arabs have been ongoing since the mid-1970s, resulting thus far in treaties with Egypt (1979) and Jordan (1994). Talks with the Palestinians began in 1991 and, at the time of writing, have proven to be fruitless. The Palestinians are showing no sincere inclinations to forge a peace with Israel.

At the July 2000 Camp David talks Prime Minister Ehud Barak agreed to cede ninety-eight percent of the West Bank, half of Jerusalem that included the Temple Mount – the most sacred site in Judaism – and to demolish most of the settlements across the Green Line.[2] Yasser Arafat turned the offer down, left Camp David and began a low-grade war that took the lives of almost two thousand Israelis and some four thousand Palestinians.

Between the years 2006 and 2009, progress was seemingly moving forward as top Palestinian negotiators regularly met with Israel's Foreign Minister Tzipi Livni, Prime Minister Ehud

Olmert, and other top Israeli negotiators in secret meetings behind closed doors. Israelis were becoming increasingly apprehensive as to what their leaders were promising the Palestinians.

Apparently, the talks between the Palestinians, Livni, Olmert, and others followed much the same lines as those of Ehud Barak, but Mahmoud Abbas, who had been Arafat's deputy, refused the offer.

Former United States Secretary of State Condoleezza Rice wrote a book entitled *No Higher Honor*, and in it she details some of the Israel-Palestinian peace talks. Rice described how Abbas rejected the terms of Olmert's peace deal. Abbas, however, denies that the conversation Rice described and quoted in her memoir had taken place at all.

In a July 10, 2012, rebuttal, Rice confirmed the accuracy of her account of a 2008 meeting with Mahmoud Abbas in which he had told her why he could not accept Ehud Olmert's terms for a permanent Israeli-Palestinian peace accord.

In *No Higher Honor* Rice records making a visit to Ram'allah in May 2008, immediately after Olmert had detailed the offer to her, during which she "sketched out the details" of the Israeli proposal, which included an Israeli withdrawal from the West Bank with one-for-one territorial swaps; the division of Jerusalem between Israel and a new Palestinian state; and an international trusteeship to control the Old City. Olmert had suggested symbolic and practical solutions to the Palestinian refugee issue, and offered to allow a limited number of Palestinian refugees (ten thousand) to live in Israel – the first Israeli prime minister to do so.

During an interview with Israel's *Channel 2* news that aired the night of July 7, 2012, Abbas denied the crucial passage in Rice's memoirs about his failure to accept Olmert's peace offer. Regarding the refugee question, Abbas said, according to Rice's account:

> I can't tell four million Palestinians that only five thousand of them can go home.

During the *Channel 2* interview, however, Abbas denied making this statement, adding that no such conversation between him and Rice ever took place.

When the interviewer, Danny Kushmaro, asked Abbas specifically about the quote in Rice's book, he responded: "I absolutely did not say that." Kushmaro then asked whether Rice was lying. "I'm not calling her a liar," the Palestinian Authority president replied. "I am saying that we never had that conversation."

In the same interview, Mahmoud Abbas also denied making a statement attributed to him by a senior United States journalist. In 2009, the deputy editorial page editor of *The Washington Post*, Jackson Diehl, wrote that he met Abbas and discussed with him Olmert's 2008 peace proposal and why the Palestinian side turned it down. "The gaps were wide," Abbas said, according to Diehl's account at the time. "I didn't say that," Abbas said in the interview when Kushmaro asked him about that quote.

But Diehl, like Rice, insists the quotes in his piece were accurate. Diehl told *The Times of Israel*:

> I stand behind the 2009 column I wrote about the meeting that my colleague Fred Hiatt and I had with Mahmoud Abbas, and all of the quotations it contains."

To put the above into perspective, readers need to understand the Arab concept of 'saving face.' It will become clearer as we deal later with some matters. Mahmoud Abbas's denials of having said things that reputable people adamantly attribute to him also involves the Islamic principle of *Taqiyyah*, or misrepresentation to achieve a higher goal.

Returning to the negotiations between the Palestinians and Israelis under Ehud Olmert, some sixteen hundred documents (known today as the Palestine Papers) detailing the behind closed-door agreements being made between the parties were leaked to the terrorist television network *Al-Jazeera*, and also to the preeminent British anti-Israel newspaper the *Guardian*, with the obvious intent of sabotaging the talks. It succeeded. *Al-Jazeera* exposed them as did the *Guardian*. If there were a single shred of decency between those media outlets they would not have exposed the contents of the secret documents at such a delicate stage of the talks. Apparently, *Al-Jazeera* and the *Guardian* were intent on sinking any chance of a Palestinian-Israel accord.

The biggest leak of confidential documents in the history of the

Israel-Palestinian conflict revealed that Palestinian negotiators secretly agreed to accept Israel's annexation of all but one of the settlements built in east Jerusalem. This unprecedented proposal was one of a string of concessions that caused shockwaves on the Palestinian street and also in the wider Arab world.

The documents – many of which were published by the *Guardian* in the succeeding days – also revealed the scale of confidential concessions offered by Palestinian negotiators, including the highly sensitive issue of the right of return of Palestinian refugees.

The documents showed Israeli leaders privately asking for some Arab citizens to be transferred to a new Palestinian state; the intimate level of covert co-operation between Israeli security forces and the Palestinian Authority; how Palestinian Authority leaders were privately tipped off about Israel's 2008-2009 Operation Cast Lead in Gaza, *et cetera*.

The documents showed the Palestinian negotiators agreeing to the annexation of all east Jerusalem settlements except Har Homa. The Palestine Papers show Palestine Liberation Organization (PLO) leaders privately suggesting swapping part of the flashpoint east Jerusalem Arab neighborhood of Sheikh Jarrah for land elsewhere. Most controversially, they also proposed a joint committee to take over the Temple Mount holy sites in Jerusalem's Old City – the neuralgic issue that helped torpedo the Camp David talks after Yasser Arafat refused to concede sovereignty around the Dome of the Rock and *al-Aqsa* mosques.

The Palestinian street was livid at the concessions its negotiators had agreed upon and Mahmoud Abbas was burnt in effigy. Unbelievably, the Palestinian negotiators denied being party to anything of what the Palestine Papers revealed, for them the documents were nothing but a bunch of lies. Saeb Erekat, the chief Palestinian negotiator, resigned in a furious mood declaring that his reputation was being blackened. He has since retrieved his former position, but has restricted himself to bad-mouthing Israel on radio and television and in newspaper interviews.

'Saving face' is very important in the Arab culture. 'Saving face' is also an integral part of Japanese culture. The difference between 'saving face' in the two cultures is that when a Japanese loses 'face' he kills himself, but when an Arab loses 'face' he kills someone else.

It seems an impossible task to negotiate a peace accord with the Palestinians. How can Israel negotiate with a side that cannot be seen to compromise or make concessions? It is apparent that following the Palestine Papers there will be no more compromising on the part of the Palestinians. The Palestinian street has shown that it will not countenance concessions or compromises, and even the negotiators do not have the cojones to stand by what they negotiate.

In July 2012, the then Foreign Minister Avigdor Lieberman blamed the Palestinians for obstructing the peace process. He reiterated his long-held view that no agreement with the Palestinians was possible while Palestinian Authority President Mahmoud Abbas remained in power. The foreign minister said in a statement to *The Times of Israel*:

> In recent months, Israel has made an effort to improve the atmosphere with the Palestinians through a series of goodwill gestures. We think we have taken some bold steps, but that the Palestinians have refused to pick up the ball, and refuse to cease behavior that we can only see as hostile.

Some of the goodwill gestures Lieberman was alluding to was the issuing of an additional eleven thousand permits for construction workers in Israel, bringing the number of Palestinian workers in Israel to more than seventy-five thousand; advancing one hundred and eighty million sheqels (forty-five million dollars) in order that Palestinian Authority salaries could be paid before Ramadan; approving an agreement to build four electric power substations in the West Bank; the removal of several roadblocks in the West Bank; agreeing to start negotiations with Palestinians and British Gas about getting the Gaza off-shore gas field up and running; the signing of an economic accord with the Palestinians aimed at enhancing trade and improving the quality of life for Palestinians; the transfer of some ninety bodies of terrorists; and the release of over one hundred Palestinian terrorists from Israeli prisons who have been held since before the signing of the Oslo Accords in 1993.

Mahmoud Abbas's response to the Israel's goodwill gestures was to write the European Union on July 24, 2012 – coinciding with the European Union-Israel Association Council meeting in Brussels – calling upon the Europeans to freeze discussions about a political upgrade in relations with Israel.

According to an internal Israeli government memo made known to the *Jerusalem Post* on August 2, 2012, the Palestinian failure to respond positively to the series of Israeli goodwill gestures shows that Palestinian Authority President Mahmoud Abbas is "unable to enter into negotiations that will require concessions."

As aforementioned, among Israel's 2012 goodwill measures to the Palestinians was the advancement of millions of dollars to facilitate payment of Palestinian Authority salaries before Ramadan. Palestinian Authority President Mahmoud Abbas and Prime Minister and Finance Minister Salam Fayyad perpetually wail about the Palestinians' financial difficulties, and are constantly begging donor countries to increase aid to the Palestinians.

In September 2012, in one of his weekly radio addresses, Salam Fayyad renewed his appeal to Arab and Western donors to provide the Palestinian Authority with urgent financial aid to ease the economic hardships. Fayyad said the Palestinian Authority has been suffering from a severe financial crisis due to the lack of international aid.

Abbas and Fayyad have somehow managed to disperse billions in aid while micro-managing a population of only two million. Abbas's estimated one-hundred-million-dollar fortune, along with individual personal fortunes worth millions of dollars held by a number of high-ranking Palestinian Authority officials may provide clues to where a lot of the aid has gone and why the Palestinian Authority is such an economic basket case.

Some donor countries that have collectively given billions of dollars and euros to the Palestinian Authority may also be unaware that Mahmoud Abbas personally authorized a percentage of the Authority's budget be paid into bank accounts of convicted terrorists serving sentences in Israeli prisons, these funds are administered by Salam Fayyad.

A September 3, 2012, *Channel 2* television report showed that thousands of Palestinian terrorists in Israeli prisons not only receive salaries, but bonuses are also paid for wives and for each child; families of suicide bombers also receive monthly salaries.

Terror is the quintessential export of Palestinians, and Abbas and Fayyad wish to reward and honor what they consider to be an admirable Palestinian quality residing in those who have killed Israelis. Abbas and Fayyad mandated an equal opportunity benefit – terrorists from Abbas's Fatah, Gaza's Hamas, and Gaza's Islamic Jihad are all treated equally – at a cost of tens of millions of dollars.

Starting in 2003, Palestinian law mandated the distribution of monthly salaries to "security detainees" in Israeli prisons. Salaries began at a monthly two hundred and fifty dollars, but in 2011 Fayyad tripled the pay. Today, salaries rise according to the severity of sentences and for years served.

Abdullah Barghouti, a Hamas bomb-maker who was sentenced in 2004 to sixty-seven life terms for orchestrating the killings of sixty-seven Israelis, currently receives a salary of fifteen hundred dollars, but this amount will continue rising.

Another Hamas terrorist, Abbas al-Sayyeed, convicted of planning the 2002 Park Hotel massacre, in which thirty Israeli civilians were killed as they sat down for a Passover meal, is paid three thousand dollars, and this also is rising.

Terrorists who may have murdered but a single Israeli, who have sat in Israeli prisons for thirty years or more, receive a basic salary of four thousand dollars.

Palestinian streets and public squares are also named after the most murderous of terrorists as a mark of respect for their accomplishments.

Palestinian news source *Ma'an* reported that Mahmoud Abbas was adamant about gaining United Nations recognition of Palestine as an "occupied state" rather than as a disputed territory. Speaking near Nablus at the Al-Najah National University, Abbas promised to continue his campaign regardless of the obstacles he may face:

> Even if this step conflicts with other parties' interests, we will not step back. Israel neither halted settlement activities, nor recognized the Palestinian territory occupied in 1967 as occupied territory. Thus, the only choice we have is to go to the United Nations equipped with a united Arab stance.

Mahmoud Abbas made his bid for recognition of Palestine at the United Nations General Assembly on November 29, 2012, against strong opposition to the move by Israel and the United States. With the overt anti-Israel makeup of the General Assembly the result of the vote was a foregone conclusion: the vote was one hundred and thirty-eight in favor, nine (the United States, Israel, Canada, the Czech Republic, Palau, Micronesia, Nauru, Panama and the Marshall Islands) against and forty-one abstentions. As former ambassador to the United States, ambassador to the United Nations, and Vice President of the United Nations General Assembly, Abba Eban, once put it:

> If Algeria introduced a General Assembly Resolution that the world was flat and that Israel had flattened it, it would pass one hundred to ten with fifty abstentions.

That is pretty much what happened in the General Assembly on November 29, 2012. And Abba Eban had been dead for ten years when the General Assembly voted to recognize "Palestine" as a non-member state.

The November 29 date was emblematic – on November 29, 1947, the United Nations General Assembly adopted the resolution recommending the implementation of the Partition Plan that was meant to lead to the creation of independent Jewish and Arab states in Palestine. Israel accepted the Partition Plan – the Arabs rejected it. November 29 is also the official United Nations annual International Day of Solidarity with the Palestinian People, a day when the General Assembly passes anti-Israel resolutions year in and year out without anyone looking at the text of the resolution. Thus, Mahmoud Abbas chose the November 29 date to go before the General Assembly to have "Palestine" recognized as a state under occupation. From that date the games really began.

(Whether by coincidence or divine machination, it is a curious fact that in 2003, when this book was just in the beginning stages, the author took photographs in the Judean Desert for use on its cover. Nine years later, when the book was finally in its closing stage and the photograph's were at last required, it was found that the date on the computer folder was 29 November 2003.)

Abbas returned to a hero's welcome in Ram'allah declaring that the Palestinians now had a state and that "Jerusalem is the eternal capital of the sovereign State of Palestine." Abbas also told his ecstatic Palestinian audience that he pledged to work toward seeking the release of Palestinian "heroes" from Israeli prisons. The "heroes" Abbas mentioned are the convicted Palestinian terrorists, murderers of Israeli civilians, some of whom had their lives snuffed out when they were only a matter of weeks or months old (in March 2001, a Palestinian sniper shot ten-month-old Shalhevet Pass in the head as she was sleeping in her stroller in a Hebron playground).

For all the grandiose speeches, the celebrations, the firing of machine guns in the air, *et cetera*, the General Assembly's vote in favor of "Palestine" changes nothing on the ground, "Palestine" as a non-member state has only symbolic value at best. The Palestinian delegation at the United Nations took it upon themselves to replace their brass "Palestinian Observers" plaque with a freshly minted "State of Palestine" plaque. United Nations Secretary-General Ban Ki-noon noticed the new plaque and knew that the official sign makers were not working that day; Ki-noon ordered the Palestinians to remove the plaque. However, *The Times of Israel* carried a report on December 25, 2012, claiming that during the previous week the United Nations officially switched from "Palestine" to "State of Palestine," and all documents and name plates at the United Nations will refer to the "State of Palestine" and President Mahmoud Abbas as "Head of State of the State of Palestine." But scholars of international law are still arguing whether Palestine can truly be considered a state, since it does not fulfill all the criteria that usually determines statehood (see below).

Like the new United Nations plaque, Abbas's Fatah faction of the Palestinian Liberation Organization (PLO) has introduced a new logo that is replete with bellicose symbols. These symbols include the barrel of a rifle (symbolizing the armed struggle against Israel); a Palestinian *keffiyeh* (male headscarf) that eliminates Israel by covering the entire territory from the Jordan River to the Mediterranean Sea; the Dome of the Rock on Jerusalem's Temple Mount (symbolizing Palestinian sovereignty over the city); a white dove in shackles (symbolizing the shacked peace process); and a door key (symbolizing the "Right of Return" for all Palestinian refugees and their descendants). The gun barrel and door key are made to form the Arabic words: "State and Victory."

The results of a December poll conducted by the Arab World Research and Development (AWAD) showed that for the first time since 2006, more Palestinians (forty-two percent) in the West Bank favor Hamas's armed-resistance policy over Fatah's political policy. Combining the poll results from the West Bank with those from the Gaza Strip, some eighty-eight percent of Palestinians favor armed struggle as the way to achieve independence.

Israel had repeatedly warned both the Palestinians and the international community that Israel would not sit idly by, but that there would be consequences if Mahmoud Abbas took unilateral action by going to the United Nations seeking recognition for "Palestine." Abbas made good on his threat and the same international community that was the "guarantor" of the Oslo Accords, under which the parties must settle all disputes by negotiation – it being expressly forbidden to take unilateral actions – voted overwhelmingly for Abbas to spurn the Accords that itself had accepted and guaranteed.

Less than twenty-four hours after the General Assembly voted to upgrade "Palestine" to non-member observer status, Israel announced plans to build three-thousand homes in east Jerusalem and the West Bank, in the area known as E-1 (East 1) that links Jerusalem to Ma'aleh Adumim, one of the largest of Israel's "settlements." Israel also announced that it would immediately withhold four hundred and fifty million sheqels (one hundred and eighteen million dollars) from taxes collected for the Palestinian Authority and put those funds toward the Palestinian

Authority's eight hundred million sheqel (two hundred and ten million dollar) unpaid electricity bill.

All told, the Palestinian Authority owes Israel sixteen hundred million sheqels (four hundred and twenty-eight million dollars) in unpaid bills. The withholding of four hundred and fifty million sheqels (one hundred and eighteen million dollars) was a warning to Mahmoud Abbas that Israel could well withhold all the taxes she collects on his behalf until the entire debt has been satisfied. Salam Fayyad, the Palestinian Authority's prime minister and finance minister was shocked – he raged against Israel to the media about the withholding of funds urgently needed for salaries (including salaries for imprisoned terrorists) and spluttered: "it's been sent to the electric company!"

There were torrents of outrage from the international community – notably from Europe – and nine countries, including Australia, Egypt, and Brazil, called in their respective Israeli ambassadors to lodge protests against the actions taken by Israel. Unadulterated hypocrisy! One hundred and seventy-nine countries treated the terms of the Oslo Accords with utter contempt when they either voted for or abstained from voting on an anti-Israel resolution to upgrade "Palestine" from an Observer entity to a Non-member Observer State. Then they have the *chutzpah* to berate the injured party for taking retaliatory action. But Europe, especially Britain, has a history of political duplicity. Belonging to the Blame Israel First Club means members never have to take responsibility for their prejudicial and myopic policies.

At the *Jerusalem Post*'s Diplomatic Conference in December 2012, then Foreign Minister Avigdor Lieberman told diplomats from around the world that:

> When push comes to shove, many world leaders would sacrifice Israel to appease Islamic radicals and buy quiet 'without batting an eyelash.'

Lieberman went on to say that:

> all the promises and expression of commitment to Israel's security from various leaders around the world reminds him of 1938 Czechoslovakia when the country, with international

guarantees, was pressured to sacrifice national interests. The
Nazis then quickly overran the country. Israel will not be a
second Czechoslovakia.

Ignoring the international community's protests, Israel fast-
forwarded a number of building projects of which some had been
placed on the back burner due to causing a near major United
States-Israel diplomatic crisis. After four days of marathon
meetings in December by Interior Ministry and the Jerusalem
Municipality's planning committees, it was decided to accelerate
the construction of some six thousand five hundred apartments
over the pre-1967 Green Line, but within the boundaries of
the city of Jerusalem; eight hundred of the homes are for Arab
residents. Jerusalem City Councilor, Yair Gabai, said:

Prime Minister Binyamin Netanyahu stopped the discussion of
these projects due to outside pressure from so many places.
The moment Palestinians went to the United Nations and went
unilaterally, the prime minister gave a green light to do all the
projects. Everything was ready years ago, we were just waiting
for a green light.

The howls of rage that came from the international community
was unprecedented. The United States spokeswoman for the
State Department, Victoria Nuland, issued an unusually sharp
rebuke and said the United States was:

deeply disappointed that Israel insists on continuing the pattern
of provocative action.

The Palestinians sought a condemnation of Israel by the
United Nations Security Council and fourteen of the fifteen
members of the council voted for a condemnation, but the United
States prevented it, forcing the four European members to issue
a joint statement lambasting Israel. India's representative read
out a similar statement on behalf of the eight Non-Aligned
Movement members of the council, and this was followed by
statement on behalf of India, South Africa, and Brazil. Despite
the unparalleled censoring of Israel's actions, Prime Minister
Binyamin Netanyahu said Israel would continue to build in her
capital; Uzi Landau, Israel's Energy and Water Minister, went
further by saying:

> Just to make it unequivocally clear to anyone: Israel will continue and do in Jerusalem what the British do in London and what the French do in Paris and what our friends in America do in Washington. We do not advise anybody what to do in their own capital and we are going to follow only our own choice regarding Jerusalem.

The condemnation of Israel by President Barack Obama and others of the international community concerning Israeli construction in Judea and Samaria is totally unfair. From the beginning of the Israel-Palestinian peace-process negotiations it was agreed between Israel and the Palestinians, and accepted by the international community in witnessing and endorsing the Oslo Accords, that the issue of settlements would be one of several issues to be negotiated in the final, permanent status negotiations. Not one of the agreements signed between Israel and the Palestinians contain any limitations on building by either party in the areas under their respective jurisdiction, and the E-1 corridor is in Area C, which is under full Israeli control. Abbas continues to sidestep negotiations with Israel so Israel continues to build.

In the same way as only Palestinian refugees receive the world's attention while eight hundred and fifty thousand Jewish refugees are ignored, so too is the building in the E-1 corridor said to prevent contiguity of a Palestinian state. No mention is ever made of the fact that the E-1 corridor cuts Israel in half. Building in E-1 strengthens Jerusalem and is essential not only for the security of the city, but also for the security of the Jewish state as a whole.

Mahmoud Abbas's unilateral move at the United Nations to have "Palestine" recognized as a non-member state set the cat among the peace pigeons. Abbas was warned that there would be consequences, but he and Fayyad said they were "only threats," but they are learning that Israel's threats can have very sharp teeth.

As was mentioned elsewhere in these pages, in November 2009, Israel succumbed to pressure from the Obama administration and announced a ten-month, construction freeze in the West Bank. The freeze was a bid to entice Mahmoud Abbas back to the negotiating table, but he refused to meet with Prime

Minister Netanyahu. Abbas refused to meet with with Netanyahu during that construction freeze and has consistently refused to meet with him until the time of writing. But when Netanyahu refused to extend the building freeze further than the ten-month moratorium, Abbas pitifully bemoaned Netanyahu's dashing of Palestinian hopes to restart negotiations.

However, the 2010 ten-month freeze on construction did not apply to Jerusalem and Netanyahu made that clear to the international community. President Obama and his administration officials made Netanyahu's life difficult over construction in Jerusalem and only in December 2012 did Secretary of State Hillary Clinton acknowledge that Netanyahu specifically excluded Jerusalem and its environs from the building freeze. In December 2012, senior Israeli government officials causticly blamed Obama for overtly encouraging the European Union to protest the latest building plans for the E-1 corridor.

Perhaps Obama and his collegues in the capitals of the countries of the European Community should read their copies of the Oslo Accords, which the head of the new Non-member Observer State of "Palestine" says "is dead." Go figure!

It was said in Chapter eleven that the Palestinian leadership only wanted a recognized state in order to gain access to the International Court of Justice and the International Criminal Court, both of which are affiliated organs of the United Nations. Gaining access to these courts will, as previously stated, allow the Palestinians to flood these Courts with legal charges against Israel. Within days of the General Assembly vote taking place Palestinian lawyers were busy preparing criminal charges against Israel, but the process may not be quite as straightforward and speedy as the Palestinians hope.

The International Criminal Court and the International Court of Justice can only hear petitions from bona fide states in good standing with the international community. The General Assembly upgrade of the Palestinians from an Observer entity to a Non-member Observer state has not made "Palestine" a state, nor did it bestow statehood upon the Palestinians. The United Nations General Assembly does not have the legal or political power to establish states, the United Nations Security Council does. Resolutions carried by the General Assembly are non-binding, they are nothing more than non-obligatory recommendations that express the political views of the states that voted for them. Therefore, upon receiving the first petition from "Palestine" charging Israel with criminal action, the Courts would first have to define what a bona fide state is and what it is not.

The Courts are legally bound to uphold some semblance of legality insofar as law is concerned, they cannot be just like the members of the General Assembly which seem unable to differentiate between chalk and cheese.

Internationally accepted requirements for statehood as laid down in the 1933 Montevideo Convention on the Rights and Duties of States include "a unified, contiguous territorial unit," which the Palestinian Authority does not have due to the Palestinian territories being divided into two areas – the West Bank and the Gaza Strip. A further statehood requirement is for:

> responsible governance of its people, and the capability of fulfilling international commitments and responsibilities.

The Palestinian Authority is totally unable to meet either of the above two requirements – Hamas is recognized by a number of countries as a terrorist organization and formed its own government in the Gaza Strip, headed by Ismail Haniya. Hamas drove the officials of Mahmoud Abbas's Fatah faction out of Gaza by force of arms in June 2007 in a brief civil war, and, according to Israeli intelligence, Hamas is preparing for a similar takeover of the West Bank. This was corroborated in a British *Sunday Times* article cited by the *Jerusalem Post* on December 23, 2012. The article claimed:

> Hamas leader Khaled Mashaal instructed the terror group's sleeper cells in the West Bank to prepare themselves for an armed struggle to take control of the Palestinian territory.

When Hamas takes control over the West Bank (it is not a matter of "if," but "when") the rocket fire upon Israeli cities will triple and Ben-Gurion international airport, along with its air traffic, will be a prime target for Hamas's surface to air missiles.

Mahmoud Abbas is the Palestinian Authority President based in Ram'allah in the West Bank and Salam Fayyad is both prime minister and finance minister. At the time of writing Abbas has not stepped foot in the Gaza Strip since before the Hamas military coup in 2007, and under the leadership of Abbas and Fayyad the Palestinian Authority in the West Bank has, as mentioned above, become a financial nightmare for its foreign donor states.

The United Nations Charter also requires that a state seeking membership in the United Nations be "a peace-loving state," which, even by stretching the imagination to the uttermost, "Palestine" certainly is not. During the past decade alone more than twelve thousand rockets have been fired into Israel's population centers by Palestinian jihadists. And three days after the United Nations voted to upgrade the Palestinian entity to Non-member Observer State, Osama Hamdan, the top Hamas official said: "A Palestinian state without an armed struggle against Israel is an illusion." Hamdan also reiterated Hamas's lifelong commitment to liberating Palestine from Israeli hands – "from the river to the sea."

Confirming what the author wrote above, on December 3, four days following the historic vote, United States Ambassador to the United Nations Susan Rice said, *inter alia*:

> a vote elevating the status of the Palestinians at the United Nations did not establish that Palestine is its own separate country.... This resolution does not establish that Palestine is a state.... Nor does passing any resolution create a state where none indeed exists or change the reality on the ground.
>
> In a one hundred and thirty-eight to nine vote, the U.N. General Assembly agreed to upgrade Palestine's status from non-member observer entity to non-member observer state – a critical distinction that technically recognizes Palestine as an independent country.
>
> Today's grand pronouncements will soon fade. And the Palestinian people will wake up tomorrow and find that little about their lives has changed, save that the prospects of a durable peace have only receded.

Despite the Palestinian celebrations, the victory speeches, and all the grandiose proclamations, the Palestinian Authority continues to exist as a mere entity and has a long journey ahead of it before it can be a "sovereign" Palestinian state.

In a Dahaf Institute Survey conducted for the Jerusalem Center for Public Affairs and published in December 2012, it was found that eighty-three percent of Israeli Jews believe that a withdrawal to the 1967 lines and a division of Jerusalem would not bring about and end of the Israel-Palestinian conflict; that sixty-one percent believes that defensible borders are more important than peace for ensuring Israel's security; and that seventy-eight percent would change their vote if the political party they intended to support showed willingness to relinquish Israeli sovereignty in east Jerusalem.

The route that leads to a sovereign state of "Palestine" necessitates the traversing of the road of negotiations with Israel. More unilateral actions by Mahmoud Abbas will be met head on by Israel. The announcement of Israel's intention to build thousand of homes in east Jerusalem and the E-1 corridor, along with the withholding of tax moneys to offset the Palestinian Authority's unpaid bills, is just a warning shot across Abbas's bows.

The great majority of Palestinian officials continue to deny the Holocaust – the genocidal murder of six million Jews by Adolf Hitler and his Nazi party. One who does not share that view is Ziad al-Bandak, a Christian and advisor to Palestinian Authority President Mahmoud Abbas on Christian affairs. Al Bandak visited the Auschwitz-Birkenau complex, laid a wreath, lit a memorial candle, and paid his respects to the dead. Approximately one million Jews were gassed at the complex. Al-Bandak visited both the gas chambers and the crematorium.

A spokesman for the Hamas terror entity, Fawzi Barhoum, criticized al-Bandak's visit to the Nazi death camp. Barhoum was quoted as saying the visit by Ziad al-Bandak was "unjustified and unhelpful." Barhoum further called Bandak's visit to Auschwitz as "a marketing of a false Zionist alleged tragedy." Islamists in general deny the Holocaust happened as part of their narrative for rejecting Israel's existence. The denials are often at the encouragement of Iranian President Mahmoud Ahmadinejad, who has called the genocidal Holocaust "a myth."

Palestine Liberation Organization Ambassador to India, Adli Sadeq, wrote in the official Palestinian Authority daily, *Al-Hayat Al-Jadida*, on November 26, 2011, that Israel is wrong if it assumes that only Hamas loathes Israel. He writes that Fatah, Mahmoud Abbas's 'moderate' faction of the Palestinian Authority, does not respect Israel either. Sadeq contends that the Palestinian Authority and Fatah utterly reject the notion that Israel has any right to exist:

> The demands of the Israeli enemy are strange and amazing demands, unique in the history of conflicts. The Israelis are not satisfied with Palestinian recognition that is a function of their state and its existence, but want recognition of the eternal right of Israel to exist. Possibly their nature will bring them to ask for compensation for the years that have passed without their state's existence, during the time it had the right to exist upon our skulls. They have a common mistake, or misconception by which they fool themselves, assuming that Fatah accepts them and recognizes the right of their state to exist, and that it is Hamas alone that loathes them and does not recognize the right of this state to exist. They ignore the fact that this state, based on a fabricated Zionist enterprise, never had any shred of a right to exist. Hamas, Fatah and the others are not waging war against Israel right now for reasons related to balance of power.
>
> There are no two Palestinians who disagree over the fact that Israel exists, and recognition of it is restating the obvious, but recognition of its right to exist is something else, different from recognition of its existence.

For decades Palestinian leaders have denied Israel's right to exist, and Palestinian leaders and official Palestinian media refer to all of Israel as "occupied," including cities like Haifa and Jaffa and places like the northern Galilee and the southern Negev.

It was postulated above that it is not possible for Israel to negotiate with a side that will not compromise or make concessions. But Israel is further handicapped in negotiations by having a side that refuses to recognize the right of Israel to even exist.

It has also been said two times previously that the Palestinian leadership desires a state only in order to gain access to the two United Nations-affiliated Courts to facilitate legal actions against the state of Israel and Israeli individuals. For the Palestinians, a state is merely a stepping stone toward their ultimate goal of eliminating Israel as a nation.

And the author has also stated before that prior to the creation of the state of Israel in 1948 there never was any such entity as a Palestinian Arab, it is a fabrication that the international community has swallowed whole.[4]

Corroborating the fictional appearance of the Palestinian nation is Azmi Bishara. Azmi Bishara is a former member of Israel's parliament (Knesset) and founder of the Balad Party – he is a Palestinian intellectual, academic, and writer. In 2007, Bishara fled Israel and resigned from the Knesset after being questioned by police on suspicion of aiding and passing information to the enemy during wartime; contacts with a foreign agent; and receiving large sums of money transferred from abroad. However, while serving as an Arab member of Israel's parliament, Bishara made a famous statement:

> I do not think there is a Palestinian nation at all. I think there is an Arab nation. I think it's a colonialist invention – a Palestinian nation. When were there any Palestinians? Where did they come from? I think there is an Arab nation.

There was never any Palestinian nation for Israel to invade, neither was there a Palestinian people who were displaced or occupied. The entire story of a Palestinian people whose supposed history travels through the sands of time is an utter hoax, a complete fabrication. Certainly, there were Arabs living in Palestine, but the land was, as a whole, barren and unoccupied. This fact has been borne out by numbers of historians and pilgrims who wrote of their travels through the centuries. Perhaps the most notable traveler and writer was American author Mark Twain, who toured Palestine in 1867 and who wrote in his distinguished book *Innocents Abroad*:

> Come to Galilee ... these unpeopled deserts, these rusty mounds of barrenness, that never, never, never do shake the glare from their harsh outlines ... that melancholy ruin of Capernaum .... We reached Tabor safely ... we never saw a human being on the whole route.

> Bethlehem and Bethany, in their poverty and their humiliation, have nothing about them now ... the hallowed spot where the shepherds watched their flocks by night, and where the angels sang, "Peace on earth, good will to men," is untenanted by any living creature ... Bethsaida and Chorzin have vanished from the earth, and the "desert places" round about them ... sleep in the hush of a solitude that is inhabited only by birds of prey and skulking foxes.
>
> Stirring scenes ... occur in the valley of Jezreel no more. There is not a solitary village throughout its whole extent – not for thirty miles in either direction.
>
> Palestine sits in sackcloth and ashes ... desolate and unlovely ... it is a dreamland.

Palestinians and other Arabs also regurgitate a myth that Jerusalem has been an Arab and Islamic city for thousands of years – since the dawn of time. However, Jerusalem is never once mentioned in the Qu'ran so, obviously, the city was never of any importance to Muhammed and his original followers. And on July 15, 1889, the *Pittsburgh Dispatch* reported that thirty thousand of Jerusalem's forty thousand residents were Jewish and that most of the other ten thousand inhabitants were Christians.

The myths and claims of Palestinian identity is another tactical maneuver in the Islamic war waged against Israel to bring about her destruction. This was admitted to the Dutch daily *Trouw* by Zuheir Muhsin, a member of the executive council of the Palestine Liberation Organization and late head of its Military Department:

> Yes, the existence of a separate Palestinian identity serves only tactical purposes. The founding of a Palestinian state is a new tool in the continuing battle against Israel. In fact, there is no Palestinian people. Only for political reasons do we speak of a Palestinian identity.

The late Feisal al-Husseini, the Palestine Liberation Organization's minister for Jerusalem and a member of the Palestinian negotiating team, said in November 1994:

Peace for us means the destruction of Israel. We are preparing for an all-out war, a war which will last for generations. Since January 1965, when Fatah [Mahmoud Abbas's 'moderate' PLO faction] was born, we have become the most dangerous enemy that Israel has. We shall not rest until the day when we return to our home, and until we destroy Israel.

Despite all the Palestinian threats to destroy Israel, the world chooses to swallow the entire pottage of Palestinian phantasms. Not only has the world proven itself to be one hundred percent gullible, but it does not even bother to make an attempt at unearthing the true facts. It does, however beat up on Israel as a consequence of its utter ignorance of the truth.

When a new, sovereign State of Palestine does come into being it will soon become a hotbed of Islamic terrorism. Any peace treaty that will have been signed would soon be found to be a worthless piece of paper and the Israel Defense Force would be forced to recapture the lands ceded to the Palestinians. Already there are the precedents of the Hizb'allah takeover of Lebanon following Israel's unilateral withdrawal from the Security Zone in southern Lebanon; the Hamas takeover of Gaza following Israel's unilateral disengagement from Gaza; and the steady terrorist Islamization of the Sinai Peninsular, from which Israel withdrew in 1979 in accordance with her peace treaty with Anwar Sadat. Each of these areas were ceded by Israel in the interests of peace with her neighbors, and each of the areas have become launching pads for terror attacks and tens of thousands of missiles against the Jewish state.

Consider the following: Until 1988 all inhabitants of the West Bank (biblical Judea and Samaria) were Jordanian citizens. At that time they were not stateless. So, had the Arabs not launched a war of annihilation against Israel the Arab residents of the West Bank would still have been Jordanians, and the territory that Jordan had annexed and renamed the "West Bank" would still have been part of Jordan. This brings us around full circle to what the author already presented in Chapter two, that in 1948 King Abdullah said: "Palestine and Jordan are one." And in 1970 Crown Prince Hassan, heir to Jordan's throne, told the Jordanian

National Assembly that:

> Palestine is Jordan and Jordan is Palestine. There is one people and one land, with one history and one destiny.

And that in 1974, Yasser Arafat, the terrorist leader of the Palestine Liberation Organization said: "What you call Jordan is actually Palestine."

And finally, in 1981, Abdullah's son, King Hussein, said: "The truth is that Jordan is Palestine and Palestine is Jordan." This he repeated in 1984. By their own actions and statements the Arabs have already established a Palestinian state and they call it Jordan.

On May 27, 1967, just nine days before the outbreak of the Six-Day War, Ahmed Shukairy, Yasser Arafat's predecessor as chairman of the Palestine Liberation Organization, thundered:

> D-Day is approaching. The Arabs have waited nineteen years for this and will not flinch from the war of liberation.

On June 1, 1967, Shukairy trumpeted:

> This is a fight for the homeland – it is either us or the Israelis. There is no middle road. The Jews of Palestine will have to leave. We shall destroy Israel and its inhabitants and as for the survivors – if there are any – the boats are ready to deport them.

It was the Arabs who launched their overtly genocidal aggression against the Jewish state, which resulted in spectacular failure, but the consequences of that failure has been forced upon Israel's head. The mortifying defeat of the multiple Arab army attack against the nascent state of Israel in 1948 is known throughout the Arab world as the *Nakba* – "the Catastrophe." The humiliating war of 1967, which was over in just six days, is known as the *Naksah* – "the Setback."

Ahmed Shukairy clearly elucidated the rationale of the post-1967 staged strategy, and the crucial role the fabrication of a "Palestinian identity" had to play in its implementation:

> For tactical reasons, Jordan, which is a sovereign state with defined borders, cannot raise claims to Haifa and Jaffa, while as a Palestinian, I can undoubtedly demand Haifa, Jaffa,

Beersheba and Jerusalem. However, the moment we reclaim
our right to all of Palestine, we will not wait even a minute to
unite Palestine and Jordan.

There we have it from the horse's mouth. To the Arabs, "Palestine" is a highly fluid geographical entity used to designate any territory where the Jews exercise control, and which Arabs have a "sacred duty" to "liberate." This is an intermediate aim in a staged strategy to eliminate the Jewish state, whatever its borders.

The goal is to make what is left of Israel's divine inheritance and the Jordanian state one entity – the true Palestinian state. And for the Arabs, fighting must continue as long as it takes to reach that goal.

In January 2012, the media monitoring group Palestinian Media Watch released a video of the Grand Mufti of Jerusalem, Mohammed Hussein, reciting a *hadith* (a saying attributed to Islam's prophet Mohammed) calling for the killing of Jews: "The day of judgment will not come until you fight the Jews," Hussein said in the clip. He also quoted another *hadith* which said:

> The Jew will hide behind stones and trees. The stones and trees will call, "Oh Muslim, Oh servant of Allah, this is a Jew behind me, come and kill him."

Mohammed Hussein, appointed by the Palestinian Authority, has refused to retract his comments, insisting he had not called for the killing of Jews, but had simply been quoting Islam's prophet, whose words he could not change and which all Muslims revere as the final revelation of truth.

On August 3, 2012, a large Palestinian flag was flown over the Temple Mount, in a deliberate and flagrant violation of Israeli sovereignty. No one could have heard about this outrageous public display of a foreign flag flying over Israel's holiest site in her capital city, or read about it in any mainstream media, because it was not reported. The incident elicited no response whatsoever. Such is the intense hostility toward the Jewish state of Israel.

Eight weeks earlier it was reported that an Israeli policeman who displayed a small Israeli flag on the Temple Mount during a routine patrol was relieved of his duties, and would face additional disciplinary measures. The Islamic clerics were enraged and the Israeli police response was swift and severe. *Wakf* (Supreme Islamic Council) officials viewed the incident with the utmost severity and spoke of it in their sermons, emphasizing that the Temple Mount – Arabic *Al-Haram Al-Sharif* – is Muslim only.

Sheikh Ikrimah Sabri was outraged and said:

> The display of an Israeli flag is an act of aggression, with the intention of applying Israeli sovereignty on the Al Aqsa mosque.

Sabri is the head of the *Wakf* and a senior preacher in the Al-Aqsa mosque. He was originally appointed by Yasser Arafat, not only to the position of head of the *Wakf*, but also as Mufti of Jerusalem and Palestine in order to gain Palestinian control of the Temple Mount. Arafat's appointment of Sabri was in opposition to Jordan, which had exercised control of the Mount since 1948.

The Temple Mount is under Israeli sovereignty, but Israeli official do not possess the cojones to enforce Israel's sovereignty for fear of Muslim anger. The Al-Aqsa mosque, the third most holy site in Islam, was originally the sixth-century Christian church of Saint Mary, which was burned and extensively damaged by the Persians in 614 and later converted and enlarged into the present Muslim mosque. Worldwide, Muslims have converted thousands of Christian churches into mosques. Muslims believe the turning of Christian churches into mosques is a display of Islam's domination and superiority over Christianity.

The Temple Mount has been a flashpoint for the venting of Muslim anger ever since Israel retook control in 1967. Prior to 1967 the Temple Mount was a little-used, weed-covered area. It was the renewed Israeli presence that spurred Muslims to proclaim the "sanctity" of Islam's holy place. Today, there can be little doubt that if the Dome of the Rock and the Al-Aqsa mosque are destroyed or severely damaged in one of the coming wars and the area falls again to the Israelis, Muslim rage will force-march itself upon Israel from the four corners of the world.

Hamas is a dedicated, fanatical Islamic terror organization operating out of the Gaza Strip. Its firing of thousands of missiles at Israel's southern cities and towns finally forced Israel to launch Operation Cast Lead in December 2008. Although Hamas suffered a blistering defeat, from which Gaza has yet to recover (widespread destruction and a kill rate ratio of one hundred to one), Hamas acts and boasts like it actually won the twenty-two-day war and is always eager for another bout with Israel.

In November 2012, in response to prolonged intermittent firing of hundreds of missiles from the Gaza Strip into Israeli cities and towns, the Israel Defense Force launched operation Pillar of Defense and heavily bombed Hamas's missile arsenals, launchers, and other military targets. More of Gaza became heaps of rubble – adding to the existing rubble from 2008-2009.

It is not that Hamas never learns, Hamas operatives actually welcome death due to their belief that dying for the cause of Allah ensures them seventy eternal virgins in the Islamic afterlife. The much higher death toll among Gaza's civilian population compared to Israel's scores Hamas points by bringing international condemnation upon Israel.

Hamas's tactics are simple, criminal, and brutal. By firing missiles into Israeli cities and towns it knows that Israel will have no option but to respond with force at some stage. Hamas hides its missiles in underground concrete bunkers hidden among the civilian population and also fires the missiles from underground. Hamas provides no shelter for the population against Israeli air attacks – Palestinian civilians are no more than human shields for Hamas's weapons caches.

Following the ceasefire that ended Israel's Pillar of Defense, Hamas's exiled leader, Khaled Mashaal, visited the Gaza Strip via Egypt. Mashaal congratulated Hamas on its 'victory' over Israel and vowed that Hamas would destroy Israel and liberate every inch of Palestine from the Jordan River to the Mediterranean Sea. According to an *Israel Radio* report Denmark, Finland, Portugal, and Ireland pressured European ministers to condemn Israel solely for her E-1 construction plans, making no mention of Mashaal's incitement-filled speech. Israel protested harshly and accused Europe of being one-sided. In the end, a brief statement that included a mild rebuke of Hamas's call for Israel's destruction was issued, but four European Union states opposed condemning Mashaal's speech. Hamas is also preventing European monitors from returning to the Rafah border crossing with

Egypt, despite and agreement between Israel and the Palestinian Authority requiring their presence at the border. But Europe looks the other way.

Despite Hamas's deliberate use of human shields in its fight against Israel, Palestinian civilian deaths are very low in comparison to other conflicts – regardless of the international community's one-sided outcries For instance, in the twenty-two day Gaza War (Operation Cast Lead), eleven hundred and sixty-six Gazans were killed. Of those killed seven hundred and nine were positively identified as Hamas gunmen – a ratio of about one civilian for every three Hamas combatants. In the eight-day Pillar of Defense operation one hundred and seventy-seven Palestinians were killed. Of that number one hundred and twenty were involved with the missile barrages – a ratio of around one civilian for each two terrorists killed. In contrast, according to a 2001 study by the International Committee of the Red Cross, there has been an average of ten civilian deaths for every soldier killed in wars fought since the mid-twentieth century. Even during the 1999 Kosovo War, North Atlantic Treaty Organization (NATO) forces killed four civilians for every Serbian combatant.

Son of Hamas is the title of a book by Mosab Hassan Yousef, the son of the founder of Hamas, Sheikh Hassan Yousef. The story of Mosab Hassan Yousef is very unusual. Mosab Hassan has a knack for controversy and has already broken every prohibition in the Palestinian book – he has worked for Israeli intelligence and converted to Christianity. Now he is working on producing a new film which is sure to be no less sensational: a biography of the life of Muhammed, the prophet of Islam.

"Islam is not a religion of peace. It's a religion of war," Yousef said on his first visit to Israel in June 2012. "Muslims don't even know the true nature of their own religion."

Mosab Hassan rejected his Islamist upbringing to help Israel fight terror. If he had the chance, he says, he'd tell his father: "Leave Hamas. You have created a monster."

Yousef broke ranks with Hamas in 1997 and began working for the Israel's General Security Service (Shin Bet). Ten years later, after helping Israel thwart dozens of terror attacks and arrest many members of his former movement, Yousef left for the United States where he sought political asylum and later converted to Christianity.

In June 2012, Yousef arrived in Israel with an invitation from the Knesset (Israel's Parliament). Yousef said he was in Israel on a personal visit "to inspire a new generation of Palestinians."

Another movie, expected to be produced before Yousef's "Muhammed," is a film adaptation of Mosab Hassan's 2010 autobiography *Son of Hamas*, in which he recounts the tale of his cooperation with Israeli intelligence. The book has already been translated into twenty-five languages and is available for free download in Arabic on Yousef's website.

Israeli officials voiced their concern about Yousef's arrival in Israel as his life is still under threat, but they arranged that Mosab Hassan would come into Israel without either visa or passport.

Hamas is a dedicated radical Islamic terror organization, but the son of its founder, Mosab Hassan Yousef, saved many Israeli lives and is firmly against the shedding of blood by either Israel or Hamas. Israel owes a large debt of gratitude to Yousef. He is truly a Palestinian that has been formed in a different mold. If more Palestinians were like Mosab Hassan Yousef, Israel would have a negotiated peace treaty by the end of the week.

Even the big boys are ganging up on Israel. According to Isabella Ginor and Gideon Remez, who provide documentation from high-ranking Soviet military officials, the Soviet Union actually orchestrated the 1967 Six-Day War with the intention of destroying Israel's nuclear reactor at Dimona.[5]

The Soviet Union was also heavily engaged in the 1969-1971 War of Attrition that was launched by Egypt against Israel along the Suez Canal in order to test Israel's ability and determination to hold onto her gains from the 1967 Six-Day War.

In a rare exposure of Soviet military activities, an article in the Soviet magazine *Ekho Planety* was cited in a July 7, 1989, *Jerusalem Post* article entitled: "Soviets say their units downed Israeli planes in War of Attrition." The report stated:

> Soviet Air Force Units and Anti Aircraft troops took part in armed clashes between Egypt and Israel from late 1969 to early 1971. Soviet anti-aircraft units, using rockets, had succeeded

in shooting down a number of Israeli Skyhawk, Mirage, and Phantom warplanes, but had suffered heavy casualties from Israeli bombing raids.

On July 29, 2012, during a brief visit to Israel, United States presidential candidate Mitt Romney called Jerusalem "the capital of Israel," which was music to Israeli ears due to Europe and its media refusing to to acknowledge Jerusalem as the capital of Israel. However, China's official press immediately leaped onto the bandwagon and said that Romney's statements "totally neglect historical facts." One can only wonder where China has been keeping its multi-thousand-year-old head during the past three thousand years? China's knowledge of Israel is known to be abysmal at best.

The Bible tells us that Israel's King David first made Jerusalem the capital of Israel around one thousand B.C. and his son, King Solomon, commissioned the building of the first temple in the city.

After the Romans crushed the Bar-Kochba revolt in one-thirty-five A.D. Jews were not allowed to live in Jerusalem or its environs. This edict held good for three years and that period was the only time the Jewish nation had been separated from its capital. And, as was aforementioned, even in 1889 the vast majority of Jerusalem's inhabitants were Jews and the balance were mainly Christian expatriates.

It is China's official criticisms of Romney's statement that "totally neglect historical facts." Romney's July 2012 affirmation that Jerusalem is Israel's capital is totally confirmed by historical facts. But, since becoming the world's manufacturing center for cheap goods, China is fast becoming the world's bully center and readily pushes its nose into other nations' internal affairs – this time it took aim at Israel.

China sided with Hamas in the eight-day November 2012 Pillar of Defense conflict; backed the Palestinians in their bid for a status upgrade at the United Nations; and condemned Israel's plans to build in east Jerusalem and the E-1 corridor. China has donated a million dollars to the Palestinian Authority and Mahmoud Abbas is seeking to draw China onto his side in his personal spat with Prime Minister Netanyahu.

With the big boys hitting on Israel, together with the great majority of the one hundred and ninety-three members of the United Nations, Israel seems to have little chance of either diplomatic or physical survival. With the continual escalation of antisemitism around the globe and the deepening anti-Israel phobia in both the Western and Islamic worlds, it would indeed seem that the solution is going be for the nations to face-off military against Israel to settle their disputes. And, as ridiculous as that may sound, that is what *"the King and Maker of Israel"* has in mind. In Joel 3:2 *"the Holy One of Israel"* says:

> *I will gather all nations, and bring them down to the Valley of Jehoshaphat; and I will enter into judgment with them there on account of My people, My heritage Israel* (Joel 3:2).

Everything appears to hinge upon Jerusalem, the city that the nations will not admit to being the capital of Israel. On January 2, 1989, Yasser Arafat appealed to the Muslim world for Islamists to come and wage jihad to liberate Jerusalem. And on October 11, 2012, Sheikh Mohammed Badie, the Egyptian Muslim Brotherhood's Supreme Guide also called on the Islamic world to liberate Jerusalem from the Israelis by jihad. The Palestinians vow never to give up the fight for Jerusalem and the *BBC*'s (British Broadcasting Corporation) Olympic website for London's 2012 Olympic Games listed no capital city for Israel, but its profile for "Palestine" showed "East Jerusalem" as its capital.

Mahmoud Abbas assures himself that he has the backing of the international community and that Israel will be forced to bend due to United Nations sanctions. It is a given that "Palestine" will eventually be recognized as a sovereign state under Israeli occupation by the antisemitic United Nations. Such recognition could trigger a resolution for military intervention against Israel to settle the Israel-Arab conflict. Possibly it will be the United Nations that will gather against Israel over Jerusalem, or it may be a confederation of armies made up from the greater part of the Islamic world. It may also be a case of 'come one, come all.' Perhaps the nations are given to thinking that the *"LORD of hosts"* was merely exhaling hot air when He said:

*Behold, I will make Jerusalem a cup of drunkenness to all the surrounding peoples, when they lay siege against Judah and Jerusalem. And it shall happen in that day that I will make Jerusalem a very heavy stone for all peoples; all who would heave it away will surely be cut in pieces, **though all nations of the earth are gathered against it** (Zechariah 12:2-3).*

The L<small>ORD</small> goes further:

On that day I will make the leaders of Judah like a firepot in a woodpile, like a flaming torch among sheaves. They will consume right and left all the surrounding peoples, but Jerusalem will remain intact in her place (Zechariah 12:6 NIV).

And it is worth repeating the Scripture used at the beginning of this chapter:

And this shall be the plague with which the L<small>ORD</small> will strike all the people who fought against Jerusalem: their flesh shall dissolve while they stand on their feet, their eyes shall dissolve in their sockets, and their tongues shall dissolve in their mouths
(Zechariah 14:12).

All the armies of the nations will be crushed and pulverized, then *"**everyone who is left of all the nations** which came against Jerusalem"* (Zechariah 14:16) will have learned respect for Israel's God. They will then come to worship the L<small>ORD</small> in Jerusalem as depicted in Zechariah 14:16. It has been said before that the nations are heading for a confrontation with *"the Holy One of Israel,"* and a reasonable assumption would be that the confrontation is sparked over Jerusalem, *"the city of the great King"* (Psalms 48:2).

A large number of Israelis venerate the Israel Defense Force and boast that it is the best fighting force in the world. Without doubt, the Israel Defense Force is indeed among the very best in the world; its weaponry and equipment are sophisticated, its men and women are brave, courageous, and daring, but were it not for *"the Holy One of Israel"* the Israel Defense Force would have no more strength to withstand its enemies than a dandelion's seed-head would have the strength to resist a strong wind.

Israel's reverence for the Israel Defense Force and her faith in it must be broken; Israel's eyes must be focused upon the LORD from whom the strength of the Israel Defense Force comes. Israel has to be brought into reality and the Israel Defense Force must be seen to be overpowered in order for Israelis to cry out to Him who created her.

In the immediate paragraphs above the author has penned much concerning Jerusalem, the city God Almighty selected for Himself – where He chose to put His name (1 Kings 11:36). It would appear that the Israel Defense Force is initially overcome in the future battle for Jerusalem, the city that has been the center of contention for millennia. It seems to the author that the battle for Jerusalem is also the catalyst for the salvation of the people of Israel.

All the nations will gather themselves against the holy city, the eternal, indivisible capital of Israel, and in the ensuing battle the Israel Defense Force is overwhelmed; half of the city is captured and looted before Israel's *"Maker"* takes up the fight. Here is the scenario in the LORD's own words:

> *For I will gather all the nations to battle against Jerusalem; the city shall be taken, the houses rifled, and the women ravished. Half of the city shall go into captivity, but the remnant of the people shall not be cut off from the city.*
>
> *Then the LORD will go forth and fight against those nations, as He fights in the day of battle. And in that day His feet will stand on the Mount of Olives, which faces Jerusalem on the east. And the Mount of Olives shall be split in two, from east to west, making a very large valley; half of the mountain shall move toward the north and half of it toward the south.*
>
> *Then you shall flee through My mountain valley, for the mountain valley shall reach to Azal. Yes, you shall flee as you fled from the earthquake in the days of Uzziah king of Judah.*

> *Thus the* LORD *my God will come, and all the*
> *saints with You.*
> *It shall come to pass in that day that there will be*
> *no light; the lights will diminish. It shall be one day*
> *which is known to the* LORD *– neither day nor night.*
> *But at evening time it shall happen that it will be*
> *light.*
>
> *And in that day it shall be that living waters shall*
> *flow from Jerusalem, half of them toward the eastern*
> *sea and half of them toward the western sea; in both*
> *summer and winter it shall occur.*
>
> *And the* LORD *shall be King over all the earth.*
> *In that day it shall be – "The* LORD *is one," and His*
> *name one.* (Zechariah 14:2-9).

Israel is to be judged by the Lord and she is being lured into a multi-faceted wilderness expressly for that purpose. Israel will pay dearly for the many sins committed against her *"Maker."* And Israel must pay double due to being the firstborn of the LORD (Exodus 4:22). The right of the firstborn is to receive a double portion of all that his father has (Deuteronomy 21:17), and Israel is the LORD's firstborn son (Exodus 4:22). Israel receives God's double portion, but He also promises to repay Israel double for her iniquity (Jeremiah 16:18), but woe to the ones whom the LORD uses as the instruments of His chastisement – it would have been good for them had they never existed:

> *the* LORD *is the true God; He is the living God and*
> *the everlasting King. At His wrath the earth will*
> *tremble, and the nations will not be able to endure*
> *His indignation* (Jeremiah 10:10).

---

[1] The web address for Jerusalem Center for Public Affairs is http://www.jcpa.org

[2] See Chapter twelve, footnote number 3.

[3] See Chapter 2 of the author's book *Philistine: The Great Deception* for the full explanation of the Arab mind and "Face."

[4] See Chapter two, footnote number 2.

[5] See the book: *Foxbats Over Dimona: The Soviets' Nuclear Gamble in the Six-Day War* by Isabella Ginor and Gideon Remez (Yale University Press, New Haven & London, 2007).

The Holy One Speaks

Having gotten the cameos and portraits of the different facets of Israel's ultimate wilderness behind us we can once again turn our attention to this book's principle Scripture – Hosea 2:14-15:

> *Therefore, behold, I will allure her, will bring her into the wilderness, and speak comfort to her. I will give her her vineyards from there, and the Valley of Achor as a door of hope; she shall sing there, as in the days of her youth, as in the day when she came up from the land of Egypt* (Hosea 2:14-15).

A brief recap of a few observations from earlier chapters may be helpful at this time, as would the full verse of scripture in English and Hebrew, together with the author's explanation.

For this book's purposes we have been concentrating upon the Hebrew text of Hosea 2:14 – the Hebrew text of verse 15 is not required.

Here once again is the Hebrew text of Hosea 2:14 (verse 16 in the Hebrew Bible) with its transliteration and the English translation from the New King James Version. The Hebrew is read from **right to left** while the transliteration is read from **left to right**. First of all, the Hebrew:

לכן הנה אנכי מפתיה והלכתיה המדבר ודברתי על-לבה

Second of all, the transliteration:

> *la'chen   hineh   unochi   miftihah   vehalachtihah hamidbar vedibarti al'livah.*

Third of all, the New King James text:

> *Therefore, behold, I will allure her, will bring her into the wilderness, and speak comfort to her.*

For readers' benefit the author has been placing emphasis on each of the Hebrew and transliterated words that needed to be explored beyond that of a customary reading, and our first Hebrew word was לכן – *la'chen,* which means "therefore."

This particular word makes clear that what is to come is the direct consequence of what had preceded it. In Hosea 12:13 the LORD says that Israel had forgotten Him, *"therefore"* He is going to act in order to correct Israel's perverse behavior. Israel's *"Maker"* is going to discipline His people punitively for transgressing His covenant, taking him for granted, and for forgetting Him – again. Only following His punitive actions is He going to bring Israel back into a restored relationship.

Our second Hebrew word was הנה – *hineh* – "Behold!" This word is meant to get the hearers' attention and is an emphatic word testifying to the certainty of what God has said taking place.

We then looked at אנכי – *unochi* – "I Myself." This tells us that it will be *"the holy One of Israel"* Himself that will take Israel into the wilderness and be dealing with her. Others may be involved, but the plans and machinations are God's alone.

Progressing on we came to מפתיה – *miftihah* – "will lure her," which is the better of the English translations and most closely adheres to the meaning of the Hebrew. It shows us that Israel will not blindly enter the wilderness by accident, but the LORD will use seductive and deceptive mediums to lure Israel into the wilderness, for it is seduction and deception that lies at the heart of the meaning of this fourth Hebrew word.

Our fifth Hebrew word was והלכתיה – *vehalachtihah* – "and bring her." Israel's *"Creator"* is not sending Israel on ahead into the wilderness by someone else's hand, it will be His own hand that will *"bring"* her into the wilderness. Other agencies will be used, but the LORD will be personally and intimately involved. The LORD will take Israel's hand and *"bring"* her into the wilderness Himself. Israel will be lured into the wilderness, enticed by her own desires – continuing further and further into the heart of the wilderness, unable to reverse unfolding events.

The last Hebrew word we looked at, the sixth, was in Chapter nine – המדבר – *hamidbar* – "the wilderness." This word means "a desert wasteland," an isolated, intense environment. In Chapters nine through fourteen we looked at some of the different facets of Israel's wilderness and through them we understand that Israel is already well into the wilderness today. Unfortunately, for Israel the wilderness will become more intense and more dangerous – it has yet to get much worse before it gets any better.

We now move on. Israel is currently isolated in a multi-faceted wilderness, but she is not alone, her *"Creator"* is with her, and here we come back to our Hebrew text.

In the original Hebrew text of the Bible past tenses are frequently used where future tenses would often appear to be more correct, and vice versa. The author feels that these instances could as easily be divine statements as be anomalies. Our next Hebrew word is an example of this peculiarity:

לכן הנה אנכי מפתיה והלכתיה המדבר ודברתי על-לבה

la'chen hineh unochi miftihah vehalachtihah hadmidbar ***vedibarti** al'livah.*

*Therefore, behold, I will allure her, will bring her into the wilderness, **and speak** comfort to her.*

ודברתי – *vedibarti* – "and I will speak."

Here, as mentioned above, is an example in the Hebrew text of the past tense being used instead for the future. The literal translation of this Hebrew word would be *"and I spoke,"* not *"and I will speak."* However, it is the author's belief that when God says He is going to do something, for all intents and purposes it has already been done. Certainly, in the mind of God it is done. Therefore, instead of the scripture saying of the LORD, *"and I will speak,"* it is actually saying of Him *"and I spoke"* – past tense – but, to the LORD, it is one and the same thing for He *"calls those things which do not exist as though they did"* (Romans 4:17).

God not only foretells the future – He also **sees** the future. For instance, God spoke with Moses out of the burning bush at *"Horeb, the mountain of God, at the back of the desert"* (Exodus 3:1) and told him to go back to Egypt and lead the children of Israel out of their bondage. The LORD tells Moses that Aaron's *"heart will be glad"* when he sees Moses, but before Moses could so much as move a foot or take up his sandals from the holy ground, God says to him regarding Aaron, who was around three hundred kilometers (about one hundred and eighty-six miles) away in Goshen: ***"look, he is coming out to meet you"*** (Exodus 4:14).

At this juncture we shall put aside the literal translation of our Hebrew word ודברתי (*vedibarti*) and stay with the widely accepted English translation – *"and I will speak."*

When God says *"I will speak"* it could be in any one of a hundred different ways. God is not limited to speaking in an audible voice:

> *God, who at various times and **in various ways** spoke*
> *in time past to the fathers* (Hebrews 1:1).

The LORD spoke in *"various"* ways in the days of yore and He still speaks in a variety of ways today. The Prophet Isaiah must have heard *"the God of Israel"* speak in a particular way, in a way other than the norm:

> *For the LORD **spoke thus to me with a strong hand**,*
> *and instructed me that I should not walk in the way*
> *of this people* (Isaiah 8:11).

The Prophet Jeremiah heard God in a similar way:

> *I did not sit in the assembly of the mockers, nor did*
> *I rejoice; I **sat alone because of Your hand**, for You*
> *have filled me with indignation* (Jeremiah 15:17).

The Prophet Ezekiel also:

> *So the Spirit lifted me up and took me away, and I*
> *went in bitterness, in the heat of my spirit; but **the***
> ***hand of the LORD was strong upon me***
> (Ezekiel 3:14).

What the prophets experienced insofar as hearing the LORD's voice on those occasions is an experience many readers have also had. When God speaks with a *"strong hand"* it generally means He speaks through the pressure of circumstances. It is a sure-fire way for the LORD to get someone's attention.

Israel is going further into the wilderness today and her *"Creator"* is already speaking to her with a *"strong hand."* It will not be the only way that the LORD will speak to Israel in the wilderness, but given enough time in that isolated, intense, and dangerous milieu, the unrelenting pressure of her circumstances will cause her to cry out to *"the holy One of Israel"* before He changes His tone.

The LORD says time and again that Israel is His *"special treasure"* (e.g. Exodus 19:5), but He is under no illusions about His *"special treasure"* – *"For Israel is stubborn like a stubborn calf"* (Hosea 4:16), a *"stiff-necked"* people (e.g. Exodus 32:9). And Moses also described Israel as people of a *"stiff neck"* (Deuteronomy 31:27).

In the wilderness Israel will be unable to escape the voice of the LORD. Her *"stiff neck"* will be bent to His yoke and her stubbornness will be tamed:

> *"O house of Israel, can I not do with you as [the] potter?" says the LORD. "Look, as the clay is in the potter's hand, so are you in My hand, O house of Israel!"* (Jeremiah 18:6).

Israel's ultimate wandering is underway. There is much she must endure. How long her sojourn in the wilderness lasts largely depends on how long she takes to bend her neck to her *"Creator's"* yoke, how addicted she is to stubbornness in the face of adversity.

sixteen

Words, Burned Into The Heart

We have now come to the eighth and final Hebrew word of Hosea 2:14 that requires examination. The author is sure to be at odds here with some other translators of our Hebrew text and for that tradition would be the most obvious reason. The author has said elsewhere that tradition is always more powerful than fact.

Translators will often opt to go with traditional renderings rather than with a literal translation. This may be due perhaps to a trepidation that by departing from a traditional rendering of a particular word or phrase it could curtail sales of the completed translation. All who have had works published by major book publishers will know that publishers' editors often insist upon changes being made to a manuscript in order to ensure a higher volume of sales. Money is not exclusively the god of the secular world, it is also the god of the commercial Christian world, too.

With only a few exceptions, the English translations of Hosea 2:14 follow closely to the author's preferred New King James Version:

> *Therefore, behold, I will allure her, will bring her into the wilderness, and speak comfort to her.*

However, nowhere does the Hebrew text say the LORD will speak comfort to Israel. This is an assumption on the part of the translators. Below is the Hebrew text, transliteration, and the New King James translation:

לכן הנה אנכי מפתיה והלכתיה המדבר ודברתי על-לבה

*la'chen   hineh   unochi   miftihah   vehalachtihah hadmidbar vedibarti **al'livah**.*

*Therefore, behold, I will allure her, will bring her into the wilderness, and **speak comfort to her**.*

Our Hebrew word is an hyphenated one, עַל-לִבָּה – *al 'livah* – literally, "on her heart." Most English translations do not even include the word "heart," which is really the crux of the text. Other translations say that God will "court" Israel; "speak tenderly to her;" "speak comfort" to her," *et cetera.* The few translations that do include the word "heart" all have the LORD speaking "to" the heart. And here the author will again find himself at odds with some translators. However, the author did come across a single English commentary[1] on the Hosea 2:14 passage that noted the more literal translation of עַל-לִבָּה – *al 'livah*, "on her heart." Please pardon the pun, but "heart" is really the heart of the matter here. And the LORD does not speak "to" the heart, He speaks "on" the heart and here again there is a major difference.

The same mistake is made in Zechariah 12:10, albeit in reverse. In Zechariah, English translations have the LORD saying:

. . . they will look upon Me whom they have pierced . . .

Here the Hebrew text literally says *"they will look **to** Me,"* but most translators follow tradition and are insistent that Israel looks upon Him. Perhaps the reason for the Zechariah 12:10 error is one of inherent antisemitism that requires the Jewish nation to physically see Yeshua (Jesus) whom they – along with the Gentiles – have pierced before turning to Him for salvation. However, looking *"to"* Him presupposes that Israel is in dire straights and is reaching out in desperation. The wilderness experience could easily force Israel to the edge of that cliff.

When Israel's *Maker* finishes speaking with a *"strong hand"* and gets Israel's full attention, He will *"speak on her heart."* Soon after bringing Israel out of Egypt God spoke to Israel and gave her His law – carved into tablets of stone. What is soon about to happen to Israel and what has already begun to happen is a rerun of that first wilderness experience – a rerun with a few refinements. The LORD repeatedly calls Israel *"rebellious," "stiff-necked,"* and *"stubborn."* Israel's *"stiff neck"* must be bent and her stubbornness and rebelliousness humbled and cured:

For rebellion is as the sin of witchcraft, and stubbornness is as iniquity and idolatry" (1 Samuel 15:23).

Salvation cannot come until Israel understands that all that belongs to her is *"shame of face"* (Daniel 9:7, 8). The LORD has said to Israel:

> *I will remember My covenant with you in the days of your youth, and I will establish an everlasting covenant with you. Then you will remember your ways and be ashamed . . . . And I will establish My covenant with you. Then you shall know that I am the LORD, that you may remember and be ashamed, and never open your mouth anymore because of your shame, when I provide you an atonement for all you have done," says the LORD GOD*
>
> (Ezekiel 16:60, 62-63).

The LORD has said He will provide an atonement and that *"I will speak on her heart."* This must surely be the fulfillment of Jeremiah's prophecy:

> *But this is the covenant that I will make with the house of Israel after those days, says the LORD: I will put My law in their minds, and **write it on their hearts**; and I will be their God, and they shall be My people.*
>
> *No more shall every man teach his neighbor, and every man his brother, saying, "Know the LORD," for they all shall know Me, from the least of them to the greatest of them, says the LORD. For I will forgive their iniquity, and their sin I will remember no more*
>
> (Jeremiah 31:33).

The covenant that God will make with the house of Israel will be put into their minds and written *"on"* their hearts. This is the same as *"I will speak on her heart."* We have already seen that God has different ways of speaking. Here the LORD is going to speak His laws on Israel's heart.

The new covenant is going to be new in every meaning of the word. It will not be like the old covenant written by the finger of God on tablets of stone – broken before they reached the bottom of the mountain. This covenant will be unbreakable, written on the individual hearts of the people of Israel – spoken and etched onto all hearts by the finger of God. That is, on all without distinction rather than all without exception.

Sins are because sin is. But God touches sin in redemption. In order to bring Israel into His salvation the LORD must reverse the bent of her nature. He must plant a new principle within her in order for her subsequent conduct to spring out of a desire to please Him and promote His honor. Israel as a nation must be born again – from above.

To facilitate this dramatic change, Israel's *"Creator"* says to His *"special treasure"* Israel, *"I will bring you into the wilderness of the peoples"* (Ezekiel 20:35), which is where Israel is aimlessly wandering today.

Israel will continue her sojourn in the wilderness until the finger of God inscribes a new life principle onto the hearts of the remnant of the people. God has promised to write a new covenant on the heart of Israel, and *"all the promises of God in Him are Yes, and in Him Amen"* (2 Corinthians 1:20). And thus the new covenant will be established:

> *written not with ink but by the Spirit of the living God, not on tablets of stone but on tablets of flesh, that is, of the heart* (2 Corinthians 3:3).

---

[1] *The Expositors Bible Commentary,* Volume 7 (the Zondervan Bible Corporation, Grand Rapids, Michigan, 1985).

— seventeen —

Lost Lands Restored

It is through the means of the second and ultimate wilderness that Israel will truly embrace the Promised Land. First of all, the fact that Israel could be lured back into the wilderness presupposes a rejection of the Promised Land, the divine inheritance given by the LORD. Second of all, Israel brought it all upon herself through her apostasy:

> *Have you not brought this on yourself, in that you have forsaken the LORD your God when He led you in the way?* (Jeremiah 2:17).

The LORD brought His people into a land *"for which the LORD cares"* (Deuteronomy 11:12), *"a land flowing with milk and honey"* (Exodus 3:8), *"but,"* says the LORD to Israel, *"when you entered you defiled My Land"* (Jeremiah 2:7).

A lengthy sojourn in an isolated, inhospitable, environment will be a time of punitive punishment; however, it will also prove to be the means of regaining all that was lost to Israel. Speaking of the wilderness God says through the Prophet Hosea:

> *I will give her her vineyards from there, and the Valley of Achor as a door of hope; she shall sing there, as in the days of her youth, as in the day when she came up from the land of Egypt* (Hosea 2:15).

In Hosea 2:14 God vows to lure Israel into the wilderness. In Hosea 2:15 He depicts Israel as singing in the wilderness:

> *as in the days of her youth, as in the day when she came up from the land of Egypt.*

We have parallels here between the first wilderness and Israel's ultimate wilderness. It was in the first wilderness that Israel expressed the desire to return to Egypt, to return to the bondage that she had endured for centuries and from which the

LORD had delivered her. Due to its lack of faith in its *"Creator"* an entire faithless generation found itself being buried in the wilderness over a forty-year period. Israel could not move on until the last corpse of that unbelieving generation was buried beneath the dust.

Now the LORD has once again brought Israel back into the wilderness – the ultimate wilderness. And just as the first wilderness prepared the Israelites for Canaan so the bringing of Israel into the ultimate wilderness will eventually bring deliverance from her enemies of today. There must, however, be a captivity and a bondage in order for the story of the first wilderness to be repeated. Nevertheless, the ultimate wilderness experience will prove as much a deliverance from Israel's enemies as it will of being a time of punitive punishment.

It is *"from there,"* from the wilderness, that the LORD will restore to Israel the vineyards and lands she forfeited through aeons of perverse behavior and apostasy. Had not the LORD said:

> *And I will destroy her vines and her fig trees, of which she has said, "These are my wages that my lovers have given me"* (Hosea 2:12)?

It is unsurprising that the LORD chose to specifically restore *"vineyards"* because in new vines the bounty of God appears when they teem with grapes. Wine represents joy and *"makes glad the heart of man"* (Psalms 104:15). *"Her vineyards"* are the vineyards which a formerly faithful Israel possessed before losing them due her unfaithfulness. A regifting of the Promised Land is alluded to in the promise to give them back to Israel.

Vineyards are not only found in lush areas. In Song of Solomon 1:14 we read of *"the vineyards of En Gedi."* En Gedi is situated in the Judean Wilderness, on the edge of the Dead Sea. The *"Wilderness of En Gedi"* is mentioned in 1 Samuel 24:1 and is one of the bleakest parts of the Judean Wilderness, with such oppressive heat that it precludes any semblance of a large population. The *"vineyards of En Gedi"* disappeared after the invasion of Israel by Muslim forces[1] in the seventh century A.D. Muslims are opposed to wine and alcoholic drink and destroyed En Gedi's vineries.

When the Lord leads Israel out of the ultimate wilderness
and back into the Promised Land her vineyards will have been
restored. It is from the wilderness that Israel will be given the
vineyards, but this should not be understood as implying that the
vineyards will grow in the wilderness where Israel is wandering.
En Gedi is an exception, the envisaged agricultural success will
be in the Promised Land, not in the desert .

The Promised Land and its heavily-laden vineyards are inter-
woven: the Promised Land is Israel's inheritance (Deuteronomy
4:20); Israel is the Lord's inheritance (Psalms 32:12); and *"the
vineyard of the Lord is the house of Israel"* (Isaiah 5:7).

When the Lord leads Israel out of the ultimate wilderness and
brings her back into the Promised Land she will once again pass
through the Valley of Achor, which means "Valley of trouble."
The Valley of Achor was the site of Achan's sin against the Lord.
The Bible informs us that an Israelite named Achan stole from
what belonged to the Lord and placed the success of the entire
conquest of Canaan in jeopardy (Joshua 7:1-12).

In our Hosea scripture the Lord alludes to the situation of
the Israelites in the first wilderness. As soon as the people came
out of that wilderness they crossed the Jordan River, entered
the Promised Land and camped inside the border, at Gilgal,
in the plain of Achor, opposite Jericho. The area was fruitful,
pleasant, and fertile. In the wilderness there had not even been a
single grain of wheat or barley, nor were there any grapes. The
wilderness had been nothing but impoverishment accompanied
by tens of thousands of deaths.

The Israelites were to first take the city of Jericho and, under
Joshua's command, the Lord caused its walls to fall down flat
and Israel destroyed everything that breathed except Rahab the
prostitute and her family. Rahab had **exercised faith** and had
hidden two Israelite scouts who had entered Jericho to spy out
the city. The scouts promised with an oath that, if Rahab wove
a scarlet cord into her window, no harm would befall her or her
family when the city was taken (Joshua 2:18).

Jericho was the firstfruits of the conquest of Canaan and
the city was doomed to destruction. Without exception, all that

breathed was to be put to the sword and all buildings were to be destroyed by fire. Only the gold, the silver, and the vessels of bronze and iron were to be saved for the treasury of the LORD:

> *And you, by all means abstain from the accursed things, lest you become accursed when you take of the accursed things, and make the camp of Israel a curse, and trouble it. But all the silver and gold, and vessels of bronze and iron, are consecrated to the LORD; they shall come into the treasury of the LORD*
> (Joshua 6:18-19).

But, unbeknown to anyone else, Achan stole from what was under the ban: a Babylonian mantle, two hundred sheqels of silver and a wedge of gold weighing fifty sheqels. After her tedious forty-year wandering in the wilderness, Israel was at the fertile plain of Achor on the threshold of Canaan, but trouble resulting from Achan's crime was about to overtake her.

Following the destruction of Jericho Joshua sent scouts to spy out Ai, the next city that was to be taken. The scouts reported back that the people of Ai were few in number and only two or three thousand fighting men were needed to overthrow it (Joshua 7:3-4). But when the men went up to battle against Ai the men of Ai struck down a number of the children of Israel and caused them to flee back to Gilgal. Joshua tore his clothes, and he and the elders of Israel put dust on their heads and lay prostrate before the Ark of the LORD.

Then the LORD said to Joshua:

> *Get up! Why do you lie thus on your face? Israel has sinned and has also transgressed My covenant which I commanded them. For they have even taken some of the accursed things and have both stolen and deceived; and they have also put it among their own stuff. Therefore the children of Israel could not stand before their enemies, but turned their backs before their enemies, because they have become doomed to destruction. Neither will I be with you anymore, unless you destroy the accursed from among you. Get up, sanctify the people, and say, "Sanctify yourselves*

for tomorrow," because thus says the LORD *God of Israel: "There is an accursed thing in your midst, O Israel; you cannot stand before your enemies until you take away the accursed thing from among you"*
(Joshua 7:10-13).

The LORD commanded Joshua to bring each tribe before Him, and the tribe of Judah was subsequently taken. The families of the clan of Judah came and the LORD took the family of the Zarhites, and they came man by man, and Zabdi was taken. Zabdi brought his household man by man and Achan the son of Zerah was taken.

Achan said: *"Indeed I have sinned against the* LORD *God of Israel"* (Joshua 7:20) and confessed to stealing the garment, the silver, and the gold because he coveted them and that the things were hidden in the earth in the middle of his tent. Joshua sent men to retrieve the articles and they brought them from Achan's tent and laid them out before the LORD.

Then Joshua, and all Israel with him, took Achan the son of Zerah, the silver, the garment, the wedge of gold, his sons, his daughters, his oxen, his donkeys, his sheep, his tent, and all that he had, and they brought them to the Valley of Achor.
And Joshua said, "Why have you troubled us? The LORD *will trouble you this day." So all Israel stoned him with stones; and they burned them with fire after they had stoned them with stones*
(Joshua 7:24-25).

Israel built a great heap of stones over the remains of Achan, his family, his livestock, and his possessions. Israel learnt through the transgression and punishment of Achan to stand in awe of God and from that time forward, being free of the *"accursed thing,"* all went well with the conquest.

The Valley of Achor is a tangible reminder to Israel that upon taking possession of the Promised Land for the second time there can be no repetition of the transgression committed in the first possession. In the first possession of the Promised Land, Israel's joy at leaving the penury of the wilderness was soon turned into heartbreak by a solitary act committed by a single individual.

Leaving the ultimate wilderness and entering the Promised Land the second time the Valley of Achor will be a symbol of better things to come:

> *Sharon shall be a fold of flocks, and the Valley of Achor a place for herds to lie down, for My people who have sought Me"* (Isaiah 65:10).

The *"Valley of Achor"* will be a doorway of hope that leads to Israel's repossession of her divine inheritance. Whereas the valley had formerly been a trough of despair, the LORD will turn it into a valley of joy, where hope dawns for a brighter tomorrow.

Modern Israel has also stolen from the LORD, perhaps not in the nature of Achan, but she has stolen from God nevertheless.

Israel is a nation set apart. In Deuteronomy 7:6: God says to Israel:

> *For you are a holy people to the LORD your God; the LORD your God has chosen you to be a people for Himself, a special treasure above all the peoples on the face of the earth* (Deuteronomy 7:6).

However, former prime minister Yitzhak Rabin was the first Israeli leader to tell the world, "Israel wants to be like other nations." It is an impossibility. Israel can never be like other nations. Israel cannot spit in the face of *"the Holy One of Israel"* and still expect His hand of blessing to be upon her forever. Apparently, the leaders of Israel have never learned from Israel's millennia of history. Time and time again Israel has turned her back upon the LORD, the *"Maker"* of Israel, and has suffered horrendous disasters in return. Israel's leaders never learn. It has been a continuation of the same old, same old.

China has a four-thousand-year history and has a population today of one billion four hundred million people. India also has a four-thousand-year-long history and at the present time has a population of one billion two hundred million. Israel, too, has four thousand years of history and her Bible instructs her forefathers to *"be fruitful and multiply, and fill the earth"* (e.g. Genesis 9:1), yet Israel today can only collectively muster no more than thirteen million Jews worldwide. This is because Israel turned and continues to turn her back upon the LORD her *"Maker"* and wants to be like all the nations, which brings sufferings aplenty from the *"strong hand"* of the LORD. The Jewish nation always blames the Gentiles for the woes that have befallen its people, stubbornly refusing to admit that it is her own transgressions against the LORD that are the cause of its suffering and isolation.

It was Albert Einstein who said the definition of insanity is: "doing the same thing over and over again and expecting different results." Apparently, Israel is insane. It is precisely because Israel refuses to consider her divinely appointed destiny that she has suffered more hardships than any other nation:

> *she did not consider her destiny; therefore her collapse was awesome"* (Lamentations 1:19).

The LORD has brought Israel into the ultimate wilderness and has, in part, withdrawn His hand of protection from over her. It was said earlier that the ultimate wilderness experience will eventually bring deliverance from her enemies. Notice that the author said the wilderness experience will "eventually" bring deliverance from her enemies. Before deliverance, enemies must be faced, and with only partial protection from the LORD Israel's casualty rate will be high.

It was said in Chapter fourteen that many Israelis venerate the Israel Defense Force and boast that it is the best in the world. Millions of Israelis say: "We have the best army in the world! We have the best air force in the world!" Such thinking leads them and their leaders to believe that it is the power of the Israel Defense Force alone that devastates attacking armies and entities.

The late Israeli statesmen, Abba Eban, a typically liberal, humanist, leftwing Israeli, disparaged God-fearing Israelis when he said: "They saw our victory not as a result of superior military performance but as a divine miracle."[2] Elsewhere in his book Eban belittles the idea of a "higher power" having had a hand in the miraculous result of the Six-Day War when he scoffs, "if you believe in a higher power."

That which held true in the conquest of Canaan must surely hold true for the modern state of Israel. Possession of the Promised Land took place over a five-year period as Israel defeated the nations squatting on her inheritance. And in the first twenty-five years after the birth of the modern Jewish state Israel took possession of large tracts of Syrian, Jordanian, and Egyptian territory due to the Israel Defense Force thrice defeating multiple invading armies from those nations:

> *For they did not gain possession of the land by their own sword, nor did their own arm save them; but it was Your right hand, Your arm, and the light of Your countenance, because You favored them*
>
> (Psalms 44:3).

In this matter Israel has been very foolish and has stolen the glory that belongs to the LORD. All the credit, the honor, and the glory for every Israeli military victory belongs to the LORD. And He will not share His glory with the Israel Defense Force:

> *I am the LORD, that is My name; and My glory I will not give to another, nor My praise to carved images* (Isaiah 42:8).

As it was postulated in Chapter fourteen, Israel's reverence for the Israel Defense Force must be broken. Reverence is due only to *"God Almighty."* Israel's eyes must be fully focused upon the LORD from whom the strength of the Israel Defense Force comes. Israel will be brought into reality in the ultimate wilderness and the Israel Defense Force will be overpowered, even if only for a brief period. And, as mentioned earlier, it would appear that the overpowering of the Israel Defense Force takes place during a major battle for Jerusalem:

> *For I will gather all the nations to battle against Jerusalem; The city shall be taken, The houses rifled, and the women ravished. Half of the city shall go into captivity, but the remnant of the people shall not be cut off from the city* (Zechariah 14:2).

As with Achan in the valley of Achor, so it must be with Israel in her ultimate wilderness. When Israel's sin is dealt with the LORD will go forth and destroy all the nations that have come against Israel. The example of Achan taught the Israelites respect for the LORD and His commandments. The example of losing the battle for Jerusalem will teach modern Israel respect for her *"Maker."* Israel will be made to understand that it is the LORD who has been winning Israel's wars and that Israel has perpetually stolen His glory, claiming it for herself. When the LORD withdraws His hand in battles against Israel's enemies, it will not be an easy time for the Jewish state.

Let us not think that those who hold Israel's vineyards are going to surrender them up without a fight. The battle for Jerusalem will be but one of many battles, but the heart of Israel's remnant will get God's law etched into it and her *"Maker"* says:

> *In that day I will make the governors of Judah like a firepan in the woodpile, and like a fiery torch in the sheaves; they shall devour all the surrounding peoples on the right hand and on the left, but Jerusalem shall be inhabited again in her own place – Jerusalem*
> (Zechariah 12:6).

Most nations of the world are gnashing their teeth at Israel today, but those nations have forgotten that the One who created

> *the heavens and the earth, the sea, and all that is in them* (Exodus 20:11)

is also the One who created Israel

> *to be a people for Himself, a special treasure above all the peoples on the face of the earth*
> (Deuteronomy 7:6).

More than three thousand years ago Moses stood before Pharaoh and told him of the terrible catastrophe about to befall Egypt from the hand of the LORD:

> *But against none of the children of Israel shall a dog move its tongue, against man or beast, that you may know that the LORD does make a difference between the Egyptians and Israel"* (Exodus 11:7).

The LORD says in Malachi 3:6: *"I am the LORD, I do not change."* Therefore only *"fools"* who say in their hearts *"There is no God"* (Psalms 14:1) will continue to harass God's *"chosen people"* (Deuteronomy 7:6). A modern Moses could stand before a Secretary-General of the United Nations and tell him of the terrible catastrophes that will soon befall the nations:

> *that [he] may know that the* LORD *does make a difference between the [nations] and Israel*
>
> (Exodus 11:7).

Israel – a people in whom the LORD will have:

> *created a clean heart and renewed a steadfast spirit within them* (Psalms 51:10

shall have no fear of the nations for the LORD is also the *"King of the nations"* (Jeremiah 10:7). To Israel's believing remnant the LORD says:

> *Fear not, for I am with you; be not dismayed, for I am your God. I will strengthen you, yes, I will help you, I will uphold you with My righteous right hand.*
>
> *Behold, all those who were incensed against you shall be ashamed and disgraced; they shall be as nothing, and those who strive with you shall perish. You shall seek them and not find them – those who contended with you. Those who war against you shall be as nothing, as a nonexistent thing. For I, the* LORD *your God, will hold your right hand, saying to you, "Fear not, I will help you. Fear not . . . you men of Israel! I will help you," says the* LORD *and your Redeemer, the Holy One of Israel.*
>
> *Behold, I will make you into a new threshing sledge with sharp teeth; you shall thresh the mountains and beat them small, and make the hills like chaff. You shall winnow them, the wind shall carry them away, and the whirlwind shall scatter them; you shall rejoice in the* LORD, *and glory in the Holy One of Israel* (Isaiah 41:10-16).

---

[1] *The Zondervan Pictorial Encyclopedia of the Bible*, (Grand Rapids: Zondervan, 1977), Vol. 2, p. 307.

[2] Abba Eban, "Personal Witness," p. 468.

Singing In The Desert

We have now come to the end of our Hosea passage and this final portion continues with an effusion of joy – the wilderness experience is all but over for the true *"Israel of God"* (Galatians 6:16). Here once again is the verse of Hosea 2:15, but we shall only concern ourselves with the latter half of the verse:

> *I will give her her vineyards from there, and the Valley of Achor as a door of hope; she shall sing there, as in the days of her youth, as in the day when she came up from the land of Egypt* (Hosea 2:14-15).

There is only once place in the biblical account of the first wilderness where we read of Israel joyfully singing, dancing, and praising the LORD *"in the days of her youth."* And recorded for us are the actual words of the song that Israel sang:

> *Then Moses and the children of Israel sang this song to the LORD, and spoke, saying:*
> *"I will sing to the LORD, for He has triumphed gloriously! The horse and its rider He has thrown into the sea!*
> *The LORD is my strength and song, and He has become my salvation; He is my God, and I will praise Him; my father's God, and I will exalt Him.*
> *The LORD is a man of war; the LORD is His name. Pharaoh's chariots and his army He has cast into the sea; his chosen captains also are drowned in the Red Sea. The depths have covered them; they sank to the bottom like a stone.*
> *Your right hand, O LORD, has become glorious in power; Your right hand, O LORD, has dashed the enemy in pieces. And in the greatness of Your*

excellence You have overthrown those who rose against You; You sent forth Your wrath; it consumed them like stubble. And with the blast of Your nostrils the waters were gathered together; the floods stood upright like a heap; the depths congealed in the heart of the sea.

The enemy said, 'I will pursue, I will overtake, I will divide the spoil; my desire shall be satisfied on them. I will draw my sword, my hand shall destroy them.'

You blew with Your wind, the sea covered them; they sank like lead in the mighty waters.

Who is like You, O Lord, among the gods? Who is like You, glorious in holiness, fearful in praises, doing wonders? You stretched out Your right hand; the earth swallowed them.

You in Your mercy have led forth the people whom You have redeemed; You have guided them in Your strength to Your holy habitation.

The people will hear and be afraid; sorrow will take hold of the inhabitants of Philistia. Then the chiefs of Edom will be dismayed; the mighty men of Moab, trembling will take hold of them; all the inhabitants of Canaan will melt away. Fear and dread will fall on them; by the greatness of Your arm they will be as still as a stone, till Your people pass over, O Lord, till the people pass over whom You have purchased. You will bring them in and plant them in the mountain of Your inheritance, in the place, O Lord, which You have made for Your own dwelling, the sanctuary, O Lord, which Your hands have established. The Lord shall reign forever and ever.

For the horses of Pharaoh went with his chariots and his horsemen into the sea, and the Lord brought back the waters of the sea upon them. But the children of Israel went on dry land in the midst of the sea.

> *Then Miriam the prophetess, the sister of Aaron,*
> *took the tambourine in her hand; and all the women*
> *went out after her with tambourines and with dances.*
> *And Miriam answered them:*
> *'Sing to the LORD, for He has triumphed*
> *gloriously! The horse and its rider He has thrown*
> *into the sea!'"* Exodus 15:1-21).

Israel's obvious joy was entirely due to the LORD having vanquished the pursuing enemy. The LORD did it completely alone. He did not then and does not now need Israel's help, or anyone else's. God does not need any of us, although He often graciously allows us to be privy to and involved in His plans.

In Chapters four through six we looked at three Hebrew words: לכן הנה אנכי – *la'chen hineh unochi* – *"Therefore, behold, I Myself;"* and we saw that the *"Maker"* of Israel had determined to take Israel into a wilderness – a metaphorical, multi-faceted wilderness that, in reality, is far more literal than figurative. It is in this wilderness that the LORD is going to deal with Israel for her myriads of transgressions against Him and His covenant:

> *Thus says the LORD God of Israel:* **"Cursed** *is the man who does not obey the words of this covenant which I commanded your fathers in the day I brought them out of the land of Egypt, from the iron furnace"* (Jeremiah 11:3-4).

> *"Behold, it is written before Me: I will not keep silence, but will repay – even* **repay into their bosom** *– your iniquities and the iniquities of your fathers together,"* *says the LORD* (Isaiah 65:6-7a).

Israel's sins are many and we saw at the end of Chapter fourteen that Israel must pay double for her sins due to being the firstborn of the LORD (Exodus 4:22). We see in the above Jeremiah passage that those who did not keep the LORD's commandments are *"cursed,"* and it is the Hebrew word ארר (*arar*) that is used, which has dreadful effects as we saw in Chapter eleven. In the Isaiah passage above we see that the LORD will *"repay"* Israel's iniquities into her *"bosom."* These two verses alone should give an indication of the trouble facing Israel prior to the etching of God's laws onto her collective heart.

It is in the ultimate wilderness where the LORD will etch His laws onto Israel's collective heart, and cause Israel to be permanently delivered from her enemies – all the nations who gnash their teeth at her today and who will come against her militarily tomorrow.

All is of God. He is not at all squeamish in the face of deprivation, death, and destruction. He has said *"I Myself"* will do it, and do it He will. Israel's salvation will be God's work alone, as will be Israel's deliverance from her enemies and from the wilderness:

> *Behold, I will do a new thing, now it shall spring forth; shall you not know it? I will even make a road in the* **wilderness** *and rivers in* **the desert.** *The beast of the field will honor Me, the jackals and the ostriches, because I give waters in the* **wilderness** *and rivers in* **the desert,** *to give drink to* **My people, My chosen** (Isaiah 43:19).*

> *For the LORD will comfort Zion, He will comfort all her waste places; He will make her* **wilderness** *like Eden, and her* **desert** *like the garden of the LORD; joy and gladness will be found in it, thanksgiving and the voice of melody* (Isaiah 51:3).

The LORD will succor Israel, His *"special treasure,"* in the wilderness – concomitant with her divine chastisement. It was said previously that the ultimate wilderness is a rerun of the first wilderness experience, a rerun with a few refinements. Both wilderness experiences are mirrored in each other. The terminal objective for the LORD in the ultimate wilderness is to win and hold the heart of Israel. The LORD longs for His heart to be fused together with Israel's. The LORD looks back to the days in the first wilderness when He first held Israel's heart:

> *I remember you, the kindness of your youth, the love of your betrothal, when you went after Me in the wilderness, in a land not sown* (Jeremiah 2:2b).

All that will befall Israel in the ultimate wilderness is deliberately premeditated to restore her love for the LORD. Those who spurn His love will have no place in the second possession of the Promised Land.

At the opening of Chapter fourteen the author said that the worst wars prophesied in the Bible are yet to come and that we only get a glimpse of the catastrophic nature of these wars from their brief biblical portraits. Three days after the Israelites fled from Egypt they saw the dead bodies of Pharaoh's army on the seashore (Exodus 14:30). Israel had passed through the Red Sea on dry land, but the LORD brought the cliffs of water crashing down upon the pursuers and destroyed them.

Following the sighting of dead Egyptians on the seashore Israel knew for sure there would be no more trouble from that quarter. And, just as ancient Israel saw the bodies of Pharaoh's army on the shores of the Read Sea, so will modern Israel see the corpses of armies of modern nations on her battlefields and know there will be no more trouble from them.

God Almighty refers to Himself as *"the LORD of hosts"* hundreds of times in the Bible. In Hebrew *"the LORD of hosts"* – ליהוה צבאות – literally translates as "the LORD of armies." Chapters 8 and 9 of the prophet Amos give us an insight into the power God wields in every area. Without needlessly going into the long scripture discourse here because for the author's purpose we need look only at the latter half of one verse, which is:

> . . . *I will **command the sword**, and it shall slay them*
> (Amos 9:4b).

Bible students are aware that the LORD commands men and armies to carry out His purposes and we know from history that they obey. For instance, king Nebuchadnezzar of Babylon, who defeated Israel militarily, destroyed the first temple, and carried away captive the inhabitants of Judah is thrice called *"My servant"* (Jeremiah 25:9, 27:6, 43:10) by the LORD. However, only in this one instance, in the book of the prophet Amos, do we see the LORD actually being in command of the sword itself.

That statement should send a shiver down every unbeliever's spine. Simply because the LORD first says:

> *"Can anyone hide himself in secret places, so I shall not see him?" says the* LORD*; "Do I not fill heaven and earth?" says the* LORD (Jeremiah 23:24).

And He then says:

> *. . . I will* **command the sword**, *and it shall slay them*
> (Amos 9:4b).

Individuals who are slated for destruction may be able to hide themselves away from the main battle, but they cannot hide away from the LORD:

> *For the eyes of the* LORD *run to and fro throughout the whole earth, to show Himself strong on behalf of those whose heart is loyal to Him*
> (2 Chronicles 16:9).

And then He *"will command the sword"* against those whose hearts are not loyal toward Him.

The firestorm of the LORD's anger toward those who will wage war against *"the city of the* LORD *of hosts"* (Psalms 48:8), will give *"everyone who is left of all the nations which came against Jerusalem"* a new appreciation for the LORD and His chosen people. It will come to pass:

> *In those days ten men from every language of the nations shall grasp the sleeve of a Jewish man, saying, "Let us go with you, for we have heard that God is with you"* (Zechariah 8:23).

The scripture says *"from every language of the nations,"* which means that innumerable nations are involved, not just the Arab nations and Iran. Many nations will suffer immeasurable losses. So, perhaps, will Israel. But the entire remnant of Israel will have gotten God's law inscribed onto its heart, and it will survive:

> *on this one will I look: on him who is poor and of a contrite spirit, and who trembles at My word*
> (Isaiah 66:2b).

All those who are too stubborn, too rebellious, and whose necks are too stiff to bend to the LORD's yoke, will perish in their unbelief in the second and ultimate wilderness – just like those who died in the first wilderness due to their unbelief.

Faith and true belief is the gateway to God's heart of blessing:

> *Abraham **believed** God, and it was accounted to him for righteousness. And he was called the friend of God* (James 2:23).

> *Therefore know that **only those who are of faith** are sons of Abraham* (Galatians 3:7).

The Bible also tells us that:

> ***without faith** it is impossible to please Him, for he who comes to God must **believe** that He is, and that He is a rewarder of those who diligently seek Him*
> (Hebrews 11:6).

The LORD says:

> *But you, Israel, are My servant, Jacob whom I have chosen, the descendants of Abraham My friend*
> (Isaiah 41:8).

The LORD sheds light upon that when He says through the Apostle Paul: *"For they are not all Israel who are of Israel"* (Romans 9:6). Only those who are of the faith of Abraham are the true *"Israel of God"* (Galatians 6:16). And if anyone, Jew or Gentile, desires to become God's friend, he or she need only believe Him.

For those of Israel that will continue in unbelief and spurn God's love, for them there will be no singing *"as in the days of Israel's youth,"* there will be no *"vineyards"* for them, and there will be no further hope or chance. Their unbelief will prevent them from walking out of the wilderness through the *"door of hope"* into the Sonlight of the Promised Land.

As is was in the days of yore so it will be in the dark days that lie ahead:

> *Not a word failed of any good thing which the LORD had spoken to the house of Israel. All came to pass*
> (Joshua 21:45).

— *nineteen* —

Epilogue Of Prayer

Father, after having looked hard and long at the biblical evidence, we want to thank You that You are in full and absolute control of world events. Nothing is going amiss. The nations may rage against Your people Israel, but it is You, the *"Creator of Israel"* (Isaiah 43:15) Who has taken her into the ultimate wilderness. The nations are unwittingly carrying out Your desires and commands.

It is Your desire that pressure is brought upon Israel. It is Your desire that she becomes thirsty for You. And it is Your desire that she suffers in her season of refining in order that she learns obedience, just as Your *"only begotten Son"* Yeshua (Jesus) *"learned obedience by the things which He suffered"* (Hebrews 5:8). But You will deliver the remnant of Israel and honor it. You will reveal Your Son Yeshua (Jesus) to Israel, and You will etch Your laws upon her heart. And, along with Your people Israel, all those who love You from among the nations will move into a glorious age where Yeshua (Jesus) is not only seen to be *"King,"* but also worshipped as such.

It is so comforting, Father, to know that everything under the sun is in Your hands – the hands of the One Who has not only foretold the future in minute detail, but Who also controls history and what the world refers to as "nature."

Help us, Father, to digest what is written on the pages of this book. Help us to take truths out from between the covers and share them with others – with our churches, families, friends, neighbors and those with whom we work.

You have said in Your Word, Father, in Isaiah 11:12, the reassembling of Your people Israel back into the Land will be a significant moment in history, a banner, a sign to the world that the end of time is drawing near. You want the nations to take notice and You call out to them:

> *Hear the word of the LORD, O nations, And declare it in the isles afar off, and say, "He who scattered Israel will gather him, and keep him as a shepherd does his flock"* (Jeremiah 31:10).

You want the nations to know that it was not, as is commonly believed, the Roman Empire that was responsible for sowing Your people Israel among the nations. But that it was You Who scattered them, vomited them out from Your land following repeated warnings concerning her unfaithfulness, idolatry and immorality. You also want the nations to know that after You bring your people Israel back to her inheritance she will never be scattered again, that You will watch over her as a faithful shepherd watches over his flock.

As redeemed children of God, through the shed blood of Yeshua (Jesus) at Calvary, You would have us loudly (and proudly) proclaim to the nations that our God is fulfilling the prophetic words recorded thousands of years ago.

Our modern world is in chaos. War and terrorism is all around us. Murder and theft, government and corporate corruption, violence, rape, child abuse, pornography, pedophilia, *et cetera*, is everywhere. Millions are dying of starvation. Millions more are dying from pestilence. Each year tens of thousands lose their lives through extreme heat and extreme cold, through floods, hurricanes, earthquakes, tornadoes, giant hailstones, avalanches and the like. But the Bible informs us that the worst calamities are still beyond the horizon.

Oh, Father, when will man learn that chaos is of his own making? When will he learn that the definition of chaos is the absence of God? But You knew all along that these things would happen because in Matthew 24:7 Yeshua (Jesus) said:

> *nation will rise against nation, and kingdom against kingdom. And there will be famines, pestilences, and earthquakes in various places.*

All these things and more are being fulfilled in our time. Yeshua (Jesus) also said:

> *there will be signs in the sun, in the moon, and in the stars; and on the earth distress of nations, with*

*perplexity, the sea and the waves roaring; men's
hearts failing them from fear and the expectation of
those things which are coming on the earth*
(Luke 21:25-26).

Many have scrambled for the best vantage points – some
flying halfway around the world – to watch recent eclipses of the
sun. And photographers went wild when blood-red full moons
appeared shortly before the turn of our new millennium.

The distress of nations is unparalleled, Father. Man has de-
generated into being a worshipper of Mammon, and of late was
hit where it hurt most when the economies in Asia, Europe and
North America either collapsed wholly or shrank to World War
II and near Great Depression levels. Untold millions of people
have been thrown out of work and for millions a lifetime of financial savings disappeared overnight. Trillions of dollars have
been lost in share values, but this is only indicative of the greater
global financial collapse. Countless millions of people have been
driven into despair and thousands have committed suicide.

Truly, Father, many hearts are indeed failing from fear and the
expectation of what is coming upon the earth. Many fear losing
their jobs and not being able to meet payments on their personal
debt. They have yet to learn that there is a higher price to pay for
materialism and greed than the actual price-tag cost.

Hearts are failing through fear of global terrorism. Airlines,
bus lines, shopping malls, and office buildings are no longer
havens of safety to be enjoyed as in yesteryear. No place on
earth is now safe. Terrorists are becoming streetwise and they
will soon have access to missiles and deadly chemicals and
biological agents that could kill thousands or millions in a single
attack. This planet, Father, has become a cruel and dangerous
playground for its inhabitants.

Father, billions of people are living in an anxious and stressed
state today due to the things happening which You foretold long
ago. However, You encourage those redeemed through the blood
of Yeshua (Jesus) to look up when these things happen:

*Now when these things begin to happen, look up and
lift up your heads, because your redemption draws
near* (Luke 21:28).

We thank You, Father, that we are living in the last days and that our awaited redemption is near at hand. We thank You, too, for Your peace, Your *shalom*, without which we could not endure living in mans' pleasure garden where morals have sunk lower than those of Sodom and Gomorrah (Genesis Chapter 19), and where violence exceeds that of Genesis 6:11-13.

You knew from day one that man would reject You, his *"Creator;"* that he would reject Yeshua (Jesus) Your Son, and that he would ultimately destroy himself and his world. You knew all of this before the foundation of the world. Knowing this, You made provision for the redemption of man at that time by giving Your Son Yeshua (Jesus) before time began (Revelation 13:8).

Too few have chosen to believe You, Father, they prefer to believe the lies (Romans 1:25; 2 Thessalonians 2:11) of the devil who is the father of lies (John 8:44). So few have accepted Your redemption by receiving Yeshua (Jesus), but two millennia ago You told us that it would be so:

> Because narrow is the gate and difficult is the way
> which leads to life, and there are few who find it
> (Matthew 7:14).

Not many have chosen to walk the straight and narrow path, Father. Salvation is so easy and free because it cost You so much, but man spurns it. Soon it will be too late. Time is running out.

You are currently brooding, hovering over Your *"special treasure"* and tens of thousands have already come to know their Jewish Messiah – Your *"only begotten Son,"* Yeshua (Jesus). You are quickly closing the gap that lies between us and the end of the age. Ere long, time, as we know, it will have ended, along with mans' last chance for redemption.

Only You know how and when the end will come, Father. You have told us what You are going to do, but we neither know how You will do it nor when You will do it. But we do know that You plan to shake everything that can be shaken in order to get mankind's attention:

> For thus says the LORD of hosts: "Once more (it is
> a little while) I will shake heaven and earth, the sea
> and dry land" (Haggai 2:6).

You are about to wrap things up for You have said:

I will show wonders in heaven above and signs in the earth beneath: blood and fire and vapor of smoke. The sun shall be turned into darkness, and the moon into blood, before the coming of the great and awesome day of the LORD. And it shall come to pass that whoever calls on the name of the LORD shall be saved (Acts 2:19-21).

Oh, that mankind would indeed earnestly seek Your face before the coming of that great and terrible Day that is so vividly described in the last book of the Bible – the book of Revelation, which in Greek is called *the Apocalypse.*

Oh, that men and women would humble themselves and come to You, trusting like children and believing that You are Who You say You are – the *"of people Almighty," "Creator"* and *"Possessor of heaven and earth and sea and all that is in them"* – their heavenly Father Who loves them so very much.

Oh, that mankind would run to You for forgiveness of sins and to be washed in the blood of Your Son Yeshua (Jesus), Who died on the Cross that man might live. Oh Father, that men and women – Jew and Gentile – would yet accept from Your outstretched hand the salvation that You so freely offer. Help them to understand that yesterday cannot be recalled and tomorrow cannot be assured, that only today is theirs. Help them, Father, help them before the final curtain falls upon the stage of this world.

Thank You, Father, for loving us who have already become recipients of Your grace and mercy. Thank You for having being so patient with us. And thank You for having accepted us just the way we are. In Yeshua's (Jesus') name. Amen.

For Your Information

Ramon Bennett, the author of this book, also writes the **Ministry & Prayer Update**, the periodic newsletter of the *Arm of Salvation Ministries*. The *Update* keeps readers informed on worldwide events that affect Israel and, also, on the ministry of Ramon Bennett and his wife, Zipporah. An annual donation is

requested for the *Update* to offset production and postage costs, which are currently costing around US15.00 per year. Amounts above this figure will be put toward the Bennetts' ministry costs and personal expenses. Donations should be made to Ramon Bennett and sent to Shekinah Books at the address below. All donations will be forwarded in full to Dr. Bennett, together with any letter or note attached.

Arm of Salvation (AOS) was founded by Ramon Bennett in 1980 and is an indigenous Israeli ministry dependent upon gifts and the proceeds from its book and music sales to sustain its work in and for the Jewish people. These are critical times for Israel so readers' support is both needful and warmly appreciated.

Copies of *The Wilderness* and other books by Ramon Bennett, together with albums of popular Hebrew worship songs composed by Zipporah Bennett, are available from:

Shekinah Books
8049 Butternut Drive
Citrus Heights, CA 95621 U.S.A.
Telephone (916) 877-0449
eMail: rose@Shekinahbooks.net.

All payments must be in U.S. funds drawn on a U.S. bank. Alternatively, visit our website: www.ShekinahBooks.com and purchase by using PayPal.

When Day & night Cease is the most comprehensive, factual and informative book on Israel—past, present and future. If you want a true picture of how Israel is falling into Bible prophecy today, look no further. You will want to read this book (306 pages).

Understand the chaos taking place around the world today! SAGA is about Israel and Israel's God; about war and judgment—past, present, and future. Nations came and went, empires rose and fell; and God is still judging nations today. A "must read" in light of world events today (237 pages).

Philistine lays bare the Arab mind, Islam, the United Nations, the media, rewritten history and the Israeli-PLO peace accord. Philistine will grip you. Philistine will inform you. Philistine will shock you. Until you read Philistine you will never understand the Middle East—the world's most volatile region (345 pages).

"They lead My people astray, saying 'Peace!' when there is no peace, and because, when a flimsy wall is built, they cover it with whitewash" (Ezekiel 13:10). Ramon Bennett exsposes the peace process for what it is, an attempt to break Israel down piece by piece (367 pages).

Halelu

A unique album of Hebrew worship songs composed
especially with translation in mind.
A beautiful dual Hebrew-English edition is the first
of a series of foreign language productions.
(CD or Cassette).

Kuma Adonai

Songs of Warfare and Worship sung by an all sabra
believing choral group. Hear Hebrew—the
'tongue of the prophets'— from native Hebrew
speakers! (CD or Cassette)

Hebrew texts, trranslation, and transliterations printed inside the jacket

Who Hath Believed?

Hebrew and Aramaic prophecies in song. Here is
the Old Testament life story of Yeshua (Jesus) the
Messiah—from His conception until His glorifica-
tion.
(CD or Cassette).

Hebrew texts, trranslation, and transliterations printed inside the jacket

Gates of Zion

The Psalms are sung again by members of Israeli Messianic congregations! This album contains some of the "golden
oldies," some of the favorite praise and worship songs of
Israel's believing community! (Cassettes only).

Hebrew texts, trranslation, and transliterations printed inside the jacket

Return, Daughter of Zion!

Zipporah Bennett's
testimony and autobiography. Read how Zipporah,
a God-hungry Orthodox Jewish girl, found the Reality she longed for. This book, often amusing, will
help the reader better understand the way Jewish
people think and feel about the "Christian" Jesus
(137 pages).